Praise for *Collabo*

"Marketing used to be about controlling the look and feel of a brand, broadcasting it. Brady gets that the new paradigm is about influencing the character of a brand—showing by doing—and that collaborations are the best way to express a brand's character."

—Jon Spear, Brand Director, La Colombe Coffee Roasters

"Consumers are more involved than ever in co-creating with the brands they welcome into their lives. Brady's thoughts on brand collaboration with customers, partners and the broader ecosystem are timely and useful to marketers of all types."

—Kirsten Newbold-Knipp, VP/CMO, Convey

"No marketer today stands a chance on their own, and everybody knows it. But true collaboration is hard. Thankfully, this new book, Collaboration is King, is a field guide for creative impact. Don't just read it—use it."

—Ross Martin, CEO, Blackbird

"Brady has beautifully laid out how collaboration is the new creativity for modern brands. Collaboration is King is jammed with insights and inspiring stories to help you amplify your brand in a noisy and saturated world. It's the book I hope my competition doesn't read!"

—Eric Ryan, method & OLLY co-founder

"No matter what you're working on, chances are you're doing it collaboratively. From GitHub to Slack to Dropbox to data.world, we're coming together in order to do more, in less time, while burning fewer resources. Brady has brought that thinking to life for marketers in a fast-paced, personal and studied look at the role of collaboration in marketing. Collaboration is King *is an entertaining and thought provoking read."*

—Robert Dowling, CEO of Hudson Cutler

"Most brands, as powerful as they are on their own, need the boost of another's DNA in order to create a truly disruptive idea or covetable product for their consumers. Ignite the power of what strong collaborations can do for your brand by following the experience of Brady Sadler in his new book Collaboration is King—*this is the secret sauce for successful brands!"*

—Laura Caszatt, Manager, merchandising / product development at The Walt Disney Company

"There's a certain alchemy that occurs at the intersection of things, when seemingly disparate worlds collide and layer to create something that feels totally new. It's inspiring, engaging, and sometimes even brings us back to that feeling of awe we experienced so often as kids, when the world was still fresh to us. Collaboration is King *reminds me that in connecting the seemingly unconnected, meaningful stories and experiences can emerge."*

—Fatimah Kabba, Brand Designer, IDEO

Collaboration is KING

How Game-Changers Create Marketing Partnerships
That Build Brands and Grow Businesses

Brady Sadler

Sol & Sonny Publishing

Copyright © 2018 by Brady Sadler
CollaborationIsKing.com
BradySadler.com

Published 2018

Creative Development Editor: Heather Doyle Fraser
Copyeditor: Bridie O'Shaughnessy
Cover and Chapter Opener Illustrations: Kyle Mosher
Designer: Danielle Baird

Printed in the United States of America

ISBN: 978–1–7324927–0–7

First Edition

Sol & Sonny Publishing — Boston, MA

To Bubbie and Zadie, thank you for making your home on Crocker Street a truly magical place. I will always cherish the love, laughter, life lessons and delicacies you so generously served up.

Contents

Introduction

THE MARKETING LANDSCAPE has changed immensely over the past two decades, and consumers now expect more from the brands they encounter.

As an executive in a marketing agency for nearly 12 years and then as a consultant, I have had a front row seat as brands of all shapes and sizes worked through the disruption of traditional advertising, the widespread adoption of digital marketing and a dramatic evolution in the way we communicate as humans.

While at the agency, our company grew from a conservative New England shop to a respected national player. We worked with businesses across a variety of industries including food and beverage, footwear and apparel, software as a service, consumer electronics, healthcare, financial services, gaming, travel and more. During this time every company in every sector had to address the shifting communications landscape or risk becoming irrelevant. Technology was changing everything, and rapidly.

Today, as this evolution continues, consumers want to engage with companies that provide more than just a product or service. They favor brands that offer functional, emotional and social benefits. In other words, brands that create value and enable connection in more than one sense.

For many years, brands could sell large quantities of mediocre or lousy products by simply spending a lot of money on advertising. Those days are clearly over, in large part because advances in technology have also democratized production and distribution. As a result, competition is fierce in every category, but smart marketers turn this into an advantage.

Instead of focusing on the confusion and clutter, or obsessively looking internally for answers, they increase their odds of winning by deliberately teaming up with other brands on various fronts.

Unfortunately, I see a lot of companies that have not adapted to this reality. I meet a lot of frustrated marketers and business leaders who are lost in data, bogged down with process, challenged by internal politics, committed to legacy practices or hyper-focused on maximizing short-term profitability. They are stuck in the sameness and the busy work that keeps the company moving. Others are paralyzed by the exponential growth in the number of brands in the market and media channels at their disposal.

I have also experienced the ways in which many of these same changes have challenged sales efforts. After all, marketing and sales are interdependent. They are both tasked with attracting, engaging and building relationships, creating value for their business and for customers.

Perhaps the most common pitfall is letting fear or greed stop us from developing relationships. In reality, mutually beneficial partnerships between individuals, departments, brands and consumers will always win over isolation, especially given our increasing connectivity.

So how do we create, or in some instances rekindle, the spark that drives inspiring work, breakthrough brands, growth and value? It takes a mix of personal passion, self-awareness, proactivity, insatiable curiosity, creativity and most importantly a commitment to overt collaboration at every level.

My "Why"

I've been fascinated by brands, particularly in sports and music, all my life. Over the years I also became obsessed with pop culture and the study of marketing, especially the fact that certain brands seemed to develop a level of cultural relevance that set them apart. The commonality? Most of the time these products and experiences were layered with storytelling, and often these same brands were connected to one another.

For the last few years I've been collecting examples of brand collaborations and realized it's more than just a trend. It's an extremely timely and effective way to market a brand. This new world of brand collaboration became most apparent to me when social media turned into a serious tool for business. Sure, it became a popular place to share content and to deploy targeted advertising, but the biggest shift ushered in by the rise of social media was the way it significantly increased our interactions with and between brands. As a result, I began to notice direct and indirect partnerships popping up more frequently across all categories, and the way they were enabling the creation of deeper relationships with consumers. That's when the new brand collaboration opportunity became clear.

Today I feel that opportunity has turned into necessity. Simply put, collaborations are essential for brand growth and evolution. And although I started writing with the intention of focusing a lot more on the business impact, this book also includes an emphasis on the individual. That's because I came to realize collaboration is a great way for marketers to employ their own creativity and jump-start personal and professional development.

This book also represents a turning point for me personally. Earlier in my career I was reluctant to share and follow through with my creative ideas because, like many of you, I wrestled with a degree of perfectionism. For a long time I didn't see it, but everyone is susceptible to this, regardless of their talent or career stage. This impacted decisions in all aspects of my life, including writing this book. I would start writing and then quickly shift to editing, in an attempt to perfect what I just wrote rather than allowing the process of creation to unfold. Eventually I realized the way I was working wasn't generating the results I wanted. Ultimately I pushed past my insecurity by committing to action, in this case writing every day. Soon after that I found a magical thing called momentum.

Another lesson that I learned along the way is that we all need a nudge and a catalyst at times. No one truly does anything completely on their own. In fact, one of the exercises that helped me gain perspective and further embrace my own creativity started with an ultimatum from my uncle, Mark Silverman, who also happens to be a professional coach, focusing on a mix of career and general life advice. One day I joined a Skype call with Mark from the Virgin Hotel in Chicago. I admired the company's founder, Richard Branson, and their airline, but I had never stayed at one of their properties.

Ever since I worked for The Walt Disney Company after college, I've paid extremely close attention to the way marketing is impacted by customer service. Therefore, it was not surprising that on this particular day I was completely geeking out over Virgin's unique take on hospitality. I couldn't stop telling Mark how impressed I was with the way their company values came to life through different aspects of the experience. He was used to hearing me rant and rave about marketing, and he had been encouraging me to share my thoughts in a more public way.

This advice wasn't random. It actually played to my passions and strengths. Mark knew that I had been interested in broadcasting since I was a kid. Among other things, I made multiple appearances on a nationally syndicated radio show at age 13, reviewed films on the local college radio station, hosted my own cable access TV segment and received high school credit for an independent study in video production. And yet, I had forgotten about these experiences and allowed the feelings of perfectionism to hold me back from creating.

I don't know why, but on this particular day Mark threw down the gauntlet and challenged me to immediately create and post a video about what I was experiencing at the Virgin Hotel. I made up excuses about lacking equipment and proper lighting, but he wasn't having any of it. I reluctantly ended my call with him, pulled the Virgin-branded phone off the wall as a prop and hit record. Two minutes later I posted the clip to Facebook and couldn't believe the response. Friends, family, co-workers, clients and strangers weighed in. The feedback was overwhelmingly positive and I decided to try it again the next week. Not long after that I committed to posting one video every week, and now over a year later I haven't missed one yet.

So why am I sharing this? The clips I posted to Facebook haven't set the world on fire or gone viral, but the experience of making and sharing them taught me more about myself and the world of marketing than I ever could have imagined. As you'll soon read, when I combined that experience with a few other mental and physical exercises I began rediscovering my own creativity, passions and convictions. It hasn't been all rosy, and I've certainly had my fair share of failures. But I now feel like I'm really in the game and I hope you are too.

Every time we push past a fear, we build up our tolerance and we unlock new opportunities. Personally, I aspire to be a connector, creator and producer, the person who brings people together and helps them find the resources to create companies, products, services, experiences, songs, shows, events, clothing and more.

I hope this book is a step in that direction. A nudge just like Mark gave me. That's right, I'm challenging myself to continue creating and now I'm throwing down the gauntlet for you too. And of course, if you want help just let me know, because what makes me feel most alive is being around people who are pushing past their fears and going for it, being themselves, building things and making an impact with their art.

Curiosity and Connecting the Seemingly Unconnected

In this book we dive into the collaboration space head first and explore the modern brand and how it has evolved, the foundation of every successful collaboration, how to make the most of collaborations and how to create a culture of collaboration in your workspace. We also introduce you to a number of modern marketers I admire who graciously shared their thoughts on the subject. Towards the end of the book, we'll walk through a DIY framework for developing and activating a brand collaboration in your world. Additionally, because none of what we do occurs in a vacuum and, as Bob Dylan said, "the times they are a-changin," we delve into ways to nurture our own passion, curiosity and creativity in an effort to remain inspired and relevant marketers, artists and entrepreneurs.

Collaborative Features of the Book

In actuality, this book is a collaboration in itself between friends, acquaintances and a variety of virtual mentors, and if you look closely you will notice collaborations taking place throughout. This also aligns with the general thesis of the book—your brand is the average of the other brands it is most associated with—which was inspired by Jim Rohn's quote, "you are the average of the people you spend the most time with."

Each chapter begins with a graphic representation of the content that will be covered in the chapter. These features, and the cover, were designed by my good friend and a talented multidisciplinary artist, Kyle Mosher. We've worked together on a number of collaborations over the years that have included indie artists, emerging brands and Fortune 500s. It's an honor to call him a friend, a collaborator and a fellow creator. Be sure to show him some love: @thekylemosher

As mentioned, you'll see the thread of music throughout the book as it plays an important role in my life. I've created a soundtrack for the book, with songs representing the different themes we cover, and you can find these on my website (CollaborationIsKing.com), along with some additional content to help you and your teammates get in the collaboration game.

If you're reading this book I suspect you're already a curious and creative person, but how do you continue building these critical marketing muscles? Throughout the book you'll find two recurring features meant to help you tap into your own creativity and the power of collaboration:

CoLAB

Chapters 2–13 will feature an experiment you can do anywhere in the world to spark creative thinking and make you a better marketer. They will touch upon four themes:

1. Personal Passion: Do What You Love

2. Self-Awareness: Play to Your Strengths

3. Curiosity: Honing Your Vision

4. Creativity: Connect the Seemingly Unconnected

MODERN MARKETERS

In Chapters 2–12 you will also get a peek inside the minds of marketers, executives and artists who have launched successful collaborations, driven results for brands and indulged their curiosity and creativity at the same time.

BUZZ...

Lastly, you will also find that I use a number of buzzwords, marked as such. Rather than pretending this isn't a challenge for me, and for our industry, I'm embracing it and I hope you'll have fun as I call myself out when I'm guilty of leaning on this language. With my "10,000 hours" in the industry, to quote Malcolm Gladwell's buzz-worthy insight, it is going to be a tough habit to break.

My friend Sonny—who happens to be a great marketer, but focuses more on management and sales in his day-to-day work for a large multinational corporation—buzzes like a bee whenever he hears my friend Taylor and I talking about marketing. Truth is, we do have a vernacular issue in our industry, with many words lacking consistency. This even confuses and creates skepticism among those in marketing.

I will commit to being more conscious of my use of buzzwords, but as an industry we should all work together to continue finding consistent meaning for the words and phrases we do frequently use. After all, these terms can be fun. Come to think of it, maybe we use lingo for the same reasons we did as kids? It becomes a creative outlet, a way to play with language and a way to be part of a club.

Now More than Ever

In reviewing the first draft of the book, a running joke became how many times I used the phrase "now more than ever." My editor and I had a good laugh every time we came across it and I looked for ways to articulate my thoughts differently. While that was a healthy exercise and helped improve my writing, I now realize the phrase turned up so much because we're in such a unique time. We really are facing more challenges, more options, more technology, more competition, more content, more media, more interactions, more alerts, more connections, more demands, more marketing messages and more brands than ever before. What we do not have is more time. And in many instances we also have limited or decreasing budgets and margins to work with. This book is meant to help all of us succeed in spite of that reality. Collaboration is not a miracle or cure-all, but it is a diverse, timely and powerful tool.

Ready to play?

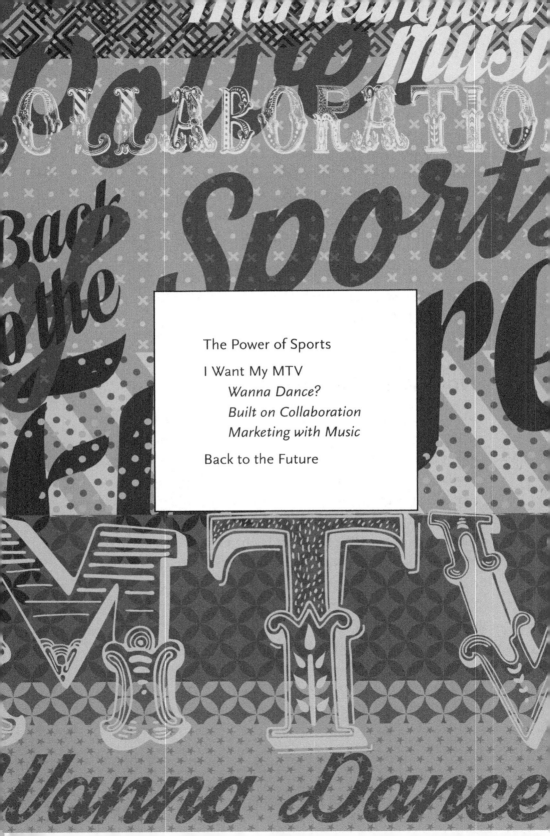

CHAPTER 1

A Product of Passion

*"The future is determined by what stories we choose
to tell and by who gets to tell the stories."*

— Juan Enriquez, author, futurist and venture capitalist

DURING THE EARLY days of my career, I changed my approach to meetings based upon my perception of each client. When I perceived clients and prospects to be more conservative, I dressed in more traditional business attire, and I avoided discussion of my fledgling side-hustle in the music business. I played to my audience. Over time though, I started to divulge more to my clients about my work in music and found that it not only helped to build deeper relationships in every sector, but was also a differentiating factor. The lesson? Embrace your passions, explore how your interests might be relevant to your business, and encourage your teammates to do the same. We all win when we bring our whole selves to the table.

It's become somewhat cliche to talk about leaning heavily on passion for career guidance, but I believe that it's worth exploring. When I speak with people who are unsure about their passions or their careers, I suggest they look back to their childhood for clues. There's usually something in our early lives we can point to as evidence of why we pursued, or dreamed of pursuing, a particular path. With that in mind, a number of the stories and examples I rely on throughout this book come from my youth. Through that exploration I've uncovered that my interest in business and marketing was sparked by a passion for pop culture and, more specifically, sports and music. After all these years, I've realized that sports and music provide inspiration that can help improve any business because they are both built on layers of collaboration.

The Power of Sports

I was taught from a young age to be a fan. More specifically, a fan of the New York Yankees. I grew up in southeastern Connecticut, a place that was geographically and philosophically split between "The Bronx Bombers" (or the "Evil Empire" if you asked the *other* guys) and what would later be branded, "Red Sox Nation." The Yankees and Red Sox made up one of the most heated rivalries in all of sports and everyone I knew pledged their allegiance to one or the other. My father was a Yankees fan, and so, unlike some of my best friends and family members, I hated the Red Sox. Not surprisingly, I jumped at the chance to debate which team had the better squad. I was truly passionate and took pride in being a part of that community, or what my favorite marketer Seth Godin calls a "tribe."

I'll never forget the first time my father took me to Yankee Stadium, just as his father had done thirty years earlier. It was a true rite of passage in our family. That morning I proudly put on my New Era Yankees hat, a Starter Don Mattingly t-shirt (he was the team's All Star first baseman at the time) and my Rawlings baseball mitt in case a foul ball came our way. We met up with a few friends and made the two and a half hour pilgrimage to the Bronx.

Needless to say, the surroundings were a lot different than what we were used to in suburban Connecticut. The experience was amplified by an orchestra of honking horns, police sirens and street vendors. When we entered the Stadium, I was over-whelmed with emotion. The energy was palpable. It became even more intense as we walked through the tunnel and I saw the field for the first time in person. The grass was a shade of green I had never seen before. It simply didn't translate through our 1980s TV. We went to Monument Park and paid homage to the great players cheered on by my father and his father during their Stadium visits. We snuck past security during batting practice to get autographs, ate hot dogs and knishes, sang "Take Me Out to the Ballgame," and cheered wildly for the Yanks. In the end we left early to beat the traffic, and listened to the play-by-play on the car radio to make sure we didn't miss any late inning fireworks. Once I was a little older my Dad agreed to stay until the final pitch so we could hear Frank Sinatra sing "New York, New York," as is the tradition at the end of every Yankees game.

Although attending the game was thrilling, it was just a small part of being a fan. We only went to the Bronx once a year, but my support for the team was a year-round commitment.

Today fans have the Yankees Entertainment Network (YES), a pioneering multimedia platform that became a sports market-ing case study, but when I was a kid we relied on a combination of print, TV and my favorite medium at the time, radio.

As Yankees fans living in Connecticut, we listened to sports radio commentary on New York's WFAN, the first all-sports station in the country. My daily ritual included listening to "The Fan" while getting ready for school in the morning and while falling asleep most nights. However, the station only had the broadcast rights for the New York Mets games, so when it came to hearing the actual Yankees games we tuned into another station, WABC. I can remember lying in bed at night listening to the "voice of the Yankees," John Sterling, calling the games. He had a classic, deep, announcer voice and became famous for his animated home run call: "It is high... It is far... It is... gone!" Unlike the ESPN and WFAN on-air personalities who mostly remained neutral, John regularly showed his Yankees bias. His passion for the team made it feel like we were in it together. This shared experience was based on a common set of values, and ultimately strengthened my connection to the Yankees brand.

At a time when there were no social media outlets through which the team could communicate, John really was the "voice" of the brand and the leader of the tribe. I remember being fascinated by this and, at the age of 13, I decided I wanted to be a broadcaster just like him.

One day I was outside playing ball—as I did almost every day—when my Dad yelled for me to come inside for a phone call. I figured it was a friend or one my grandparents, but instead I picked up the phone and heard a man with a familiar deep voice say, "Hello, Brady." It was none other than John Sterling.

Like many Yankees fans, my father felt a connection to John. He had actually listened to him on a different station years before John started calling Yankees games. In fact, my father even wrote him a letter explaining how he had followed and admired his career. I don't want to discount the contents of the letter, especially since my father happens to be a talented writer, but I'm guessing that John didn't get a lot of fan mail at the time. Not only did he call our house to say thanks for the letter, he invited us to visit him at Yankee Stadium!

On our next trip to the Bronx we met up with John for a tour of the press box, where he introduced us to the other media personalities, including the legendary Phil Rizzuto, and gave us a tour of George Steinbrenner's office. George was the controversial owner of Yankees, later portrayed as George Costanza's boss on *Seinfeld*. At the time he was in the middle of a league-imposed suspension which meant he was not allowed in the ballpark. I could tell John got a kick out of walking us through George's private office while "The Boss" was away.

For a few years, visiting John became a part of our Stadium ritual and I'm extremely grateful for those priceless experiences. Although I decided not to pursue broadcasting, I can still see a clear connection between what John represented as the voice of the Yankees and my work in marketing.

The interactions with John may have played a role in shaping my career, but like millions of other sports fans, it was a combination of factors that bred my passion and loyalty for the Yankees.

When I take a step back I see that sports are filled with stories, personalities, history, heritage, traditions and experiences. Teams provide endless opportunities for fans to engage, including a wide array of content, merchandise and events. Perhaps most importantly, sports provide a platform for connection, emotion, pride and an opportunity to be part of a community. Every company would like to develop a brand that harnesses the power of sports, and although we may not have the resources of a professional team, we can all apply these lessons in our own way.

Another factor that played a role in building my loyalty for the Yankees was the ecosystem around the team, which included a variety of supporting brands. There were the media brands that covered the games and those who sponsored the broadcasts. The brands that advertised in the stadium and those that sponsored the giveaways. (I'm still not sure "Bat Day" was a great idea since the Stadium could get rowdy, but someone sponsored it.) The brands that made the uniforms, equipment, hats and other merchandise that enabled us to rep our favorite teams. The brands of baseball cards my friends and I tracked, traded and sold as if we were stock brokers. And last but not least, there were the players, who sat in the middle of everything with their own complex personal brands.

I gave up my early dream of becoming a sports broadcaster like John, but I did end up working in professional sports for a few years as a sales and marketing exec. While there, I learned even more about the power of collaboration as I activated sponsorships for Dunkin' Donuts, Harley Davidson, Miller Light, Kia Motors and dozens of others. The marketing agency where I worked next also produced numerous segments for *Sportscenter,* the show I watched religiously as a kid and once dreamed of working for as a broadcaster. Things have a funny way of playing out when you develop the right collaborations.

I Want My MTV

As a young kid in the 80s, you belonged to one of two households—those that allowed MTV and those that did not. Guess which one mine was? When talking about my passion for music, my mother likes to reminisce about the day she walked into the living room to find me jamming out to MTV. Knowing it was banned in our household, I pointed out that she said I couldn't *watch* MTV, but she didn't say anything about *listening* to it. I had used the contrast knob (remember when TVs had knobs?) to blur out the picture in an attempt to get around her rule. But why would I bother doing that? What drew millions of people just like me to the channel in the first place?

It turns out that MTV marked a pivotal moment in the evolution of media and branding. Not only was it a visually appealing medium that played right into my short attention span, but from a business standpoint it was also the first mass media channel to completely blur the lines between content and commerce. This created a complex ecosystem and an ideal platform for brand collaboration.

Every music video on MTV—in addition to being highly entertaining and cutting-edge in terms of creativity—was essentially an advertisement for an artist and an album. Just like sports announcers, video DJs—or VJs—became the voice of the MTV brand, providing commentary on videos, interviewing artists and reporting on the news.

Consumer brands quickly adapted their approach and made advertisements that resembled music videos. By leveraging the same tone, style and often collaborating with the same artists, brands became an integral part of the viewing experience and less of an interruption. Whether you had an artist in your advertisement or not, being on MTV meant you were collaborating with their brand. It allowed you to co-opt some of the cool and feed off the rebellious nature of the channel that turned on young people and turned off most parents.

Wanna Dance?

In the early days no artist stood out more on the MTV platform than Michael Jackson.

With the help of MTV, Michael Jackson built an empire that redefined the meaning and impact of personal branding in entertainment. He was already famous, but he took full advantage of the new music video platform to take his career into the stratosphere. He captivated us with his songs, dance moves, style, eccentricity and his use of visual storytelling. I'm only slightly embarrassed to admit that I had a make-your-own studded glove kit and mimicked his dance moves in my living room. Jackson's brand grew as he released a string of hit records and collaborated with a variety of other brands to amplify his reach and raise their relevance at the same time.

One such brand was Pepsi. Their main competitor, Coca-Cola, had built a global following that benefited from a variety of collaborations with brands like McDonald's and successful advertising campaigns that focused on friendship and happiness. To win, Pepsi had to carve out a more youthful and edgy position. Michael Jackson and MTV were the perfect partners. The Pepsi tagline, "The Choice of a New Generation," tapped into the idea that the product—just like Michael's image and MTV—was not for everyone. This was a bold move because, on the surface, it alienated people and limited the brand's appeal. However, savvy business leaders and marketers know it is always better to be some people's number one than everyone's number two.

The brand took things even further when they commissioned Jackson to rewrite his hit song "Billie Jean" for a commercial, and hired legendary advertising exec-turned-filmmaker Bob Giraldi to direct the spot. At the time Bob was known as one of the directors driving the new music video genre ushered in by MTV. He crafted the commercial to resemble Michael's "Beat It" video, which he also directed, and featured a gang of kids mimicking the King of Pop's dress and dance moves while the he sang, "You're a whole new generation, you're a Pepsi generation, taste the thrill of your day and taste the Pepsi way." Bringing all of those elements together was a monumental marketing moment. The collaboration took on an added layer of virality, long before what we know as viral today, when Jackson's hair caught fire during the filming of the campaign's second spot. Eventually it premiered on MTV as part of a special prime-time program, resulting in one of the first instances of a commercial running as actual content.

Built On Collaboration

While Michael dominated the early days of MTV, and I practiced my Moonwalk, the relatively new music genre of hip-hop was also emerging, and it was literally built upon collaboration. First and foremost, the music itself often layered one record over another or new lyrics over audio snippets of existing songs. This foundational element set a tone and led to more artists working together in this genre than any other.

My friends and I were completely obsessed with hip-hop from the moment we heard it. I'll never forget the first time I saw the Parental Advisory stamp on a cassette tape that I was probably too young to listen to. Of course, just like my mom's short-lived MTV ban, the label made me even more curious. At first we relied on each other to discover new artists, but soon we began looking more to the artists themselves to connect the dots and expose us to their contemporaries.

When artists formally teamed up as part of a group like Wu-Tang Clan, they had a better shot of breaking out than they did as solo performers. Although each individual member was unique, they typically shared a common style, their own version of buzzwords, and in many instances a hometown or region. Most importantly, they shared the spotlight on the same songs and albums. Even if an artist wasn't officially part of a crew they could quickly become associated with one if they were featured in a song. For example, I first heard Snoop Dogg when he was featured on the song "Deep Cover" with Dr. Dre, which was also Dre's first solo song after leaving the group, N.W.A. Snoop was just one of many superstars Dre would go on to collaborate with and introduce to the world, including Eminem, 50 Cent, The Game, Kendrick Lamar and others. Even Dre's labels—Death Row Records and later Aftermath—were collaborations with his longtime partner, Interscope Records executive Jimmy Iovine.

As this collaborative formula proved successful, it was emulated by more artists. Once Snoop was established we were introduced to his crew, Tha Dogg Pound. Many artists took this a step further and began launching their own record labels. Eminem created Shady Records, another imprint of Iovine's Interscope, relying on the same theory of collaboration by introducing his crew D12, not to mention the business benefits that come from owning more of your own intellectual property.

Collaborations in hip-hop continued to evolve and even some of today's biggest stars in other genres owe their continued relevance to the world of hip-hop. Take Justin Timberlake, whose foray into becoming a solo artist was ushered in by a collaboration with the rap group Clipse and production from Pharrell. This was masterfully executed to help him evolve from his boy-band branding into a pop star.

A similar collaboration phenomenon also played out in hip-hop and other genres through sampling: the art of taking pieces of songs and using them like instruments to construct new tracks. By sampling, an artist reveals something new about themselves and their brand. This holds true when an artist quotes an existing lyric from another song, and even when an artist or band performs a cover song. These associations make statements and inform how brands, in this case personal brands, are perceived.

Christopher Wallace, better known as the Notorious B.I.G. or Biggie, applied all of these tactics to launch his career. He first came to the attention of most fans through his feature on the song "Flava in Ya Ear" by Craig Mack, a popular rapper at the time and a fellow member of Bad Boy, a record label with a variety of artists.

Although Biggie was later shot and killed, allegedly as a result of an ongoing battle with west coast rappers, the lyrics and hook on the first song of his first album were each sampled from the king of west coast hip-hop, Dr. Dre. In doing so, Biggie was paying homage to an artist he admired and revealing his taste to fans. And in giving listeners something familiar, a point of reference, he also made his music and his personal brand more approachable. Familiarity, trust, respect and admiration can all come from producing and experiencing a thoughtful collaboration.

Biggie's producer, Sean "Puffy, Puff Daddy or P Diddy" Combs, was a student of music and a great marketer who took the art form of sampling to a new level. Although many would challenge his assertion, Combs claimed that he invented the remix. As documentary filmmaker Kirby Ferguson established in his 2010 film *Everything Is a Remix*, artists have been stealing from each other forever, but Combs and others in hip-hop made it a deliberate part of the art form.

Today two of the most popular places to discover new music are YouTube and Soundcloud, especially when it comes to hip-hop. There we find another example of branding and collaboration playing out. As young artists create music, they often collaborate on the production, and in many instances they do it virtually. In fact, an entire economy has been built around marketing and selling instrumental beats over the internet.

Bedroom and basement beat makers sell creations on social networks and within communities like BeatStars and MyFlash-Store, where anyone can listen to, license or outright purchase the music. Like any growing marketplace, it's getting crowded and becoming difficult for newcomers to stand out. In an attempt to overcome this and attract attention, many producers create type beats, as in Drake-type-beats, or beats that sound like the artist Drake. This illustrates one of the same principles that drives collaboration: association.

As Biggie and Puffy did before them, by tying their product to an existing artist and personal brand, these producers create a familiar reference that increases awareness and consideration for something new. Artist A$AP Rocky even admitted to sourcing the beat for one of his songs by searching A$AP Rocky-type beat.

Marketing With Music

Just as they do in sports through sponsorships and a variety of other products, services and media, brands also play a huge role in music. While every genre gets in the game, and this is not a new phenomenon, the most creative brand partnerships have always been in hip-hop.

One of the first and most famous examples grew out of the track "My Adidas" by Run-DMC. As the song gained popularity in July of 1986, the month I turned seven years old, the group's management invited adidas representatives to a concert at Madison Square Garden. On that night the band prompted fans to literally put their shoes in the air when they performed the track, further demonstrating their influence.

Music manager, label exec and founder of Translation—an advertising agency focused on being a bridge between culture and corporations—Steve Stoute shared his interpretation of what unfolded that night in his book *The Tanning of America,* "When adidas execs witnessed twenty thousand young urban fans jubilantly holding their brand aloft, they immediately saw the incredible economic potential that this new, raw form of entertainment possessed."

The overall awareness and commercial impact of name-checking brands in music cannot be overstated. Most of these branded lyrics began as unofficial endorsements by artists who were unprovoked and unpaid. Still, it didn't take long for brands like adidas to quickly realize the potential impact, embrace the phenomenon and begin paying artists. After that evening at Madison Square Garden, Run-DMC ended up with a seven-figure payday and their own sneakers, making them the first nonathletes to secure this kind of deal. Perhaps fittingly, Run-DMC was also the first group to blend hip-hop and rock when they teamed up with Aerosmith and produced "Walk This Way."

> *"For anyone at any level of commerce, from corporate execs to aspiring entrepreneurs, from marketing directors to college students who will soon be entering the working world, this is theretofore a cautionary tale: Ignore the globalization of popular culture at your own peril."*
>
> —Steve Stoute

Back to the Future

So why all this history and nostalgia? I find it's incredibly helpful to look back in order to understand current and future trends. Just like they were for me as a kid, sports and music are arguably two of the most pervasive parts of our culture today. In fact, while television viewing has been moving to on-demand, streaming, and time shifting, the two things that are still consistently viewed live are sports and entertainment industry award shows. This viewership, and the layers of collaboration we see in sports and music, provide a stark reminder that brands must be part of our culture if they expect to be part of our conversations. And if they are not part of our conversations then their products will not be purchased.

When you combine this with the fact that individuals are more empowered to communicate through technology, build their own communities and influence one another, it's easy to see why the brands that invest in collaboration to gain cultural relevance tend to win.

Today brands and products show up in sports and music all the time, but just as brands need to continue taking collaborations further to make them more creative and impactful, athletes and artists are doing the same. In some instances they create completely new brands and products that run independently and then form collaborations with known brands, while in others they launch with the help of a core brand partnership.

Dr. Dre and Jimmy Iovine built an empire with their headphone and speaker company Beats by Dr. Dre, which relied heavily on artist and athlete endorsements and, along with the streaming service Beats Music, sold to Apple for a reported $3 billion. Sean Combs turned Ciroc vodka into a juggernaut. Rihanna launched her Fenty Beauty line of products exclusively with retailer Sephora in the U.S. and also has a popular sneaker line with Puma. Jay-Z, her longtime mentor and collaborator, has also been a prolific brand creator, partner and ambassador. In addition to running his own management company, and brokering deals between artists, athletes and brands, in 2018 he was personally named the President of PUMA's resurrected Basketball division. Drake created his own brand, OVO, then grew it through collaborations with Nike's Jordan brand, Canadian Goose, Timberland, Clark's, the Toronto Raptors and fellow Canadian artist The Weeknd, who, in turn, launched brand and label XO in partnership with retailers H&M and Puma. Perhaps one of the most popular and impactful uses of personal branding and collaboration came when Kanye West helped adidas regain relevance, just as Run-DMC had done 30 years earlier, with the launch of his Yeezy Boost line of sneakers.

But these collaborations must be created thoughtfully and *fit* into a consistent brand story if they are going to be perceived favorably. It is not enough to simply insert your brand into culture without considering whether or not the alignment reflects shared values and goals. In the coming chapters we will explore how to find this *fit* and how to act upon it once you do.

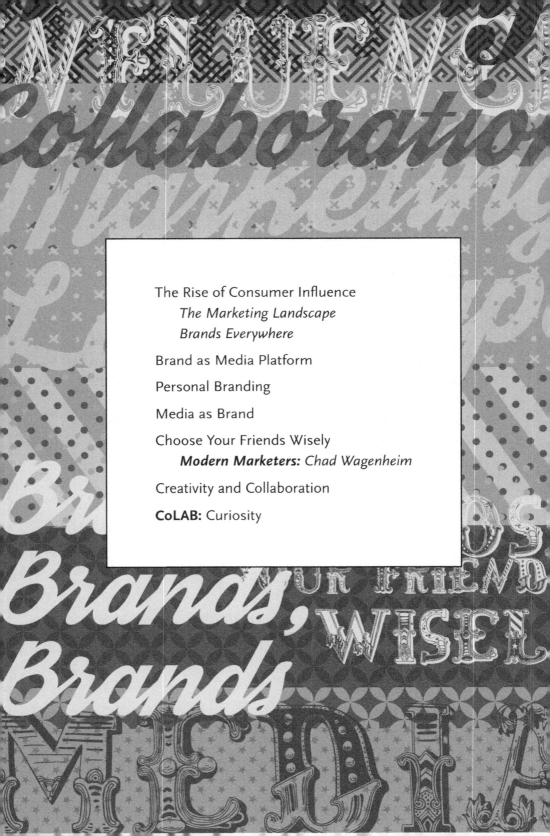

CHAPTER 2

Demands of a Modern Brand

"Marketers ruin everything."

— Gary Vaynerchuk

IT'S ALMOST IMPOSSIBLE to avoid brands in our modern culture.

Look around right now and count the number of brands in your orbit. Your computer, phone, bag, car, jewelry, clothes and shoes each represent one or more brands.

Some brand interactions are based on deliberate choice, like the media channel you select and the show that's airing, while some are more adjacent or circumstantial like the commercials or the products featured within the show.

If you're watching TV you're engaging with a furniture company, TV manufacturer, a cable company or streaming platform, a network or publisher, a show, actors and actresses. If you're eating ice cream and checking Facebook at the same time you can add a few more brands to the list.

Let's unpack that scenario.

The decision regarding the purchase of the couch may have been made years earlier by a roommate, while other choices are more personal and immediate, like grabbing that pint of Ben & Jerry's ice cream on your way home from work. Perhaps you like Cherry Garcia, the flavor named for the lead singer of the Grateful Dead, yet another brand.

The point is there's an ecosystem of brands around each and every one of us. While some feel random and others more deliberate, brands are in our lives because of the decisions we make. Where we live, work, play, shop and travel; what we consume; and who we spend time with all impact the brands that are in our orbit. While we have always had some control over the brands we associate with, today there are more to choose from and increasingly new ways to engage with them.

The Rise of Consumer Influence

Until recently a brand could hide behind a miniscule address or 1–800 number on the label of a product. I remember my mother peering at a product with a magnifying glass and then diligently sending a letter to the company with a complaint. Unfortunately, I don't think she ever received more than a generic thank you message and a coupon to purchase the same product she found to be flawed. We thought it was amazing that the company was even willing to do that. The bar was low.

So how did brands succeed in spite of this lackluster customer service? For many years there were a limited number of competitors in each category and only few mainstream media channels where products vied for attention. This allowed large brands to control their image and buy market share and shelf space. But more importantly, brands took advantage of the fact that consumer influence was extremely limited. If you had a bad experience you could only tell so many people. Basically, a company could ignore you with little consequence.

Today, due to the impact of technology, the proliferation of social media and a highly competitive marketplace, consumers have more direct influence and increasingly complicated relationships with brands.

The Marketing Landscape

Technology and the internet changed the marketing world more than anything in the last fifty years. We know this intuitively, but what were the key factors driving this shift? For one, consumers now have the ability to directly engage in a dialogue with brands, and with each other, on a global scale. When my mother has an issue or a compliment today, thanks to social media she can let the company and all of her friends and family members know with a few simple keystrokes. While she only has a few hundred people in her social network, many individuals have built vast online audiences that rival large media companies. Study after study shows that consumers trust recommendations from friends, family and perceived experts more than traditional advertising, so brands must adjust to this new reality.

With individual influence at an all-time high, your customer service must be on point. But it's not enough to be reactive. Your brand runs the risk of being hijacked if you don't proactively develop a marketing strategy that takes the rise of consumer influence into consideration. The good news is, these same trends have created an environment where brands can thrive.

As marketers, it is part of our job to find ways to exploit media in pursuit of consumer attention and attempt to harness their influence. Wherever people spend time, brands will follow and try to insert themselves into conversations. However, these attempts don't always make strategic sense, especially if we are merely interrupting people to sell something.

Of course a commitment to doing more than just interrupting requires an investment, and some legacy brands are struggling to adapt. One example of a traditional marketing practice that can be problematic is the tendency to invest in campaign ideas that roll out for a few weeks or months, at the expense of building long-term relationships and reputations. Campaign concepts are often created in a vacuum to support a specific initiative, then handed over to partners and forced in front of people through paid media. Brands do this. Agencies do this. Brands ask agencies to do this. And sometimes it works. But too often the dollars are disproportionately allocated to these initiatives.

When media was limited to TV, radio, print, outdoor and banner ads, one big idea could be developed and then adapted to each medium. And many campaigns are still developed in this TV-centric manner. It seems to be driving a return for brands that spend tens of millions of dollars, but for most companies, today's marketing landscape requires a more thoughtful approach than the linear nature of conventional campaign development and the limited channels they typically utilize.

Instead of, or in addition to large campaigns, more work must go into ongoing marketing efforts that consider the entire customer experience. Even when brands adopt more progressive practices, long-term success remains dependent upon how these companies consistently deliver value and build lasting relationships, not how efficiently they reach people or convert an impression into a click or purchase. We can think of this as the difference between a one-hit wonder and an artist or band that has a passionate fan base and long career.

But my goal is not to rail against advertising or minimize the complicated nature of marketing. These changes are extremely difficult to address and often require new personnel, partners, perspectives, processes and offerings. These changes and challenges are also the reason so many new brands are succeeding. They don't have legacy practices to shift, expectations to reset, or layers of politics to navigate. Instead they build their companies around values that take into consideration the entire customer experience and then execute accordingly. However, even these new companies can struggle as they attempt to grow. The pressure to capitalize on success and increase profits often threatens the same values and related practices that customers find so appealing.

So how do successful brands, old and new, think about marketing in this context? First and foremost, by developing exceptional products and services. Next, by constantly analyzing and improving the customer experience—before, during and after a purchase—with an emphasis on delivering value. Entire books are written on every aspect of the marketing funnel and customer journey, but here we're focused on one theme that can and should be applied across the board: collaboration. How so? By viewing the increasing number of brands (products, services, media, individuals) as potential partners and avenues for connection.

Constantly seeking out partners that *fit* with your brand, and developing creative collaborations, can result in new offerings, experiences or content. But regardless of what you produce together, or how ambitious the effort is, a successful collaboration always provides a unique way to deliver value. As we'll now explore, collaborations also result in stories that are ripe for marketers to creatively leverage.

Brands Everywhere

Well before collaborating, brands need to clearly define their reason for being and the value they deliver, as well as what makes them different from their competition, and what audiences they hope to serve. This provides an opportunity to then craft an authentic voice, brand narrative, and visual identity that reflect their values. With these elements in place, brands can develop marketing plans to reach and engage consumers. While all of this is critical to successfully marketing a brand, today it takes even more creativity to build a comprehensive strategy that drives results.

This is because the number of brands and media channels competing for attention have increased exponentially. As noted, until relatively recently, marketing was limited primarily to paid advertising through print, radio, TV, billboards and direct mail. But now the list of options for paid media alone could fill an entire book. Add to that all of the owned channels that brands can exploit, including assets such as websites, email, text messaging, podcasts, mobile applications, loyalty programs, private communities, physical locations and events. Then there are all of the shared channels such as Facebook, Snapchat, Instagram and other platforms where brands can develop their own presence within large communities that have been built for interaction and collaboration with consumers. As we are beginning to see with Amazon Echo and other devices that are becoming smart for the first time, the Internet of Things will surround us with even more opportunities, or points of entry, to engage with brands in ways that resemble media.

This begins to explain why consumers have trouble recalling most marketing messages, and why advertising often goes unseen. In fact in 2017, Procter & Gamble—one of the largest advertisers in the world—pulled over $100 million in online advertising because of concerns over fraud, viewability, brand safety and return on investment.

The average attention span has also decreased from approximately twelve seconds in the year 2000 to eight seconds (one second less than a goldfish) in 2015, according to a Microsoft consumer study. Mediums are also blending together, a trend that's been exacerbated by the number of brands producing content and considering themselves publishers. At the same time, traditional media companies are beginning to produce more of their own products and brand platforms. All the while, individuals now create an immense amount of their own media. This also leads to questions about who and what to trust, especially given the cultural skepticism and polarization surrounding the news and social media.

With this backdrop, modern marketers must be extremely creative and deliberate about how and where their brands show up. To navigate all of this, the most effective brands develop partnerships that allow them to stand out, share their values and reinforce their value proposition through a variety of different outlets.

As we'll explore throughout this book, now that every brand is capable of being a publisher, brand partnerships are becoming increasingly powerful tools for engaging and influencing consumers. When appropriately aligned, brands can work together to create the kind of novelty and authority, through stories, content, promotions and new products and services, that it takes to stand out in today's cluttered and sometimes confusing world. By aligning, brands can also rely on one another to provide the digital and physical street cred that comes from teaming up with a brand that is already viewed favorably.

Subscribing to this approach also acknowledges that consumers now have the power to program their own lives. They make choices to invite things in and edit things out. If brands want in, they must demonstrate value. And, given our collective attention deficit, brands must do so efficiently and respectfully because time can never be replaced.

> *"The nut of it is that we, today, human beings, we're just absolutely saturated with media. Literally as I'm talking to you, out of my right eye I see one screen and out of my left eye I see another and there are two more screens there. And what that's done is, it's sort of refined our bullshit detectors to a degree that, if it's bullshit or it smells at all, we don't see it; we ignore it. And I always say: the only thing worse than bad is invisible. That's how I describe 99.9 percent of all advertising; it's just invisible. You didn't even see it. You didn't even know it existed. So in order to be effective, you have to penetrate that."*

— Casey Neistat, YouTuber, from the book
Streampunks: YouTube and the Rebels Remaking Media, by Robert Kyncl with Maany Peyvan

 Cutting through the clutter has become a popular phrase in the marketing industry to explain the intention of not getting lost in the flood of content and marketing messages we all face. It speaks to the attention challenge outlined above and that many people deliberately ignore or pay to avoid advertising. For example, at this point we all know that traditional TV advertising does not have the reach and impact it once did. But the same holds true for many traditional online ad units, as the

P&G budget cut proved. The classic pop-up banner ad was an attempt to cut through, yet in reality it simply interrupted what people were actually trying to do. Those ad units have become less popular, but the replacements haven't been much better. Does anyone like the full page takeovers or pre-roll ads that we are forced to look at for a few seconds while we wait for our article, video or podcast, especially when we're shown the same ad over and over?

I realize repetition can make something memorable, but that doesn't mean the memory is pleasant. Yet the marketing industry gets excited about advancements in how we use technology to automate the purchase of these same ad units in a more targeted manner. Digital advertising can be extremely effective, but in many instances we are just annoying people in new places. As we have established, consumers are now more in control, so an interruption can feel even more intrusive.

That said, we should rethink what we mean by cutting through, and maybe even do away with the phrase. Cutting is rarely a positive thing, so perhaps it's fitting that we use it for something one-sided that benefits the brand and interrupts the consumer. Think back to being a kid. I feel like my elementary school teachers were constantly reprimanding someone for "cutting" as we lined up to go from one activity to another. We even made up different types of cuts that were negotiated when the teacher wasn't looking, like back-cuts. Sometimes we let someone cut to curry favor, but just like advertising that simply interrupts, that was self-serving and annoying. This isn't the only example of the word "cut" having a negative connotation. You never wanted to cut the grass, get cut from the team or get caught cutting the cheese. Even haircuts are scary at first. Paper cuts are the worst, and nobody wants a budget cut.

But if cutting was frowned upon as a kid, and is still avoided in most instances by adults, why is it something we aspire to do as brands and marketers? The answer is that we do not really want to cut through. We want to join, be invited to share something, or inspire others to share on our behalf.

I know it is unrealistic to think we will do away with interruptive advertising. However, we also need to keep it real, recognize that people intuitively know the difference, and increasingly mix the messages we push out with ones that consumers hopefully pull, or invite, into their lives. And there are many examples of marketers, agencies, brands, media platforms and technologists who are making great strides in this area, creating campaigns that educate, inspire, entertain and add value. The case that I'd like to make in this book, with the help of the Modern Marketers featured throughout, is that collaboration is a bridge that leads to more positive and effective marketing.

But before we dig into the brand collaboration space in more detail, let's explore what it means to be a brand today and the different types of brands that now exist, so we are all speaking the same language, even if we have to use a few buzzwords to do it.

Brand as Media Platform

Modern marketers must embrace the idea that every brand has the ability to become a publishing platform. This not only creates new channels to push messaging through, but also invites interaction and relationship building. Marketing used to be a one-way street, as illustrated by my mother's experience reaching out to 1–800 numbers and P.O. boxes, but those days are long gone. Today every brand is much more accessible, and each one must have an ongoing dialogue with consumers if they expect to succeed and hold or grow their market share.

By building up a variety of channels, in social media and beyond, brands can communicate a strong point of view and directly engage consumers. And, just like any worthwhile use of time, consumers expect value in exchange for their attention. When brands forget this and use these channels to simply sell products or interrupt, people tune out.

In order to create value, top brands have started taking a more journalistic approach by regularly producing and distributing content that would have previously been left to proper media companies.

Red Bull is the classic example of a brand as media platform. They don't simply sell beverages. They also own a record label, magazine and a TV channel—one of the only branded stations outside of media companies and traditional publishers delivering content directly through channels on platforms like Apple TV. Red Bull creates, sponsors and distributes content through these channels, all with an eye towards engaging consumers around a set of beliefs that align with the brand. They want to give people the literal fuel (their product) and the inspirational fuel (their content and events) to tackle life head on.

The most ambitious example of Red Bull's approach was its sponsorship of a space jump, during which millions watched as a man literally leaped from a platform beyond Earth's atmosphere and returned to Earth. The stunt gave new meaning to the tagline, "Red Bull Gives You Wings."

The brand's commitment to content has become a classic marketing case study, but a quick glance at Red Bull's Twitter presence shows that in addition to publishing, the brand also embraces the opportunity to directly engage in conversations with consumers.

Most productive interactions with brands mirror those between people, and so in order to provide a positive experience and create a meaningful connection, empathy and clarity are essential. This is the kind of thinking that guides customer service for brands, but it can become challenging when it happens in public through social media. Thoughtful brands get ahead of this and develop social media guidelines that create consistency in their values, voice, tone and style, turning these interactions into positive brand building experiences.

The marketers running Red Bull's Twitter account not only reply to almost every Tweet that mentions the brand, they also start conversations with people who are posting about situations where a boost from Red Bull might be beneficial. This often leads to the question of whether or not the consumer has tried Red Bull. If the answer is no, the brand points them to a landing page that makes it easy to sign up for a free case.

In just a few posts the brand creates awareness, collects consumer data and initiates a sampling opportunity. They also show anyone that happens to see the exchange how they treat people. Very few brands engage this deeply, which makes the entire experience even more refreshing. While it can be challenging to directly quantify social media ROI, this is a great example of a brand connecting social media conversations to product consumption.

As we will discuss in Chapter 13, when technology makes it more realistic to automate conversations, and artificial intelligence closely mirrors human interaction, savvy brands will not only be prepared with actual humans who can jump in when needed, they will leverage collaborations with other brands to improve these customer experiences.

Personal Branding

> While brands are becoming more human, humans now
> have access to the tools needed to brand themselves.

Individuals have always had personal brands, otherwise known
as reputations. The difference is, before the internet we lacked
the tools to efficiently build our brands and communicate
broadly without permission from traditional media gatekeepers. Even when someone experienced their 15 minutes of fame
and received media coverage, it was often contained within a
15-mile radius.

When I wasn't listening to John Sterling calling the Yankees
games on WABC, or timing commercial breaks in an effort to
record songs to cassettes from our local Top 40 station Q105,
my preferred radio signal was 660 WFAN. As I noted earlier,
WFAN was the first all-sports station in the country, based in
NYC, and I was just close enough to get a fairly clear signal
where I grew up in Connecticut. The station's programming
kicked off every day with *Imus In The Morning,* a show that
mixed shock-jock humor with politics, sports and pop culture.
Many years before Don Imus was rightfully kicked off the air
for making racist remarks, he was giving Howard Stern a run
for his money and commanded A-list guests.

Imus and his brother Fred had their own side-hustle selling
branded tees, mugs and other novelty items they promoted on
the air. I decided to purchase a few items for a Father's Day
gift and after weeks without anything arriving I called Imus to
complain. I dialed the only publicly available number I could
find repeatedly until I reached the producer Bernie and gave
him my pre-rehearsed schtick. He laughed, told me to hold

and then put me through to Imus. Without further warning we were immediately live on the air and he introduced me as "13-year-old Brady from Connecticut." I was nervous, but as a regular listener I knew exactly how to get a rise out of the host and his crew, so by all measures the call went well. However, what happened next took me by complete surprise. Imus made it clear we were done talking, and while still on the air told his producer to give me the direct phone line so I could call in again. I was blown away. It felt like I was being invited to sit on the couch by Carson after doing stand up (a highly coveted sign of approval from the original king of late night TV).

After calling into Imus again, the local newspaper decided to do a story on my appearances. An incredibly embarrassing picture of me, with braces in full effect, ran on the front page. This was my 15 minutes of fame as a teenager. And while most people I knew locally read the piece, the news stopped there. Not even my out-of-town relatives knew until we mailed them the article.

Contrast this with the weekly video musings I currently post on Facebook, which accumulate hundreds of views and comments from friends, family and strangers who all live outside of my town. This is a very small example of a very big shift in media and the way information travels.

Brands should be respectful of every consumer, regardless of their influence, because it is the right thing to do. But they should also be aware that every individual now has the ability to quickly capture and share their experiences with just a few keystrokes. It is easy to think of instances where a brand or brand representative forgot about this and caused a major PR issue. We no longer need 15 minutes of fame to make an impact. Today it is more like 15 seconds.

While the power of personal brands can have a negative impact, companies can also tap into this same phenomenon and use it to their advantage. By collaborating with specific individuals who have built their own audiences and influence we can create awareness, reinforce a brand's point of view, promote a product or service and directly increase sales. Not to mention doing so in a way that recognizes the fact that consumers trust individuals over brands, as we cited earlier. At the same time, Edelman's 2017 Trust Barometer global study shows that individuals feel a company's social media is more believable than advertising by almost two-to-one, even though social media interactions are often the result of paid efforts given the decline in organic reach.

Today because of personal branding, there are numerous ways to activate an endorsement, and exponentially more individuals for brands to consider teaming up with. Hiring a spokesperson is not a new idea, but prior to social media these relationships were predominantly based on the use of "name and likeness." An artist or an athlete would show up in an advertisement endorsing a product or service, and possibly make an appearance on behalf of the brand. Typically it stopped there.

However, if brands frame their work with individuals as collaborations, rather than just transactions as they did for most of the last century, they will be more successful. As we touched on in Chapter 1 with artists and athletes, and as we will explore more in Chapter 5, associating with a specific personal brand sends a message to consumers and directly informs their perception, especially when it comes across as a partnership and not just an attempt to shamelessly reach people.

Media as Brand

To bring this meta-marketing party full circle, it's important to note that media channels and traditional publishers have become powerful brands in their own right. Because audiences have increasingly limited attention, and unlimited choice, media companies must work harder than ever to establish platforms that stand for something and consistently deliver value. Although not always the case, most media brands also need to build up a variety of channels to distribute content, engage in conversation and build community rather than relying on a single destination or distribution point. This has created opportunities for upstarts and has forced legacy brands to rethink everything.

Bleacher Report is one of the most popular new media brands today and a go-to resource for young people seeking sports news and entertainment. When most thought it would be a fool's errand to take on ESPN, the "Worldwide Leader in Sports," they developed a massive audience by creating a unique voice, perspective and embracing the overall marketing ecosystem, especially digital. Today they reach more fans through social media than their own website and they've taken quite a bit of attention away from the established players. They've also attracted marketing dollars from brands who are beginning to realize Bleacher Report not only has reach and attention, but also influence.

Additionally, media companies like Bleacher Report develop collaborations that blur the lines between content and commerce to complement the traditional advertising model. Content, like their co-branded animated series with Nike *Small Ball,* is shared through social channels and cross-promoted on TV during NBA games. This branded content offering is treat-ed like any other original animated show, and includes personal brand collaborations in the form of celebrity guests voicing characters, such as *Saturday Night Live*'s Michael Che.

Even though upstarts like Bleacher Report are challenging individual Disney-owned properties like ESPN, they are not holding back legacy media brands like Disney from aggressive expansion and progressive marketing. Disney's presence, impact and influence span the media spectrum and challenge all conventional wisdom in terms of defining a brand. As we'll explore in the next chapter, they have a history of collaboration, rooted in exceptional storytelling capabilities, that continues to drive their business today. In fact, their current "digital" offering to other brands says it all. According to their website, "Disney Digital Network creates high quality, digital-first stories and delivers them to Gen Z and Millennial audiences through the platforms and influencers they know best. Add a touch of magic to your next marketing campaign by combining your story with some of the world's most powerful brands."

This evolution of branding in media has created an entirely new environment for product and service-based brands to navigate. When they associate with a media brand in any way, even if they are simply purchasing advertising space, and especially if they are engaging in the more blurry branded entertainment or native content, it reveals something about their brand to the consumer.

In other words, context is increasingly important. It must be thoughtfully considered by both parties and deliberately aligned just like any collaboration. According to the Forces of Change study from Wharton Business School and media buying agency Hearts & Science, "70% of Millennials and Gen X won't like, recommend or purchase products from a brand whose ads appear alongside derogatory, hateful or offensive content." They have even created a name for this type of problematic association: "Negative Reach."

This new reality and importance of context, or juxtaposition, reinforces the value of true partnerships and bespoke marketing programs. Leading companies understand this emerging dynamic and rely on it to entice brand partners. Once again, Disney shows their aptitude in the way they communicate this in their branded entertainment messaging: "We understand how important it is to protect your brand's integrity. By partnering with Disney, your customers will associate your company with one of the world's most trusted brands."

It's also interesting to think about the evolution of personal brands within the evolution of media brand building. We knew Ted Turner was behind CNN, which now owns Bleacher Report, but he wasn't typically front and center. More recently, Arianna Huffington created a media brand around her personal brand with the Huffington Post, although a key differentiator was their large contributor network. And while she's moved on in many ways, and very few stories are associated with her, she continues to create content and develop her personal brand in a way that reflects the values of the platform. One of the Huffington Post's most popular sections is about mindfulness and healthy living, which launched on the heels of Arianna's book about finding balance after she fell during a particularly stressful time in her career.

Another individual who has built a series of media brands in concert with their personal brand is Bill Simmons. When Bill started writing his Page 2 column for ESPN, what stood out most was his use of pop culture. He was the only person who had the confidence, foresight and ability to weave things like *Beverly Hills 90210* into articles about sports. He used these references, and his unapologetic bias for certain teams—his first writing moniker was "The Boston Sports Guy"—to distinguish himself and develop a personal brand that was arguably more relatable than anyone in his field.

Beyond personal branding, he launched a series of new brands in and around ESPN including Grantland and the award-winning 30 for 30 documentary platform. After a political battle with the powers that be at ESPN, Bill left to launch a new media brand, The Ringer. Interestingly, he started the company with a unique combination of media platforms: an email newsletter and a series of podcasts that he personally hosted or appeared on. Bill has now surrounded himself with a team of individuals, including some with their own emerging personal brands, but make no mistake: The Ringer is inextricably linked with Bill's personal brand.

In the convergence of personal branding and media we also have The Player's Tribune, a platform founded by former New York Yankee Derek Jeter that allows athletes to cut out journalists, author their own articles and speak directly to fans through a channel that feels more like a traditional publication than social media. Lebron James has launched his own athlete-driven media platform, Uninterrupted, and put himself front and center, especially when it comes to working with brands. One of the early features was a branded series about finance created in partnership with Chase. The show's theme song, Jay-Z's "Dead Presidents 3," name-drops Lebron and a phrase that became the title of this Uninterrupted series: Kneading Dough. The result is an effort that checks a number of boxes—value, values, believability, culture and collaboration.

To further illustrate this evolution and convergence, many of the top media companies have actually created or acquired advertising agencies and digital marketing firms. The New York Times Company operates T Brand Studio and their tagline illustrates the value proposition they hope brands will buy into: "Stories That Influence The Influential." These and other entities like Virtue, the in-house agency of Vice Media, focus on creating branded content for advertisers that feels more authentic to the platform and arguably connects better than the content an outside agency might develop.

Media publishers are also tapping into their own archives for creative ways to build their brands and find new revenue streams. For example, in 2017 *The Washington Post* announced a partnership with Storied Media Group, which now represents their intellectual property in Hollywood. This creative approach to business doesn't come as a surprise especially when you consider the publication's enterprising ownership. After generations of management by a single family, in 2013 the paper sold to Amazon's founder and CEO Jeff Bezos.

While we're on Bezos, he also owns the go-to media brand and platform for streaming video game play, Twitch. If you're still wondering why people watch others play video games, get over it. This phenomenon is not only here to stay, it's evolved into a legitimate profession with eSports players, teams and leagues commanding sponsorships from the likes of Axe, Coca-Cola, Geico, Nissan, Intel, T-Mobile, Sour Patch Kids and many more. This is yet another media platform where personal branding plays a huge role, as eSports athletes are inherently connected and digitally savvy. While there are formal teams, just like in music, players also form alliances that resemble hip-hop collectives.

One of the most popular groups in eSports is known as FaZe Clan, with dozens of members including those who compete and others who simply create content to keep fans entertained. In hip-hop, for example, we have A$AP Mob and their artists A$SAP Rocky, A$AP Ferg, A$AP Ty Beats and others.

FaZe Clan has FaZe Timid, Faze ClipZ, FaZe Rug and the list goes on.

In addition to Twitch, live events and podcasts, much of the eSports action takes place on YouTube, where these influential personalities build their own channels and nurture huge audiences. Beyond brand sponsorships, FaZe Clan also has an extensive collection of their own apparel, including a limited edition t-shirt collaboration with the Pittsburgh Steelers wide receiver JuJu Smith-Schuster. This is the kind of progressive collaboration that remains below the radar, relatively speaking, but is poised to become more common. There's *fit* because JuJu is an avid gamer and an extremely savvy marketer with his own popular YouTube vlog. Given this digital presence, it's not surprising that his jersey sold more than any other NFL rookie in 2017. He had a great season, as did his team, but he also plays the personal branding and collaboration game extremely well.

Media companies are also monetizing their brands through new products and services. One example is *The New York Times,* which now offers luxury travel accompanied by journalists with trips topping out at over $100,000. They have lower priced items too, including t-shirts, water bottles and notebooks. When it comes to further diversifying revenue and monetizing their intellectual property (IP), the Times also offers niche content subscriptions that provide access to archives of content, including recipes that have been repurposed and reorganized.

In an even more overt connection between content and commerce, the magazine-driven media conglomerate Condé Nast was the lead investor in the popular global shopping platform Farfetch. After their own attempts to build out a concurrent ecommerce business under the Style.com banner, they sold that domain and the related IP to Farfetch in a separate deal from their earlier funding. The intention is to find ways for brands like *Vogue* and others across the Condé Nast portfolio to monetize content with the help of Farfetch. In a Business of Fashion article announcing the deal, Jonathan Newhouse, chairman and chief executive of Condé Nast International, said, "As an early investor in Farfetch, this partnership is the next step in our evolving business relationship. It further unites two leaders in their respective sectors, combining best-in-class content with the world's leading online luxury shopping destination."

Vogue magazine has also experimented with their own branded products, primarily through collaborations like the one launched with Kanye West's former creative director and designer/owner of the brand Off-White™, Virgil Abloh. For this effort Abloh, a formally trained architect and multi-disciplinary artist who received a Grammy nomination for designing Kanye and Jay-Z's *Watch The Throne* album, developed a line of clothing for Burton that was also co-branded with Vogue. There's no doubt Vogue is an iconic media brand, but it was a coup for them to be overtly featured in a collaboration led by a designer with as much youthful buzz, social clout (1.4 million Instagram followers) and credibility as Virgil. (Off-White™ won the 2017 British Fashion Award for "Urban Luxe Brand," among other industry honors.)

The reality is, legacy media brands like Vogue need collaborations like this to stay relevant. The timing also proved to be fortuitous, as just a few months after the debut of this collaboration Abloh was named the next artistic director of men's wear at Louis Vuitton. For Burton, this partnership also reinforces an extensive collaboration strategy and platform, which we'll discuss more in Chapter 8.

Recently an issue of another Condé Nast property, *Bon Appetit,* showed up in my mailbox. It was labeled "Special

Issue" but looked fairly typical. When I flipped open to the first page I was met with an ad from Google explaining that the entire issue was special because it was branded. "The kitchen is a place to question and experiment. How can I make this tastier? Healthier? It's this freedom of imagination—the courage to do things differently—that Google strives to embody. That's why Google is bringing you this issue of *Bon Appetit,* which boldly challenges how we see, eat and experience food from around the world."

There were no traditional magazine ads in this issue, just a few pages where Google's Pixel 2 phone was part of the food content. And even these pages were created in collaboration with three food influencers—a food artist, a chef/author, and a creative pasta maker—who each have their own audiences.

To make things even more confusing in the land of media, we now have agencies creating and purchasing publishing brands such as Cycle Media, which is owned by the agency Laundry Service, which, in turn, is owned by the holding company Wasserman Media Group, a company rooted in sports with a history of brokering lucrative partnerships and venue naming rights. The tagline showcasing Cycle's hybrid of consumer media channel, influencer network, production company and branded entertainment offering sums up many of the themes we've covered thus far: "Cultural Relevance. Premium Content. Guaranteed Reach." Oh, and the word that Cycle uses in the navigation of their website—where most, including Disney, say "Advertise With Us"—is "Collab."

This is just a small sample of the changes taking place in media and branding. If it feels a bit random, that's intentional. It's the wild west y'all.

Choose Your Friends Wisely

As this overview of the current brand landscape illustrates, brand affinity is extremely complex. Yet, in many instances it can be boiled down to one idea: individuals associate with brands they identify with. In other words, they feel certain brands reflect or reinforce their own stories. The stories they tell themselves about who they are, who they want to be, what they believe in and how they want others to view them. Essentially, brands are like badges that inform an individual's identity. This is why a product may be seen favorably when it is introduced through a team, player, artist, trusted individual or another brand. These can provide familiar reference points that create awareness and often change the way brands are perceived.

Consumers also seek out brands that stand for something or provide benefits beyond the product or service. As Simon Sinek explained in his often-cited TED Talk and books, "People don't buy what you do, they buy why you do it." They want to engage with brands that evoke an emotion, brands that are increasingly human, culturally aware, proactive and collaborative.

With this backdrop, it now takes a certain type of marketer to succeed: one who understands technology, is comfortable analyzing data and is accountable to the bottom line, but also one who pays close attention to culture and knows how to develop a brand with a sense of humanity and purpose that people can connect with.

It may sound simple, but we have the opportunity to inform all of the above, the way brands are created, promoted and experienced, by overtly developing a collaboration strategy. This approach creates additional points of entry, leverages related references that lend credibility, provides opportunities for interaction and shapes an ecosystem for a brand to exist within. Yes, just as we see in sports and music, brand collaborations are the modern marketer's equivalent of a Swiss Army knife. Collaboration has infinite possibility and it can make or break a brand.

Motivational speaker Jim Rohn famously said, "You are the average of the five people you spend the most time with." This now holds true for brands.

When marketers understand the dynamics at play within the new and expanding marketing landscape, they realize proactively aligning with other brands is critically important.

Spending time with other brands correlates to who you partner with for promotions, the banner next to yours in a sports arena (not to mention the sports team you're sponsoring), the athlete you are endorsing, the charity road race you're supporting, the tortilla chips you're using to sample your salsa, the sneakers paired with your denim brand in a photo shoot, the photographer, the Instagram influencer you invited on set and even the location of your photo shoot. Each of these has a "brand" that reveals something about yours. Though some of these may look like simple adjacencies, context is critically important and informs the way your brand is perceived. As we'll explore later, you can take these partnerships even farther with more overt collaborations like co-creating and co-branding.

At this point you may agree with the collaboration thesis, yet feel that other pressing matters must be prioritized. If this is the case, know that when a brand refrains from collaborating it doesn't get a pass. The brand simply leaves it up to the consumer to decide which brands they are associated with. In other words, the way you are perceived is directly impacted by the other brands you are aligned with and surrounded by, regardless of whether you lead or let the consumer choose their own adventure and make assumptions about where you *fit* into culture and their lives.

> That's why today it's not about whether or not brand collaborations should be a part of your strategy, it's what brands to align with and how to bring these partnerships to life.

MODERN MARKETERS: **Chad Wagenheim**

For the most part we'll talk about collaboration from a marketing standpoint, but let's keep in mind that brand partnerships are driven by a variety of factors, including operations, manufacturing, distribution and of course sales. In terms of the latter, a popular and proven path to increasing revenue is brand licensing. Based on the increasingly broad definition of a brand, as outlined above, if you're in the business of licensing, or considering it, it's time to evaluate opportunities through the lens of collaboration. Even if licensing is not something you're working on, or plan to explore, the discipline involves layers of collaboration and creative business practices we can all learn from.

With that in mind, I connected with Chad Wagenheim, EVP Strategic Development & Operations, for Sequential Brands Group, Inc. Sequential Brands Group promotes, markets, and licenses a portfolio of consumer brands including Martha Stewart, Emeril Lagasse, Jessica Simpson, GAIAM, William Rast (co-founded by Justin Timberlake), AND1, Avia, Joe's Jeans, Revo and more.

When you are seeking or evaluating a brand extension, collaboration or licensing partnership that involves two brands presented side-by-side to the consumer, what criteria do you prioritize?

The key with co-branding is always to ensure that the brands complement rather than compete with each other as best as possible, and that they share a consistent strategy in terms of where to play (tier, pricing, target demo, etc). With any co-brand or license opportunity, we prioritize the same diligence process to ensure that the other brand or license has the following: best-in-class sourcing and/or manufacturing capabilities; the highest standards with testing and consumer safety standards; an excellent and proven distribution model; proof that the business is well-capitalized; and finally, confidence in management.

What are the benefits of exclusive retail partnerships, like the one between Martha Stewart and Staples, as opposed to creating and distributing a branded product line more broadly?

There are many benefits to taking the DTR (direct-to-retail) path versus the third-party manufacturer/supplier path. First, you are going to be much more important to the retailer under a DTR scenario because they will treat you like their own private label brand, versus a regular vendor. This usually means more shelf space and more marketing support, and of course because of the nature of your relationship they are cheering for you to be successful. Another benefit is that DTRs are typically longer in term. If you have the right partner and structure, you work together to build something for years to come. Any DTR deal should be entered into with the mindset that the business will last for at least 5–10 years if done right. Finally, while most retailers aren't a sure bet in this environment, DTRs usually come with the assurance that your partner has A+ credit.

What led to the Emeril Lagasse acquisition on behalf of Martha Stewart Omnimedia?

We were looking at 2–3 other brands as well as Emeril at the time that we decided to buy his merchandise and media businesses. We saw it as a terrific opportunity to simply "bolt on" his business to our platform. He had products in the food, kitchen and housewares spaces, as well as a media business with TV and books, just as we did. We inherited his top line revenues, and took on minimal costs beyond that, so it certainly improved our overall margin structure. We were well positioned to grow his business based on our retail relationships and in-house design, creative and content production resources. We certainly believed that we had a great platform to increase his business from a promotional perspective, as we had him on Martha's NBC live show on a regular basis and also added a column for him in our Martha Stewart Everyday Food Magazine, as examples.

A number of your brands collaborate with celebrities, creators and influencers, such as recent partnerships between Joe's Jeans and models Bella Hadid and Taylor Hill, as well as NFL athlete Julian Edelman. How can brands minimize risk and maximize exposure and influence when developing collaborations with individuals?

For the names you listed, we have traditional spokesperson/brand ambassador deals in place. Meaning, they partner with us to help promote our products and have some involvement with the design process. It's critical to find someone who has a good track record of being a solid brand partner and stays away from bad PR. From there it's all about the contract, which has highly negotiated terms in it covering everything from term, requirements for service days (press, production, in-store, photography, etc.), definitions for exactly what a service day entails, approvals over usage of name and likeness, approvals over where and how the talent's IP can be utilized, and non-competes, among other things.

Today a key element is a specific schedule regarding exploitation of the talent's social channels. You minimize risk by having a great partner, a great contract with clear deliverables, and a strong relationship. Another important item with a traditional spokesperson deal is to be careful not to reach too high and pay too much for someone who may appear to be an amazing person for your brand, while in reality the money is so small for them compared to other projects that they will end up not prioritizing your partnership.

We are also starting to do more non-traditional spokesperson deals. For these we really involve our celebrity partners even more in the design process, as we want them to be invested in the product and feel great about wearing it and talking about it. The prize is when your celebrity partner goes above and beyond their contractual obligations. If someone wants to get involved with trend direction, design process, etc., we love that as it means they really want to be a part of the business.

Many of your brands have develop multi-tiered partnerships like the one between Martha Stewart, Marley Spoon meal delivery service, and AmazonFresh. Are there specific market forces driving the opportunity for unique opportunities like this where more than two brands are strongly aligned?

For us it's all about brand monetization, wherever it makes sense, while always ensuring that we preserve brand vitality. The deal between Martha Stewart, Marley Spoon and Amazon-

Fresh is an example of us wanting to play in a category (meal kit delivery) and knowing as a pure-play licensing company that we needed a partner to get into the business. We met with all of the players in the space and felt that Marley was the right partner for us. After about 6–9 months of business together, we saw AmazonFresh as a terrific way to gain market share. They allowed us to go after a different customer with a similar product offering. Our strategy is to make ourselves available wherever and however the customer is shopping.

Outside of the Sequential portfolio, are there any brands you admire for their creative approach to partnerships?

Nike is always top of mind as the best in the business when it comes to maximizing the promotional power of their brand partnerships. The authentic and emotional connection between their brand and their celebrity partners which is always on display through all of their creative assets is always a winner in my book.

▼ ▼ ▼

Creativity and Collaboration

I heard a quote recently by the author and poet William Plomer that speaks to the power of collaboration and why it will always be important:

> "Creativity is the ability to connect
> the seemingly unconnected."

Plomer's take on this was an a-ha moment for me. Collaborations are often rooted in connecting the seemingly unconnected, or unexpected, which makes them inherently creative. The novelty of a collaboration also generates feelings of intrigue and excitement. It can make discovering and experiencing a product or service even more fun.

I was personally inspired by the fact that this theory of creativity and connection reinforces the value of collaboration for everyone, and that it complements the classic definition of the word "collaborate" from Merriam-Webster: "to cooperate with an agency or instrumentality with which one is not immediately connected."

The origin of the word collaboration comes from the Latin word *collaborare*, which translates into "to labor together." How fitting that the word ends in *rare*, considering the result of a collaboration can only come from the brands that have created it. Just as every fingerprint is different, so are collaborations. They are truly collabo-RARE.

Unfortunately, people are often afraid to do rare work and champion the idea of a collaboration within their organization. It requires leadership and vulnerability. It means stepping up and selling people internally and externally on your vision. But we also need to build a culture of collaboration in and around the marketing function and recognize that it is critical for every business. We'll dive into the personal side of collaboration and creativity more in Chapter 9.

CoLAB: *Curiosity*

If you are still with me and excited about collaborations, try the experiment below and explore the brands that you have already invited into your life. Then read the next chapter on the roots of brand collaboration in entertainment and the underlying principles that make collaborations impactful.

Dig into your own habits and the brands that live in your personal ecosystem. You won't have to go very far; start by taking a walk around your living spaces including your kitchen cabinets, refrigerator and freezer. Do you notice any themes?

Now take a look at your closet and your garage. Again, what themes or patterns are you seeing?

Next, survey your social media channels. Is there a theme to the things you share and talk about?

Now take a piece of paper and list out all of these brands. I know—this may be a long list. Can you group them in any way? What do these brands have in common? How are they different?

When you think of these brands as they are part of your life, what do they say about you?

CHAPTER 3

Foundation for Collaboration

*"I used to be embarrassed because I was just a comic-book
writer while other people were building bridges or going on to
medical careers. And then I began to realize: entertainment
is one of the most important things in people's lives."*

—Stan Lee, Marvel Comics

"DAD, WILL YOU please tell me a Batman story? I promise
I'll go right to sleep after that."

Bedtime was typically a negotiation in our house. Although
I enjoyed reading books—more like having them read to me—
there was a phase where all I wanted to hear was one of my father's improvised adventures. They were always built on a similar formula where Batman would find himself in a predicament
and then I would be worked into the storyline to help save the
day. Sometimes he would weave in other friends, family members or characters from pop culture. I can distinctly remember
how thrilling it was to be a part of the action and to see who
else would show up.

I didn't realize it until recently, but this is my first memory of what it feels like to experience a brand collaboration and where my fascination with this phenomenon started. I now see how my father used familiarity, creativity, connection and storytelling to capture my attention, and how the same formula, though not always overtly called out as collaboration, has been deployed by brands time and again to pique my interest.

Synergy: Opposites Attract

When everything you know about one brand or personality crosses over with another, it creates something completely new. If the two are strategically aligned, this cross-pollination is extremely valuable. It is similar to the idea that the whole is greater than the sum of its parts (1+1=3). The association also reveals more about each respective brand and their values. This is why proactive collaboration is such a powerful mechanism to reinforce the way a brand is perceived. It takes the idea of guilt by association and turns it into a positive.

But you can't just throw anything together and expect a favorable outcome. That's where the phrase "seemingly unconnected" from Plomer's theory of creativity that we discussed in Chapter 2 becomes important. For a collaboration to be truly effective, brands have to complement each other in some way and ultimately create mutual benefit. Brands also need to be sure the collaboration story is effectively communicated so the benefit to the consumer is clear.

Like any creative endeavor with a specific goal in mind, collaborations require a mix of art and science. A little tension can be positive and generate intrigue, but too much may mean the brands are not a true *fit* and the story lacks believability.

When we look at brand marketing through this lens, we can say that a successful collaboration is based on synergy. That's a fancy word often thrown around conference rooms, but it's actually quite practical. According to our old friends Merriam-Webster, synergy is "the increased effectiveness that results when two or more people or businesses work together." This definition reminds us that collaborations, just like great partnerships, have to be win-win.

Combine this with the fact that today marketers have the opportunity to be even more creative given the variety of channels and unique ways brands communicate, and you can see why it's such an exciting time to be in the space.

As we explored in Chapter 2, brands have been humanized, and in many ways humans have become brands. Both are now capable of reaching huge audiences, rivaling what only traditional media was capable of for decades. The idea that product-related and service-related brands, as well as individual brands, can now engage in so many different mediums also increases the options for collaboration. Add the sheer number of brands that now exist, and the increasingly global nature of our economy, and it's easy to see that opportunities for creative partnerships are infinite. However, these changes also make it difficult for brands to reach people and hold their attention. That is why the collaboration must be communicated and launched with a comprehensive campaign that relies on a variety of different tactics or activations that tell the story. Activations equate to all of the different touchpoints, or points of entry, where consumers encounter a brand. Whether online or offline, the more interactive and engaging these experiences are, the better.

A fall 2017 study on millennials and the luxury goods market, authored by Claudia D'Arpizio of Bain & Co., explained how Gucci has adopted a variety of new practices including unique activations in-store that keep people coming back. "The store has become like the theater where the brand's creativity is living and taking place, where you come for the different stories that the brand is telling," she said of Gucci in a 2017 Bloomberg article about the study. "You want to go there many times to see what's next, what's different."

Gucci has also relied on a number of collaborations, including a 2017 partnership with streetwear pioneer Dapper Dan, whom we'll talk more about later.

When Everything Old is New Again

The Batman stories deliberately represent a subtle example of collaboration from my youth, but I believe studying these entertainment-based subtleties can help us all hone the skills we need to identify synergies, tell great stories, and successfully execute marketing collaborations for our own businesses and brands. This is especially true now, when so much of the work brands do must treat marketing like theater, just as Gucci demonstrated in the example above.

Advertising and entertainment have always gone hand-in-hand. If you're a baby boomer then you probably remember the first instances of brands sponsoring TV content. This actually looked a lot like the public radio "support" that brands still provide on NPR. In fact, some of the first soap operas were originally radio programs sponsored and produced by Procter & Gamble to promote their household goods. It was believed this form of entertainment was appealing to the same audience, and with content "brought to you by" a brand like Oxydol soap, P&G hoped the commercial messages would be seen as a reminder that they were adding value by enabling the show to exist, rather than simply interrupting programming.

This early form of what we now call sponsored content or branded content adheres to the synergy rule—value is created for both parties. In this case the product and the entertainment brands both cater to the same audience. Rather than relying on the typical commercial format, sponsored and branded content allows commercial brands to take credit for delivering entertainment, escapism, education or inspiration to the audience, while gaining positive awareness with new potential customers and reinforcing their value to existing ones. I call this a collaboration because both parties are directly linked. If the commercial brand isn't seen in a positive light, it calls into question the value of the entertainment brand. Alternatively, if the entertainment brand isn't actually entertaining, then the perceived quality of the commercial brand may decline.

I was not alive when the first soaps aired, but I was born just in time to experience the impact of another storytelling platform that was supported by stellar marketing: Star Wars. The franchise was a true phenomenon that touched our lives in many different ways. This played out in movie theaters, on TV, on the playground and at the top of my holiday wish list. All of it was based around the exciting story that piqued our collective imaginations and transported us to another galaxy. It was intoxicating, and created a brand platform that is as popular today as it was back then. From a marketing standpoint, Star Wars allowed us to discover and engage with the brand through various points of entry, and it became part of our culture, just like sports and music.

Not to take anything away from the films, since they can certainly stand on their own, but it's important to remember that Star Wars has always relied heavily on merchandising and licensing to increase reach and relevance. Star Wars action figures were prized possessions that I dragged my parents around searching for. These toys and accessories were often in demand because of slight variations to each collection, character and packaging, based on different storylines. However, in addition to selling branded products like toys in traditional retail environments, successful entertainment brands like Star Wars also develop collaborations that create connections in unexpected places.

Delivering the Unexpected

Around the same time that Star Wars entered the cultural zeitgeist, fast food chains such as McDonald's and Burger King began an era of aggressive expansion and marketing.

One part of the strategy became framing a visit to their restaurants as a reward for kids, and a convenient and inexpensive tool for parents.

As fast food brands became synonymous with fun and socializing, they became a popular partner for entertainment brands. Each chain offered commemorative co-branded glasses, special-edition action figures and other tchotchkes with the purchase of kids meals. Through "limited time" promotions, these brands challenged kids and adults to "collect* them all," which translated to even more demand, or nagging if you were a parent. I was a bit too young to recall the Star Wars Burger King glasses, but I distinctly remember collecting a number of Muppet-themed toys at McDonald's when my Bubbie, aka grandmother, and Aunt Etta would routinely take me there after nursery school. Their friend Edna worked at the local McDonald's and made sure we didn't miss any of the toys.

Collect can be an interesting spin on consume. It implies demand, value, repetition and it bakes in an element of creativity into the purchase. It gives the consumer permission to covet something and attempts to shape it as a productive outlet. As we will explore later, brand collaborations often benefit from the same layer of scarcity, or merely the perception of it, to create additional demand.

It's fair to challenge and debate the ethics of a brand like McDonald's and their use of toys to lure in kids and parents, but from a marketing perspective their entertainment-based collaborations were undeniably effective. These pairings also worked because McDonald's was positioned as an entertainment brand itself, not just a place for food. They had their own platform that was ripe for other brands to join, including characters like Ronald McDonald and my favorite, the Hamburgler. All of this came to life through their advertising and in the restaurants, which felt like a combination theater and amusement park. Everything tied back to an overarching value proposition and supported the same story, including the co-branded toys and games. This created mutually beneficial relationships, as McDonald's and the entertainment brands were borrowing from one another.

McDonald's attached themselves to reward, adventure, imagination and celebration. They also relied on these collaborations to extend engagement with their brand beyond the five minutes it took to scarf down a burger and fries. Similarly, the entertainment brands benefited by inserting themselves into a fast food ritual that was developing across the world, not to mention the exposure they received from McDonald's advertising.

But Hollywood licensing deals and brand collaborations went far beyond film and fast food. It became a lucrative business, and a great way to market, that continues to expand today. In 2017, *Star Wars: The Last Jedi* aligned with some of the usual subjects like Lego, Campbell's Soup and Nissan. However, it also teamed up with fashion brands Rag & Bone and Po-Zu footwear; the U.K. postal service; NVIDIA graphics cards; and smaller companies such as Brooklyn-based Ample Hills Creamery for limited edition ice cream flavors and a 12-person German beverage startup called Drink Department One on a sparkling juice.

Collaborating With Character

One day while watching an episode of *Scooby-Doo* I realized my father didn't invent the idea of worlds colliding in the way they did in his made-up stories. Shaggy and the gang were up to their usual antics when all of the sudden a few new characters entered the scene. They had never been on the show before, but they were extremely familiar. It was The Harlem Globetrotters. Turns out they had their own animated series in the early 70s, but I only knew them from my love of sports and their live tour. The intersection of these two entertainment brands was exhilarating. In later *Scooby* episodes The Addams Family, The Three Stooges and my old friend Batman all made appearances.

As I reflect on this I'm reminded that the World Wide Wrestling Federation was another place where collaborations played a huge role. When I was a kid Hulk Hogan was by far the most popular character. He was one of the "good guys" and his brand extended into action figures, clothing, movies and cartoons, much like the Star Wars cast. When he teamed up with Randy "Macho Man" Savage, another one of my favorite wrestlers, to form the tag-team group the Mega Powers, I felt that familiar sense of excitement that only comes from collaboration. Now that I think about it, every tag-team pairing was rooted in the principles of collaboration, and the best ones were also unexpected.

Even sitcoms got in on the act. When I was about ten years old the highlight of the week was TGIF, a lineup of Friday night shows. I'll never forget when two of my favorites, *Full House* and *Family Matters*, crossed over characters. It captured my attention and sparked my imagination in ways that rarely happened while watching the shows individually. The only other episode of *Full House* that comes close to being that memorable was the one when The Beach Boys showed up.

If you're a comic book fan, you know that your favorite superhero periodically makes an appearance in a completely separate series, tapping into this same entertainment trick. Just like the guest appearances on *Scooby Doo*, the entire world of comic books relies on collaboration as a key ingredient to maintaining the intrigue that continues to drive the platform's relevance today. For example, the film *Batman vs. Superman*, although not well received by critics, paired two comic book icons and led to a record grossing opening weekend. *Justice League*, *Fantastic Four* and other franchises draw on a similar formula. In even grander collaborative fashion, Marvel, one of the largest publishing companies in the comic space, was acquired by Disney.

The Business of Synergy

No matter what age you are, you're familiar with Disney and their endless sub-brands and characters. This is a company that has mastered collaboration and has an entire department dedicated to synergy.

The brand itself holds the same name as its founder, Walter Elias Disney, who started the company as a cartoon studio and early in his career created one of the most famous characters in entertainment history, Mickey Mouse. Around the same time an enterprising movie theater owner decided to develop a kids club around a Mickey Mouse films, complete with membership cards and special screenings. This turned a trip to see Mickey on the big screen into a chance to be part of a community. It didn't take long before you could find Mickey and his animated friends on every toy, game, article of clothing and household product—including an entire line of branded food. In addition to licensing the brand, Disney also worked on a number of co-branded products including Donald Duck's Nabisco Cheese Quackers.

Walt built his own personal brand alongside the characters by hosting a TV series called *The Wonderful World of Disney.* Content like this drove brand recognition through the roof, especially since in the 1960s and early 1970s there was still a limited number of channels from which to choose.

Although Walt was clearly the voice of the brand, Disney relied on many different voices to engage audiences. Through the creation of movies, TV shows, books, toys and theme parks, Disney literally and figuratively created a world of their own. Each of these entities included distinct yet complementary brands in the form of properties, characters and other unique story elements. The Disney brand was truly an ecosystem that provided endless opportunities to cross-promote their own brands and add value for outside brands. Of course this was all predicated on the value the brand created for consumers in terms of entertainment and experiences, or "magical moments" as we called them when I worked for the company.

MODERN MARKETERS: **Laura Caszatt**

I connected with my friend Laura Caszatt, the Manager of Merchandising/Product Development at The Walt Disney Company. Laura also worked on the expansion of the Star Wars brand after it was acquired by Disney, and I wanted to get her take on the collaboration space and how she keeps the creative juices flowing:

Laura, why do you think collaborations are powerful?

Collaborations are powerful because consumers are constantly expecting something new, unexpected, and disruptive in order to convert to purchasing. Most brands, as powerful as they are on their own, need the boost of another's DNA in order to create such an idea, message, or product. "White space" is now becoming more and more difficult to find and fill, so in order to achieve something unique you really need to reach out and combine forces with the right partner to reach your ever picky consumer. Collaborations can also result in speed to market because both companies bring to the table what they do best and that can speed the process along.

Collaborations are powerful when they are limited and create scarcity. Consumers need to feel like if they don't get it now, they may miss the opportunity. You want your consumer hungry for the next collaboration and your next big idea.

Do you have any favorite collaborations that you've been involved with and what made them successful?

I have had the opportunity to work on many collaborations while working for the Disney Parks. Dooney & Bourke & Disney accessories have become one of my favorites because of the huge fan base and hearing directly from them on their favorite bags. This collaboration was necessary for Disney because we are not experts in leather or premium accessories. Dooney & Bourke was interested in collaborating with us because we have amazing storytelling opportunity and far reaching IP that can create beautiful prints for their bags. I have enjoyed watching the guests create their own Facebook and Instagram pages where they share their bags "in the wild". We collaborate with Dooney at their New York fashion week to ensure we are using the latest shapes, colors, and techniques, and we bring creative content that we feel will our guests will love.

What has made this collaboration successful is that from the beginning we blended storytelling with quality. Dooney is known for their quality of leather, and they register every bag so that if you have any damage to your purchase you can return to them and they will either send you a new bag or repair yours and return. Disney is known for their heritage and creative storytelling so there has been an endless supply of content to create the latest handbag for a Disney lover. We have also been successful because we pay attention to the details and think through every pattern, leather color, etch stain, closure, and print. We have also partnered together on marketing and communication so guests know about launches, special events, and one-time launches that create a high demand and scarcity of the bags.

Any advice for marketers to help make the most of their attempts at brand collaborations? Where to begin, best practices or common pitfalls?

From a marketing perspective, I think the best advice is to know who your consumer/demographic is and ensure you are communicating to them the way they best receive information. Some of our guests do not want constant social media updates, but they would rather have emails that provide a link to our website to purchase new collaborations. We use our Disney Parks blog to ensure our Disney guests are up to date with all new products, and we have a consistent person who writes that communication. He has become popular with guests in his own right, but I think what makes it successful is the consistency. Guests know what to expect and they look forward to hearing from him.

For retailers—my best advice is to not try and collaborate with everyone, but to really choose meaningful brands that are the right *fit* for your product or message. We have created filters that we internally use anytime a brand approaches us to collaborate, and we also use the same filters when we are deciding who we want to approach. At the core of our filter system is the theory that the brand we collaborate with has to elevate the Disney brand in some way that we cannot do on our own. It needs to be a relevant brand that is already known in the market, and not emerging but already established themselves in the marketplace and to our guests.

I have found common pitfalls are to move too quickly and not ensure the proper legal documents are signed so that both companies' trademarks are protected. It is important to always ensure that both companies understand the process and the timeline for the project and that the creative teams are trained on how multiple brand names can be used on the same item or marketing.

What do you do when you're looking for creative inspiration?

My creative inspiration changes regularly but I currently love Instagram for instant creativity when I need a mind break. I love following my favorite brands and fashion icons, and I look for images on trending colors, brands, fonts, and silhouettes that I can send to my team.

I love to read magazines and I subscribe monthly to many that I flip through for inspiration on a daily basis.

Another source of inspiration for me is food. I love trying new restaurants and looking for ways to relate trends in food to trends in retail. Currently the "farm to table" trend can be found in boutiques where people want to know where their products come from, and they also expect to see something different every time they shop.

We also encourage our teams to get out and explore. Recently we have started a new monthly secret shopper program where we send groups out to our own stores and others to really learn who the consumers are and to use the information to find scalable ideas for the future. I find so much inspiration from just watching our guests explore, have fun, and watching them use the products that we develop. The best inspiration comes from your own consumers, you just have to listen to them.

▼ ▼ ▼

Most Valuable Marketer

After Disneyland became a clear success, Walt launched a separate company, WED Imagineering, that focused on new ways to extend the brand and push the limits of creativity and technology. This new entity took on nontraditional projects and worked with other brands, enabling them to tap into some of

Disney's creative thinking and engineering talent. This work was prominently featured at the 1964 World's Fair, where WED was contracted to create experiences including the Ford Magic Skyway; the General Electric Carousel of Progress; and the Pepsi-Cola Pavilion, which featured It's a Small World, created for the nonprofit UNICEF.

The corporate investments allowed Walt and his team to experiment, and after the Fair most of the attractions were moved to Disneyland. For Walt, who was quietly planning an east coast version of Disneyland, this was also an opportunity to show off Disney's capabilities to his future audience, develop new experiences and create intellectual property. Doing so by partnering with, and receiving funding from, some of the largest companies in the world was a win-win-win for Walt, his clients and the consumers who enjoyed the innovative and entertaining experiences.

In the 1980s the Disney brand became even more ubiquitous as they launched a cable channel and a chain of retail stores. Most of this activity pointed directly or indirectly to one thing: Disney Theme Parks.

Going to Disneyland or Disney World was the ultimate aspirational vacation and kids begged their parents to take them. And while Disney had kids hooked with so many different ways to engage, the brand always needed a complementary marketing strategy that targeted parents. One way they accomplished this was through a collaboration with the NFL, arguably the most powerful brand in sports. At the end of every Super Bowl, the biggest night in advertising, as millions of fans, young and old, watched the MVP celebrate on the field, a reporter was prompted to ask what they were going to do next. Each superstar, often with their kids on their shoulders, echoed the same five words year after year: "I'm going to Disney World."

This was a brilliant activation on two levels: first, the personal brand collaboration between Disney and the NFL athlete in their ultimate moment of glory and popularity; and second, the sponsored, or native content, which integrated a marketing message into the telecast itself rather than the commercials. The brand was part of the story and a cultural moment.

Those promotions made an impression on me and I too begged my parents to take me to Disney. They did, and our trips fueled a lifelong affinity for the brand. After college I spent a short time working for Disney and became even more impressed with the company. I'll never forget when my roommate at the time, Anthony, came home after seeing Tom Brady being ushered down Main Street in the Magic Kingdom following his first Super Bowl win. Since then I have watched closely as the brand has become even more dominant. Disney now owns Star Wars, ESPN, Hollywood Records and Marvel, as mentioned earlier. They have solidified their position in our culture through not only original content and experiences, but also endless collaborations that celebrate new and old characters. To understand just how iconic the brand has become we can point to the fashion space, where everyone from Pharrell's Bathing Ape to Gucci, Coach, Dooney & Bourke, Kenzo and dozens of others have joined the party by teaming with Disney.

Get in the Game

Disney's Super Bowl campaign was extremely powerful, but it was a more recent big game moment that served as a tipping point for modern brand collaborations.

The Super Bowl is the one night every year when my obsession with marketing is a bit less obvious since everyone is critiquing the commercials. Over the past decade the marketing activity has expanded beyond TV as brands leverage the web to create additional engagement. And while traditional advertising can be cost-prohibitive, smart marketers have taken advantage of the Super Bowl spotlight by focusing their efforts on original content and social media.

When the lights went out in the Superdome during Super Bowl XLVII, Oreo was quick to react. In addition to their traditional TV ad during the big game, they had a team of marketers working to create real time content that was posted in social media. As fans and players waited approximately 30 minutes for things to brighten up, the brand seized the opportunity and posted an image of a cookie with the caption, "You can still dunk in the dark." This took the internet by storm, ultimately garnering over 500 million media impressions.

While this viral hit is credited with kicking off a wave of real-time and reactive content, I found Tide's effort the following year even more exemplary of how marketing has evolved. Tide decided not to purchase a traditional TV spot, but instead shifted all of their efforts to social media.

During the game, Tide started interacting with other brands by posting content and comments with the hashtag #GetsItOut. For instance, after a Cheerios commercial featured a family getting a new dog, Tide Tweeted, "Adding a puppy to the family @Cheerios? Beware of puppy stains. @Tide #GetsItOut #SB48," and linked to a video that featured both brands. This showed Tide's personality, sense of humor, humanity, and other traits we expect to see from modern brands.

This also marked a relatively new and important evolution in terms of the way brands show up in the world. Cheerios and other brands that Tide engaged had no control over the content. Some would even say Tide hijacked the other brands. But that is illustrative of the brave new marketing world we live in. There's nothing you can do to stop this, but you can counter it, and inform the way you're perceived, by developing your own proactive brand collaborations.

Another recent watershed moment in Super Bowl marketing came in 2017 when Doritos* decided not to air any commercials during the game for the first time in years. However, Doritos found their way into the conversation that night by negotiating a deal that made them the featured product in a commercial for Amazon Echo. Through collaboration, they had a nontraditional presence on the biggest night in traditional advertising.

---

*   *Doritos were actually invented at a Disneyland restaurant before they were turned into a packaged goods brand by Frito-Lay.*

The following year Doritos decided to come back with their own spot, but they did so by sticking with the collaboration theme. This time they worked with Mountain Dew, a brand owned by Frito-Lay, a wholly owned subsidiary of Doritos parent company, PepsiCo. During one of the first commercial breaks *Game of Thrones* star Peter Dinklage appeared, took a bite of the new Doritos Blaze chips and then walked through a room lip syncing to Busta Rhymes. The tight shot of Dinklage expanded to reveal various things catching fire, interspersed with Busta himself in a picture frame rapping along. The spot ended, or so we were made to believe, with Busta's voice-over—"Doritos Blaze a bold new flavor that brings the heat"—a product shot and the hashtag #SPITFIRE on screen.

At the exact point you'd expect the next commercial to begin, everything in the Doritos shot began to freeze. Next a mix of snow and wind swept the entire screen to one side, revealing a shot of Morgan Freeman standing in a similar position as Peter was in the beginning of the previous spot. Instead of a bag of Doritos, Morgan was holding a Mountain Dew Ice. He twisted the cap, took a sip and began lip syncing Missy Elliot's classic "Get Ur Freak On" as, you guessed it, Missy rapped along from in a framed picture as Busta did. Morgan closed the spot with a voiceover about the new Dew and the hashtag #ICECOLD. After that we saw Freeman and Dinklage face off and quickly trade breaths of ice and fire.

For those paying attention to the social media accounts of either brand, this battle, playing off the idea of a traditional rap battle, had been brewing for a few days. While Missy and Busta were hamming it up and trading barbs on Twitter, they were also promoting their new song together which launched a few days before the big game. The brands also released a ton of ancillary content, provoked fans to engage and sponsored Snapchat filters where fans could join the battle and show off their own skills on the mic.

This campaign had a little bit of everything including timely cameos by popular actors, appearances and music by familiar artists timed with the release of a track they are both featured on, a call to action via social media, consumer interaction and engagement, bonus content and a humorous tone that was perfect for the Super Bowl. However, the most unique aspect of this campaign was the way the two brands teamed up and shared the spotlight. We rarely see brands literally split an ad, especially when the stakes are this high.

It would be easy to chalk this up as one clever idea, but in reality it was the culmination of years of progressive marketing and experimentation with collaboration by both brands. As an example, Doritos managed one of the largest crowdsourced video contests ever and tied it to their Super Bowl advertising for years. Mountain Dew has sponsored a platform for music, art, sports and fashion called Green Label since 2008 and worked with a variety of emerging artists and superstars like Lil Wayne with their high profile "DEWeezy" campaign.

Another big winner in the 2018 Super Bowl, while also leaning heavily on collaboration, was Tide. Whereas most brands invest in one concept and one commercial, Tide ran a series of commercials, and created a theme that made viewers wonder each time if they were watching an ad for another product or a #TideAd. In the first quarter the concept was introduced when *Stranger Things* star David Harbour appears in what looks like a stereotypical car commercial. The scene then shifts to what looks like an ad for beer, then diamonds, then razors and even the Amazon Echo, while David explains that what makes it an ad for Tide are the clean clothes. The spot ends with him posing the question, "Does this make every Super Bowl ad a Tide ad? I think it does. Watch and see."

Throughout the game he appears in what looks like an ad for various other products, including Old Spice (also owned by Tide's parent company Procter & Gamble), before each time revealing that it's yet another spot for the detergent. By playing off of these familiar scenarios, and using the context we've come to know from typical ads in each category, this became a sneaky example of collaboration that in some ways represents an evolution from the brand hijacking approach they pioneered during the Super Bowl years earlier.

The key message here: if you want to steer your brand, get in the collaboration game.

It's unlikely you'll have a breakout moment overnight, but if you build upon these principles and stick with it you'll win over the long term. These examples also illustrate the need to build a culture of collaboration within your organization. Without it these more audacious campaigns would not be possible.

You might be playing along at home and thinking, this makes sense for Disney, Amazon, Oreos, Mountain Dew, Doritos and Tide, but those are some of the biggest brands in the world. What about a smaller brand? The good news is that the principles are the same, and later we will explain why and how collaborations allow companies of any size to create a bit of the magic these brands have demonstrated.

License To Brand

Before we move on and explore the ingredients of a successful collaboration, let's talk about the distinction that's often drawn between collaboration and licensing.

Entertainment brands like Disney helped create the licensing industry in the early- to mid-20th century when they began working with other companies to produce the ancillary products like toys and household goods described above. Licensing is essentially renting brand assets (name, logo, characters, etc.) to another entity with a set of parameters. This is typically done when a brand wants to take advantage of the manufacturing, distribution or other unique resources that outside entities can bring to the table.

This is a form of collaboration, although it's rarely labeled this way and it may not be apparent to the customer. Beyond the fine print, it can be difficult to know if you're buying something directly from a brand or from a licensee. Assuming licensed products and services maintain a consistent standard, it's a net positive. But to ensure this the licensor must be selective about who they work with and deliberate about the terms of every deal.

Licensing becomes even more relevant in terms of collaboration when a deal results in the licensor's brand showing up next to another brand; otherwise known as co-branding. As we've explored, and as Chad shared in last chapter's Modern Marketers, one of the most important principles of collaboration is recognizing that each brand is a reflection of the other, which is why it is always important to choose your friends wisely. However, brands often overlook the fact that every co-branded piece of content, experiential activation, product or service is a form of collaboration in the eyes of the consumer.

Furthermore, even when a deal lacks overt co-branding, there's often an element of contextual collaboration similar to what we explored in the last chapter with paid advertising. In this case I'm referring to a retailer or another sales channel where the product is sold. For example, the impact on a licensed brand is quite different when their product shows up at Target vs. JCPenney. Haphazard licensing, typically done in an effort to aggressively drive revenue, is a surefire way to water down a brand. By more frequently viewing licensing as a form of collaboration brands have a better shot at protecting and building long term value.

CoLAB: *Creativity*

It's time for some outside research—and you can take this literally to mean go outside, or just virtually get out of your regular routine. The choice is yours.

Take a walk through a shopping district, or browse your favorite multi-brand shopping website, and try to spot an unexpected collaboration that might look like mismatch on the surface due to the size and stage of the businesses. Essentially you are looking for one large established brand that has teamed up with an earlier-stage, independent, or simply lesser-known brand.

Now attempt to break down the collaboration:

- Do the brands appear to share the same values? How can you tell?

- Think about how they are both showing up. Does it reflect positively on both brands?

- Is it clear why they teamed up? Can you now see the synergy?

Next consider where you discovered this. Does the context or environment reinforce the believability that these two brands genuinely wanted to work together?

From a value standpoint, what might you gain from purchasing this product? Is it clear that by teaming up these two brands have become even more appealing or entertaining?

CHAPTER 4

Establishing Fit

"It Takes Two To Make A Thing Go Right"

—Rob Bass and DJ Easy Rock

WITH SO MANY brands, how do you know which ones to collaborate with? First, let's think back to why consumers favor certain brands before we prioritize our potential partners. Remember, marketing is a mix of art and science.

Barry Schwartz, Professor of Social Theory and Social Action at Swarthmore College, developed a now infamous theory known as the Paradox of Choice. It's based on his study of the feelings people have about decision-making and options. Conventional thinking is that individuals want more choice, but he found this actually brings about negative feelings because it becomes harder to make, and stick with, a decision. This theory also proposes the inverse is true, and individuals are typically more satisfied with less choice.

Prior to Schwartz's work, back in the 1950s, scholar Herbert Simon studied the idea that people do not always seek out "the best" because they don't have the time, knowledge or inclination to do so. In those moments, Simon says, people are "satisficers" ("satisfy" + "suffice") who are fine with "good enough."

In other instances they are "maximizers" who attempt to find the best option.

But the best option is impossible to define, especially given the relatively endless choices we have in any given situation. Therefore, maximizers are ultimately less satisfied with their decisions because they can't forget about the other options they have yet to explore or even know about. They second-guess themselves. Sound like any shopaholics you know?

When I was growing up I regularly heard the cliche, "the grass is always greener on the other side." Basically, it was a reminder to be grateful for what you have and recognize nothing is perfect. This is how a satisficer looks at the world, and Simon argues they are happier with their decisions.

Today, thanks to the internet and other advances in technology, choice is on steroids. In a sense you might say we are all forced to become maximizers, but it can be overwhelming.

So what do we do? Both deliberately, and in many cases subconsciously, our brains look for shortcuts. Psychologists call the mental habits we use to evaluate things heuristics. Essentially, we create certain rules, like the Paradox, that allow us to more efficiently make decisions. And often these turn into questionable judgments, also known as cognitive biases. When we're in a rush, overwhelmed or just trying to process the endless messages and choices we're forced to contend with, we rely on this kind of thinking to get through the day.

In his book *Thinking, Fast and Slow*, psychologist and Nobel laureate Daniel Kahneman breaks down our decision-making into two buckets: "reflexive thinking" or "Thinking Fast," and "reflective thinking" or "Thinking Slow," with the latter requiring more brain power. He explains that our brains constantly go back and forth between the two depending on the situation. In both instances we use the thinking process to create meaning and attach it to the things around us, including brands. Over time we develop built-in biases about certain ones that can impact how we perceive new things we're presented with.

It's easy to go down the rabbit hole on the science, and there are over 200 documented cognitive biases to dig through. Fortunately Buster Benson, formerly of Twitter and now Platform Product Lead at Slack, analyzed and painstakingly grouped them into "the four conundrums of the universe that lead to all biases." Here's how the challenges break down in Buster's epic Medium post, along with his summary on how we react to each one:

1. **Too much information.** Information overload sucks, so we aggressively filter. Noise becomes signal.

2. **Not enough meaning.** Lack of meaning is confusing, so we fill in the gaps. Signal becomes a story.

3. **Need to act fast.** We jump to conclusions. Stories become decisions.

4. **What should we remember?** We try to remember the important bits. Decisions inform our mental models of the world.

If you're ready for a deeper dive, I encourage you to Google Buster Benson and explore heuristics, normative marketing, elaborative encoding and semantic processing. The psychology behind neuro-marketing is fascinating and studying this will become increasingly important as more brands rely on algorithms and artificial intelligence to drive consumer engagement.

However, for the purposes of this book and brand collaboration, the take-away is that we constantly and often unconsciously look for short cuts, points of reference and trusted resources to inform our decisions.

Just as we trust certain friends, experts and influencers, we trust the brands we have an affinity for. And when a new brand collaborates with a trusted brand, we are more likely to engage with that new brand. Even if we've never seen it before, this new brand—or brand that is new to us—has a head start in the race to earn our attention and respect. The likelihood that we also give this new brand our money, loyalty and advocacy depends on where it fits into our life, the value it provides, our own values and the stories we tell ourselves about the world.

$$\text{FIT} = \begin{cases} \text{Shared Values } + \\ \text{Shared Goals } + \\ \text{Shared Target Audiences} \end{cases}$$

Shared Values

As I ate my way through my favorite trade show, the Natural Products Expo, sampling a different organic treat every five feet, I noticed something I had never seen before. One brand began popping up in booth after booth: Sir Kensington, producers of "better for you" condiments.

I first encountered Sir Kensington's branded condiment dispensers at the Teton Waters Ranch booth as I pumped their ketchup onto a grass-fed burger. It was delicious, but more than the taste I was impressed by the alignment of these two brands. I stood there and watched as, one after another, trade show attendees grabbed a sample then reached for Sir Kensington's. Booth space is notoriously expensive at this B2B (business-to-business) trade show, so brands are justifiably territorial. Why would a brand welcome another into their valuable space?

I continued navigating the show floor, "thinking slow" and analyzing every brand message, I soon ran into another Sir Kensington's dispenser, this time at the Alexa French Fries booth. At this point I realized the brand had developed an overt collaboration strategy, and I decided to visit their booth to find out more. That's where I met Patrick Jammet, Sir Kensington's Director of Marketing, who told me they had six different partnerships at this one event.

"It was a strategy that we started at last year's Expo," Jammet explained. "We know that our brand and product is best introduced to people through trial by taste. We always look to acquire as many taste buds and eyeballs as possible, especially at a show like Expo. This was a low-cost, high-reach way to do that."

I asked Patrick if he used any criteria to determine which brands to associate with.

"At Expo West, it's much easier to find brands and products that align or fit with our mission. We always look to align with brands that are disruptive to their category and either natural, non-gmo, or organic."

As Patrick and the Sir Kensington's team demonstrated, every successful collaboration is rooted in shared values. When that is in place, and you add shared goals and a common target audience, you have true collaboration *fit*.

"Don't become a wandering generality.
Become a meaningful specific."

— Zig Zigler

From a values standpoint, it's critically important that your brand has a set of beliefs and a point of view that guides decision-making. The more direct your point of view, the easier for people to decide if they are on board. As we discussed earlier, passionate brand support is developed by clearly articulating why your brand exists, not just what it offers or how it delivers. This kind of clarity in your values and your why helps you identify who to align with for collaborations.

In the case of Sir Kensington's, a core value, and therefore a key criteria when evaluating partners, is clean ingredients. They define this as either natural, non-gmo or organic. They also value the entrepreneurial spirit that it takes be a "disruptive" brand. This is reflected in their packaging, as it looks professional but also feels more handcrafted than the well-known leader in the ketchup category. While in this instance, disruption was coming from an early stage brand, large established players are increasingly recognizing the need to shake things up too. In fact, in the time since this event Sir Kensington's was acquired by the Fortune 500 company, Unilever.

The volume of acquisitions in the food and beverage category has made it more challenging for consumers to know what company they are buying from. Over time, competition and access to information about brands will increase, making the source of ingredients, business practices and ownership more transparent. Collaboration between brands that truly share the same values will become even more important given this new reality. Like any industry shift, this will benefit some and leave others exposed.

Consumers are incredibly savvy when it comes to interpreting marketing messages. After all, we're marketed to constantly from the time we are small children. When you layer that on top of the increased transparency and choice now apparent in the market, it's easy to see why authenticity is so important, even if the term itself is overused. As noted above, our brains have been trained to spot marketing messages and we intuitively know a values mismatch when we see it. That's why a collaboration is meant to promote or reinforce values that are already true for both brands, not to turn a brand into something completely new.

When it comes to values and alignment, another question marketers often ask is whether or not both brands need to share the same tone and voice in terms of their communication style. The answer is that brands can have different personalities as long as they share values and collaborate in a way that is complementary. But how is this achieved?

Shared Goals

What are we hoping to achieve by working together?

To define shared goals, remember that all successful collaborations are mutually beneficial. In the Sir Kensington's example, each brand wanted to introduce their product to retailers and other Expo attendees in a way that mirrored how people actually eat. Teton Waters Ranch knows that people want ketchup on their burgers, so teaming with Sir Kensington's makes sense.

This sounds simple, but that is the beauty of collaboration. Sometimes the best partnerships are straightforward. It may not take much to find common goals that make your combined efforts more compelling than your independent marketing.

Even though collaborations can be simple and straightforward, they can become complex when marketers are more ambitious. The rewards may also be greater, but the execution will only pay off if all relevant players have clearly identified and communicated what they hope to achieve. Additionally, both brands must have the same expectations about the level of effort and resources they will commit to the partnership. It's important to make sure the goals and resources line up. Does one of you have certain manufacturing resources or expertise, a network of passionate ambassadors in key markets, relationships with key retailers? Will these factors allow you to get to market faster, more efficiently or more effectively with the collaboration?

There is nothing wrong with dreaming big and brainstorming all the possible ways brands might be able to work together. However, in my experience it's also beneficial to get a win under your belt in the form of a more temporary collaboration, like an event-based activation, which allows you to build momentum before teaming up on something more complex like co-creating a new product. This is especially helpful if your brand has limited experience with collaboration. In Chapters 10–12 we will explore this in more detail and share a framework for the development of a collaboration. We will also look at collaborations that support specific products, events, seasonal promotions, corporate social responsibility programs and philanthropic endeavors.

R.E.S.P.E.C.T.

If brands have established *fit* in the form of shared values and common goals, and all partners have clear expectations about their contribution, a strong foundation for collaboration is in place. However, a few more ingredients are still required to make the partnership a success.

As the Queen of Soul declared decades ago, respect goes a long way. This means coming to every conversation, brainstorm, production meeting, marketing jam and status call with reverence and appreciation for your partners. Assume they are working just as hard on their own career, brand and business as you are. They likely have bosses, board members, investors, teammates or family members who they are trying to support. Your partners may also be under pressure to deliver results that do not seem linked to your work. They may be nervous to even pitch the collaboration idea, so be a true partner on every level and provide them with guidance, resources and rationale.

"If you're interested in doing good work, the important thing is not to be fearless, the important thing is to be brave. To do it even though you are afraid."

— Fernando Machado, head of brand marketing at Burger King (recipient of the 2017 Cannes Lions Marketer of the Year award)

Delivering Value

We started this chapter with the idea that it takes two to make a thing go right, but it actually takes at least three. That is because when it comes to successfully planning and executing a collaboration, brands must look beyond their own needs. The effort must add value for all of the participating organizations and the audiences they serve.

This is the ultimate litmus test for a successful
collaboration: how will it positively impact the consumer?

As we explored in Chapter 3, brand collaborations set out to
achieve synergy. Regardless of the specific metric, this means
their collective efforts increase their effectiveness. This can be
measured in a variety of different ways, but essentially it boils
down to either adding value for existing customers and/or creating value for new customers.

One way to measure value is to look at the functional, emotional and social utility a product or service provides.

Brands that focus on functionality are relatively easy to
identify. To determine this, ask yourself if the product or service helps you achieve a core task. In his "Jobs to be Done"
theory, author, consultant and professor Clayton Christensen
suggests that brands examine the "job" that consumers are interested in "hiring" a solution for. In other words, examine why
we invite something into our lives and what we expect it will do
for us. This is one way to think about how an existing or new
product or service can deliver value.

In many instances we hire brands to educate us, inspire us
or entertain us. But we also hire for distinctly emotional jobs
like aiding self-expression and gaining confidence. Then there
are things we hire for even more deliberate social impact like
enabling us to be part of a cause or community. As we talked
about earlier, sports and music are inherently communal, and
in some ways we hire teams, players, bands and artists to do
various jobs for us as fans.

When it comes to shopping, most purchases are based on
satisfying, or attempting to satisfy, a combination of needs.
As Clayton explains in his book *Competing Against Luck*, Mc-
Donald's realized commuters hire their breakfast smoothies

because they not only taste great, but the product fits perfectly into the cup holder, requires less juggling than a bagel, leaves no immediate garbage like a banana, doesn't make them feel as guilty as eating a candy bar and the drink lasts for most of their ride.

Brands should never underestimate the impact that comes from making an emotional or social connection, even if their primary goal is functionality. Since the beginning of time, one of the best ways to convey emotion and create connection has been through storytelling. As evidenced by the massive global impact of Hollywood and all of the supporting products, promotions and partnerships, our appetite for stories that spark emotion seems to be insatiable. As we will explore in the next chapter, the most successful brands in the world have developed compelling narratives that communicate their value proposition and increase their appeal.

Customer value can take many different forms, which means it can also be created by brands at any stage, from the initial launch to much later when a brand is established or even iconic. However, age and stage is often a leading indicator of where brands may be strong and where they may be vulnerable. For example, early stage brands rarely have large audiences, so they tend to rely on their youthful voice, tone or style, their cachet as a disruptive force, their roots in a specific geography or the passionate support of a small tribe. All of this can be appealing to established brands that are looking for fresh ideas, access to younger audiences and cultural relevance. At the same time, the established players may have reach and resources that early stage collaborators find appealing. In Chapter 8 we'll look more into collaborations between emerging and established brands, including how these collaborations impact innovation and product development.

Fit On Display

Now that we have established a basic foundation for finding *fit* between brands—shared values, shared goals and shared target audience—let's unpack a few more fun and straightforward collaborations to understand how they applied these principles.

Shortly after Nestlé purchased DiGiorno they decided to cross-promote the two brands by packaging them together in a frozen pizza and cookie dough combo pack. For many consumers the synergy is clear and it checks the functional and emotional boxes. Although you could eat it by yourself, the packaging also implies social value. Who wouldn't be excited if you showed up with pizza and cookies? The collaboration allowed the brands to offer a simple story of convenience and indulgence, reinforcing what they already stood for. The synergy is clear for the brands and the value is clear for consumers.

In this instance, the brands focused on core competencies and simply layered in a new way to merchandise their existing offerings. But what if you want to reach your audience and add value in a completely different way?

After years of listening to customers say how much they loved the smell of their laundry, Charmin decided to seek out a new way to deliver this fresh scent into homes. They approached Air Wick, who then licensed the Charmin brand to create the "Familiar Favorites" line.

That same line includes a scent that is co-branded with the fast food company Cinnabon. For their own efforts in the collaboration world, Cinnabon has expanded to completely new distribution channels through deals with Pinnacle Vodka, Taco Bell, Burger King and Pillsbury.

While Cinnabon could have invested in creating and launching their own vodka, for example, they chose to work with an existing brand that brought resources, expertise, distribution, existing customers and more to the table. Partners like Pinnacle benefit from Cinnabon's brand awareness and clear value proposition—almost everyone has seen, or smelled, Cinnabon in malls, airports and highway rest stops—while adding variety to their own product offering.

In every instance, successful collaborations are born when brands look at where they have existing traction, equity, or value in the eyes of consumers, and then use partnerships to expand the ways they deliver it.

This brings us full circle to where the collaboration work really begins. Brands need to be clear about who they are, who they want to be, why they do what they do and how they deliver value. They need to understand where that value is being realized today and who else might appreciate it. Only then can they begin to think about the other brands that consumers might associate with a similar value proposition.

Marketers can also think about potential partners through the lens of adjacency. Meaning, what would be an extension of your brand that is closely linked to where you show up today? Jumping from the dessert freezer over to frozen pizza is not a huge leap. Neither is going from detergent to air fresheners. Like almost everything in life, there are exceptions but even sweets and vodka are fairly straightforward to connect. These brands also work with many of the same retail partners, so from a contextual standpoint they are already showing up near one another.

Be sure to reflect on adjacency, but remember it's a tool for jump-starting ideation, not a rule that must always be followed. Certainly consider the more obvious extensions for your brand, but also remember what Plomer taught us about connecting the seemingly unconnected. That might seem contradictory, but the idea that marketing is a mix of art and science, as we explored at the beginning of this chapter, is popular for a reason. Both are needed to be successful in our game.

Collaboration requires vision, creativity and leadership, but mining data can certainly provide inspiration and sometimes explicit direction when it comes to identifying partners.

An example of delivering customer value through collaboration is the partnership between ride-sharing company Lyft and fast-food giant Taco Bell. Lyft noticed that riders were gushing on social media when their drivers agreed to take them through the Taco Bell drive-through on their way home, especially late at night. After watching this activity for a while the two brands decided to pilot a new co-branded service explicitly designed to deliver on this drive-through use case. Customers in the test market saw taco icons in their Lyft app, letting them know that drivers were available for rides that include a Taco Bell pit stop. For their part the fast-food giant promoted the partnership and offered riders a special discount. Later we will take a look at the other ways Taco Bell has become a modern master of collaboration, as this is just one of many innovative partnerships they have formed.

As I alluded to in the first few chapters, technology now makes it possible to identify and engage with consumers in ways that were unimaginable until relatively recently. As Lyft and Taco Bell proved, mining data—in this case, carefully paying attention to social media—has also become a great way to identify partners who are a natural *fit* in the eyes of your customers.

Coming Together & Finding *Fit*

The Boston-based apparel and accessories brand Ball and Buck was built with clear brand values and a clear direction in terms of target audiences. The brand's founder, Mark Bollman, started the company in college with just one product, a t-shirt. Like many entrepreneurs before him, including fellow Boston-based t-shirt impresarios and Life is Good* founders Burt and John Jacobs, Mark initially traveled to different college campuses to sell his wares. However, Mark put his own unique spin on the business by offering students the option to customize each t-shirt pocket with different fabrics, colors and patterns. This approach to customization is really a form of collaboration between an individual customer and a brand. It is sometimes referred to as co-creation, a topic we will dig into more in Chapter 13 as we discuss the future of collaborations.

* *LIG is a fascinating example of a brand that stays true to its core values and creates a deep emotional connection. The brand makes people feel good, allows them to be part of a tribe and provides a brand badge that says, "I'm an optimist."*

Eventually Mark opened a retail store in Boston's North End and filled the space with a collection of products from like-minded brands. His criteria for the brands he featured, or curated, started with one key value: the products had to be made in America. In addition to these products, Mark slowly developed the Ball and Buck brand into more than just t-shirts. I remember Mark explaining to me how difficult it was to source every single item from America, especially things like buttons and tags. He was not willing to compromise on this core value as it created a key differentiator that helped the brand establish itself and build a core base of loyal customers.

Because it took a long time to design and manufacture his own products, in the early days he developed a collaboration strategy that enabled him to offer a variety of Ball and Buck branded goods without having to own the production process. These co-branded products created a bridge between his small range of completely original products and the curated goods from other brands that he offered. He developed and sold co-branded jeans with Tellason, a small selvage denim company from San Francisco; boots with Danner, a well-respected outdoor brand from Oregon; and sneakers with New Balance, another Boston-based company with a dedicated production facility in New England. The latter were by far the most popular. And while both brands call Boston home, there's much more to why these brands *fit*.

New Balance is a 110+ year old global brand, and Ball and Buck is a relative newcomer best known in Boston. On the surface that might seem like a mismatch, but remember, size is never a deal-breaker. In fact, a mismatch like this can work to the benefit of both brands. The rationale for this follows many of the marketing trends we discussed in Chapter 2, especially the need for brands to directly engage with consumers more frequently.

Developing a personality can also be challenging for large brands, as opposed to small ones that have visible and active founders like Mark. For example, Mark personally told the story of why he started the company and what drove him to create their first dress shirt in a campaign launch video. He also engaged consumers by continuing to leverage the co-creation process he began on college campuses, initially offering these dress shirts for the first time through Kickstarter, a crowdfunding platform where individuals can pre-purchase or back items they believe in. This is a powerful tool with a built-in marketing function that aids in the development of a brand's voice and story, while allowing consumers to take ownership and feel connected to a brand.

In some instances, large brands have trouble dedicating resources to smaller collaborations like this one because they are hyper-focused on revenue. This is why it's important to clearly define and agree internally at your company, and with your collaboration partner, on the goals and key performance indicators (KPIs) that will be used to measure the success of a collaboration.

Contrary to what Puff Daddy said, it can't be all about the Benjamins all the time. Don't get me wrong, collaborations can drive substantial revenue. However, any successful marketer, entrepreneur or business leader knows that some resources must be allocated to activities that support a brand's long-term vision. That might feel risky, but marketers need to embrace this and executives need to encourage it. Collaborations are not considered part of the classic marketing mix, so they are easily overlooked and underfunded. Hopefully you're beginning to see why that's a mistake you need to help your organization overcome.

> *"We need leaders who realize that empowered*
> *creators, in a network, are able to make*
> *a huge dent in the status quo."*
>
> — Seth Godin

One way to build value beyond revenue with a collaboration is to deliberately limit the quantity of items sold. Just as we touched on with the McDonald's toys I coveted as a kid, large brands, especially in the footwear space, have relied on scarcity for many years to increase short- and long-term demand. In almost every instance they have the capacity to create more of these products, but psychologically most of us want what we can't have, so this strategy works incredibly well when it comes to creating buzz and justifying higher prices. This is exactly what Ball and Buck and New Balance achieved by offering a limited number of collaborative sneakers.

When the product launched it sold out within hours and received media coverage in publications ranging from *GQ* to dozens of "sneakerhead" websites. The two had clearly established *fit* and launched in a way that resonated with audiences. In this case, Ball and Buck benefited from the kind of much-needed exposure that early ventures crave, and the validation that a big brand collaboration can provide.

For their part, New Balance used the collaboration to express their brand personality by hanging with a cool upstart, reinforced their U.S. manufacturing story, generated coverage in fashion magazines, and garnered much-needed street cred with lifestyle enthusiasts. That last item was extremely important to the New Balance brand, as they have primarily been known for their performance footwear and sometimes overlooked by the lucrative fashion footwear category. When brands crossover and find relevance in both areas, as competitors Nike and adidas have done so masterfully, sales soar. Ironically, it is the performance side of New Balance that really makes their brand a *fit* for Ball and Buck since so many of Mark's products are functional.

Next Level Collaboration

When you have clearly defined who you are and why you exist, and you tell that story consistently through quality products, content and experiences, there's a good chance you will build a strong audience that rallies around your brand. You will also become a sought-after collaboration partner.

It was clear from the early days that Mark at Ball and Buck understood all of this deeply, even before he began manufacturing his own products. The brand positioning, the other products he curated, the initial co-branding and the experience walking into his shop were all thoughtfully executed. When he eventually decided to manufacture his own products he simply doubled down on what he had already created. This all manifested in the story he told consumers and the way he followed through.

Mark also does a great job personally living the brand and showing the products in the field through social media. Not a day goes by without a shot of Mark or a friend of the brand with one of their products in action. Nothing looks staged because it is not. This is what marketers really mean when they talk about authenticity.

From a values standpoint, customers can count on the brand to introduce them to like-minded brands that also embrace quality and attention to detail. Mark also went on to partner with hundreds of brands outside of Ball and Buck's collaborations by creating American Field, a platform that features emerging and established brands through a variety of channels, including a series of "Pop Up Markets." These events have grown in attendance every year, driven in large part by the collective collaboration of all the brands that are involved.

Is there room for you to establish a leadership position by developing a collaboration platform like American Field in your industry? Remember it must be built on *fit,* meaning every brand that's invited must share a similar set of core values, goals and target audiences.

MODERN MARKETERS: **Mark Bollman**

I connected with Mark to reflect back on the growth of Ball and Buck, the role of collaborations and the power of building a community around a brand:

In your experience, what makes collaboration a powerful tool for brands?

When you are a young brand most people don't know you. So, one of the stronger things you can do is associate with a brand people are familiar with. That baseline of personal trust and brand alignment provides a strong foundation for connection. Think about it as if a brand was your friend, you can reasonably expect consumers to view your brand in a positive way because they are already "friends" with a common brand.

When Ball and Buck collaborates with another company, we look to build upon a product they are already well-known for. That's why I like doing collaborations with iconic and well established brands that make iconic product styles. By building upon these iconic styles consumers have a baseline expectation of what that product normally is, which helps to highlight the design elements that are modified—thereby highlighting your brand DNA.

Although I typically recommend building a collaboration upon a well-known product in circulation from an established brand there is one exception. Bringing back an authentic style from a brand archive is also very interesting. Assuming that the two brands align overall, and the specific bring-back style or product makes strategic sense, the resulting product can exude your brand DNA in an even more powerful way. We did this when we were the first ever to collaborate on the New Balance 585 style and its trifecta makes for a great collaboration.

What makes the collaboration between a large and small brand mutually beneficial?

For a small or emerging brand, being able to associate, co-market and have a partnership with a larger brand is important. Larger brands have a significant following but often less freshness and relevance. The partnership is mutually beneficial because smaller brands can bring their authentic story and relevancy into a collaborative product that can be promoted by the larger reach and budgets of the bigger brand. Through this the small brand gains exposure, and the large brand builds relevancy and authenticity.

How do you decide what to create yourself and what to work on with partners?

My rule is always that we should only collaborate on a product if the result of the collaboration is better than the product we could have made independently. That philosophy has really defined what we've done as a company. We don't make shoes, we're not good at making them and we don't plan to make them. There's a technical expertise that we're not set up to do, and if we tried it wouldn't be as good as what is currently on the market. Instead, we offer shoes through collaborations with those who do it really well like Danner Boots, New Balance, and PF Flyers.

How have you seen collaboration impact product development?

Brands are rightfully protective of their look and overall presence, but that often manifests in a level of rigidity that doesn't welcome much room for innovation. However, when a third-party like Ball and Buck enters the equation it's more of a limited liability opportunity to expand, not reset the internal rules. That gives far more freedom for design.

We're always doing new things that push brand design limitation, so often large brands will test-kitchen features on collaborative products with Ball and Buck. It allows a brand to limit their risk while testing something new. The added benefit is that it opens the door to explore new features and design styles that might not be given the green light internally (normally) because of time, resources or existing brand standards. If it does go well, then they might apply similar styles to other products in their core offering. For example, with the New Balance 574 they hadn't really done a camo on a shoe until we did it together. It sold it out and now they've launched, and I own, probably ten other versions of similar styles or other colorways we worked on with them.

Do you have a favorite collaboration outside of Ball and Buck that you've admired? What made it stand out?

Between 1975 and 1986 Jeep offered a collaboration with Levi's on a CJ5 (now called the Wrangler). Looking back now, it was one of the most prominent and successful collaborations that have ever been done, taking a lifestyle brand and integrating it into an automobile. I think that's really interesting. There are few cars more recognizable than the classic Wrangler. So when they added the special blue denim upholstery it gives you the clear expectation that it's the Levi's edition. To this day on forums and in the resale market there's still buzz, brand recognition and exposure to market 40+ years later. From the standpoint of return on investment, that is a tremendous number impressions and word of mouth exposure. You wear a pair of shoes for a year, you wear a wax jacket for hopefully five or ten years but you have a car for maybe 50 years if it's a collectible.

That makes this a staple in the history books in terms of presence and awareness.

You've always leveraged crowdsourcing and recently launched a collaborative platform to co-create products with customers. Can you share a few insights regarding that philosophy?

Integrating our product development lifecycle directly with consumers' is very important. At the end of the day we want to make great products, but the goal of the brand is to have those products actually used. We want people to build experiences in their products making them a living canvas that reflects their lifestyle.

We've always been committed to a process that takes existing product and makes it better. In our first few years the products were specifically dictated by my personal experiences and discoveries in the field and city, as well as my interactions with other brands products. Now that we have a large community of consumers who have become part of our brand family, we can turn to them and ask what they really want. With our crowd funding platform "The Hatchery" we provide a platform for us to pull back the curtain and allow people to be part of the design/development process. It's very difficult to create and manufacture product and do it well, but since we have that expertise we are able to leverage that together with the great ideas of our community to make even better products. In a way, it's a microcosm of a large-scale collaboration as it's an individual to company project instead of small brand to large brand.

▼ ▼ ▼

Think Slow, Act Fast

Every so often a collaboration launches and generates negative press, resulting in cynicism about the brands' intentions. This is typically because the collaboration seems like nothing more than a stunt. When there is a complete disconnect, as opposed to one that is just seemingly unconnected, and the brands have not made it clear where the logical connection lies, there is no clear value being created. This makes the effort feel lazy and opportunistic. It reflects poorly on both brands and the collaboration space.

The footwear and apparel company Supreme is one of the most respected streetwear brands of all time and they are known for unique collaborations. These efforts always create buzz, but when the brand worked with high-end fashion label Louis Vuitton on an entire collection it also generated a lot of debate. Journalists questioned if LV risked losing some of its cachet since Supreme was not a traditional European fashion house. And while that may be true, it proved to be shortsighted as the two were actually a great *fit*.

Working with Supreme may have been unexpected and seemingly unconnected, but that's also why it worked. For one, it's clear the brands appeal to some of the same audiences. To connect the dots look no further than Supreme's long-running tradition of teaming up with artists in jazz and hip-hop. Now look at one of hip-hop's biggest names, Kanye West, and his nickname "the Louis Vuitton Don." Of course Kanye gave himself this nickname, and it does not represent any formal affiliation with the brand, but it no longer matters and consumers use this as a heuristic to link the two. Kanye has also done his part to blur the lines by formally taking on an apprenticeship at Fendi.* Since then we have seen many more high-profile collaborations between hip-hop artists and iconic fashion houses.

* *Kanye worked at Fendi alongside his longtime collaborator, Virgil Abloh who we profiled in Chapter 2. In the spring of 2018, Abloh, who is also a part-time DJ, was named the new artistic director of men's wear at LV.*

While Supreme broke ground with this collaboration, streetwear has actually been impacting the overall fashion landscape for decades. In the 70s and 80s a designer in New York named Dapper Dan created an entire business doing essentially the same thing Supreme and LV did. Dan's custom clothing took high-end fashion brand logos, patterns and materials and created clothing and accessories that resembled the style of popular streetwear and athletic brands.*

* *If you're interested in learning more about hip-hop fashion I highly recommend the documentary* Fresh Dressed.

Although technically illegal, this renegade creativity is something brands should continue paying attention to. It reminds me of the early days of MP3s and Napster. If record companies had embraced digital music and collaborated with technology companies instead of suing them, they may have changed the trajectory of the industry and avoided a decade of declining sales. Smart marketers see inspiration, a connection to culture, and opportunity for collaboration, not the short-term dollars that may be lost.

To bring this example full circle, in 2017 Gucci recognized the cultural impact of Dapper Dan and the opportunity to support his creative approach to design thanks to a connection made by Steve Stoute, who we discussed in Chapter 1. This time rather than trying to thwart Dap with lawsuits, as so many brands had done, they made him the face of a campaign and in early 2018 they teamed up with him to reopen his boutique in Harlem for the first time since it closed in the early 90s.

Partnerships that push the envelope like the one between Supreme and LV, or Gucci and Dapper Dan, will always cause some to question their value and intentions, but as long as they are based in sound strategy that benefits consumers, they have a shot at resonating. In fact, the connection between brands that seemingly appeal to different audiences has become an entire niche within collaboration, characterized as high and low. As we'll explore in Chapter 8, brands like Target have made this a consistent part of their strategy by bringing high-priced or exclusive designers to the table, resulting in much lower-priced items.

Pay Attention to the Fundamentals

While I am a fan of the high-low concept, and the Supreme and LV collaboration, I do wonder about any brand with as much hype as Supreme. Every Thursday when they drop new products there is a long line of people waiting outside of their NYC flagship, not to mention the online attention. Their consistent limited-release strategy creates an interesting mix of anticipation and scarcity, but it also makes me question how long they can keep it up.

Last time I walked by to catch the Thursday scene there were a number of individuals immediately reselling the items on the street for a profit. Other products show up on Ebay for big bucks. What happens if the line becomes filled with more flippers than actual fans? As a brand marketer and leader you have to consider things like this and take steps to ensure a brand does not lose its way. You can also develop collaborations to offset the more mainstream buzz when it begins to develop. At all costs, you want to avoid surface-level collaborations that might cause your audience to question your values.

With that in mind, I do see a few signs that perhaps the Supreme brand may be reaching a bit too far. Let's juxtapose the LV collection with Supreme's recent New York City MTA Metro system collaboration. While the former relied on creativity, history, design and craftsmanship, the latter involved the Supreme logo on Metro cards and nothing else. There was no promo event, no story about why the two teamed up, no special ride to be unlocked and no related content other than a few straightforward social media posts announcing the product. There was absolutely no functional utility, except for those who flipped their cards for a profit, and the emotional value was limited to bragging rights and perhaps a more pleasing aesthetic for the few seconds riders have their cards in hand. This just looked opportunistic. There were so many interesting things they could have layered into this collaboration, but they chose to do nothing. Most of the buzz was negative and coverage primarily consisted of fights on subway platforms and comments noting the lack of substance.

I'll admit, I'm a marketer so I pay closer attention than the average consumer. But so do the influencers and modern socialites who have the power to make or break a brand.

Only a few months after this incident Supreme t-shirts began showing up at Kmart. Yes, the same shirt that sells for about $40 was selling for $4. This was likely triggered by American Apparel going out of business and liquidating their inventory, including products created for other brands. As a result we are reminded of the fact that we pay considerably more for the same product by simply adding a logo. This speaks to the idea that even manufacturing partners may be seen as collaborators in the eyes of consumers.

Before we move on the to the next chapter and continue exploring how to make the most out of a collaboration, let's look at another example of a fashion partnership with the City of New York that had a little more substance than the Supreme and MTA Metro collaboration.

Heron Preston represents a new breed of creative entrepreneur who cannot be defined by any traditional labels. He received a BBA at the Parsons School of Design and parlayed that into work as a global producer for Nike, a creative consultant to Kanye West, and the head of his own fashion label HPC Trading Co. He is a self-proclaimed "cultural icon in youth culture" and, according to his website, "finds particular joy in the unexpected; taking conventional themes and reinterpreting them."

Guys like Heron do not engage in surface-level collaborations. They go all in, just as he did when he teamed up with The City of New York Department of Sanitation. After literally brushing up against a plastic bag while swimming he decided to do something that would make a statement about the environment. At the same time the Sanitation Department was launching a new campaign and nonprofit to promote sustainability and bring attention to the efforts of sanitation workers to keep the city healthy, safe and clean.

Heron took used Sanitation Department uniforms and redesigned them. He combined the existing materials with donated clothing and design elements and the launched the line, dubbed UNIFORM, at one of the Department's salt sheds. According to Heron, "UNIFORM's ideology redefines fashion, and brings awareness to DSNY's service to New York City, without which street culture would not exist." A percentage of all proceeds from the line went to the Department's Foundation.

As my friend Taylor, author of *Ballgames to Boardrooms*, is fond of saying, go one more step. That's just what Heron did when he decided to turn his outrage into a creative endeavor that provided value on many levels. That extra effort may be the difference between two brands merely fitting together and a collaboration that truly flourishes.

Behind every successful collaboration is someone like Heron who decided to step up, conceive and lead. Later we'll explore the most important part of a collaboration: you. While this may sound egotistical, you're going to be the one that drives this conversation in your organization, and it takes a certain type of thinking to kick this off in a productive and creative way.

CoLAB: *Curiosity*

As brand clutter makes it even more important to filter out unwanted marketing, and technology makes it possible to automate most purchases, we will inevitably establish and maintain more ongoing relationships with brands. Of course, we will initially select them based on what we perceive to be a strong *fit*, but if they don't deliver and continue demonstrating value we'll replace them.

List all the brands you have ongoing relationships with today and rank the brands in terms of who you have been engaged with the longest.

Do you remember how you first learned about these brands?

Did they align with your values then and do they still resonate as you audit them today? Or have you stuck around out of convenience or necessity?

Do any of these companies rely on collaborations with other brands to keep their relationship with you interesting or to upsell or cross-sell you new things?

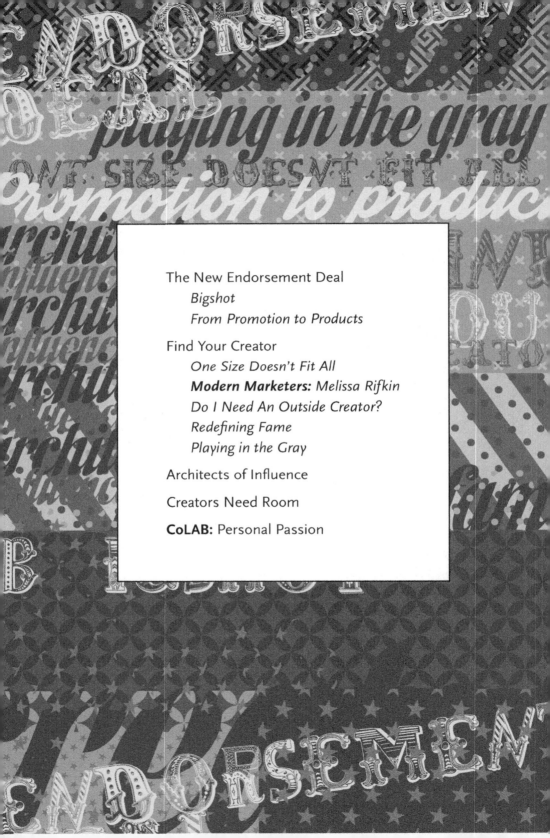

CHAPTER 5

Personal Brand Collaborations

"Future marketing will be more about technology and sociology, and less about reach and communication. Strategy will shift from directly influencing consumers to mediating the influence consumers will have on each other."

—Arun Sundararajan, NYU Stern professor and author of *The Sharing Economy: The End of Employment and the Rise of Crowd-Based Capitalism*

SINCE WE ARE now connected through our devices at all times during the day, we draw less of a distinction between who we are in and out of work.

When was the last time you left your house without your cell phone? Do you remember how it felt when you realized it wasn't by your side? I'm guessing the degree of panic that you felt was in direct correlation to the distance you had traveled and your ability to go back and retrieve it.

The moral of the story is that we are constantly in communication with our friends, family members and any of the brands we have invited into our lives via email, text, apps or social media. Of course, we can also proactively engage with brands through our phones in a variety of ways. While many jobs frown upon this activity during the workday, it's almost impossible to completely cut yourself off from these outside influences. This is especially true for marketers who are encouraged to stay relevant by exploring digital media and other trends.

This constant connectivity means that we are no longer a different type of consumer inside and outside of the work environment. Instead, we can think of ourselves as always-on consumers. And most importantly, our attention is in extremely short supply.

Even though certain transactions can now be automated and many products are self-service, we must keep in mind that a purchase process begins well before the transaction. Choice, access to information and peer influence give more control to individuals. Even when people buy from brands using technology, their purchase decisions are often impacted along the way by individuals. This is why tapping into personal brands has become a popular way to introduce or reinforce a brand narrative, bring personality to companies in every industry and impact the way brands are perceived.

The New Endorsement Deal

Even brands that have historically relied on a mascot or spokesperson must now supplement this approach with a distinct human voice they can use to interact. Do you want to talk about ingredient sourcing or a product recall with the Pillsbury Dough Boy, the Keebler Elf or Kim Kardashian? The latter might actually be fun, but her brand deals would be a lot more costly if she was periodically taking customer service calls.

And while every modern brand needs to develop a thoughtful approach to online interactions, this doesn't diminish the opportunity to also align with a spokesperson or a group of individuals for marketing purposes.

In fact, the media trends forcing product- and service-based brands to rethink their marketing strategies are also empowering individuals to create media platforms and strong personal brands. This is because the same tools that enable more efficient communication between consumers and brands have armed individuals with the tools they need to produce and distribute content. In the battle for attention, some voices are losing reach and relevance, including many media outlets that dominated for decades, while others are rising to the top and wielding their influence in a variety of new ways.

> What's important to note from a collaboration standpoint is the blurring line between product and service brands, personal brands, and what we traditionally think of as media brands.

Like him or not, Kim's husband Kanye West may be one of the most influential personal brands on the planet today. After breaking into music by making beats for Jay-Z, Kanye proved himself to be a great rapper too. It became clear that he wasn't going to stop there, and the outspoken artist began aligning with a number of brands, especially in fashion as we touched on in the last chapter. In doing so, Kanye built up his global influence through traditional media and social media.

Kanye first stepped into the sneaker game through a collaboration with Nike, until he ditched the brand in a very public way and landed a deal with adidas. That collaboration resulted in the "Yeezy Boosts," which sold out in minutes and became a status symbol. The alignment with Kanye has been lucrative for adidas, and many look to this collaboration as the halo effect that drove the brand's overall growth over the past few years. (In the fall of 2017 it was announced that adidas had grown to become the number two best-selling footwear brand.)

It remains to be seen what adidas's alliance with Kanye will mean for the adidas brand over the long term. Will Kanye drop them like he did Nike? Will adidas drop him over controversy he stirs up on Twitter or elsewhere? Therein lies the risk that all brands must consider when they collaborate with personal brands. All the legal protection in the world can't stop an individual from intentionally turning on a brand or encountering personal drama that brings with it negative consequences.

Bigshot

Brands have developed partnerships with famous athletes, artists and actors since the early days of advertising. At first most brands simply negotiated the use of "name and likeness" so they could feature images or quotes from these individuals in radio, print and TV ads. These deals were dubbed "endorsements," as brands often tapped into the implied expertise of these individuals to gain credibility.

But like any successful collaboration, endorsements work best when they are based on genuine *fit*, meaning the expertise of the endorser makes them uniquely qualified to evaluate the merits of a product or service, and in turn reveal something truthful about the brand.

An early example of this functional endorsement came when PF Flyers, a popular sneaker brand and precursor to Converse, hired pro-basketball superstar Bob Cousy. Bob, aka

Mr. Basketball, aka the Houdini of the Hardwood, was known for his ball handling and passing skills, which made his claims about the shoe's support and comfort more credible. This first-of-its-kind collaboration set off a huge trend and an intense competition between brands for deals with top athletes.

However, in the example above, the impact of the collaboration was limited by the fact that Bob's personal brand, and his reach, were in many ways out of his control. Bob's exposure was primarily contained to the media coverage of his on-court performance and the advertisements in which he appeared. If he wanted to reach fans, he relied on the traditional media and the brands he endorsed. There were no options for individuals to build their own media, making personal branding more predictable and limiting the risk of an endorsement for a brand.

In the more than 50 years since the PF and Cousey collaboration, endorsements have become much more nuanced, and in many ways the evolution of these deals ran parallel to changes in media. This is especially true in sports and music, where dedicated platforms like ESPN and MTV gave athletes and artist more exposure. Most of these outlets were also built with advertising in mind, as we discussed in the first chapter, creating an ideal environment for endorsements.

One of the most dramatic changes in the size and scope of an endorsement came when Michael Jordan stepped into the national spotlight. The timing was perfect as the ubiquity of cable TV mirrored Jordan's rise to greatness.

Nike, at the time a relatively fledgling brand mostly known for running shoes, took a different approach to the partnership with Jordan from day one, long before anyone knew he would become the greatest player ever. Although he described himself as an "adidas-nut" prior to the deal, Nike made a compelling case and won his allegiance. By truly collaborating with him to design a signature line of sneakers and apparel, they created what would quickly become an aspirational brand and a status symbol both on and off the court. Michael's basketball dominance lent credibility to the quality of the shoes, and the entertaining and inspiring commercials gave the brand even more appeal.

"Every version of the Air Jordan was influenced by the desire to always be better and to reach higher levels. He inspired me to be better every single time because frankly he got better every year."

— Tinker Hatfield, Nike designer and Jordan collaborator

I'll never forget how it felt to put on my first pair, the Jordan IVs. Kids and adults around the world wanted to "Be like Mike" as he racked up championships, MVP awards and numerous endorsements from brands including McDonald's, Gatorade, Wheaties and Fruit of the Loom. The Jordan brand became a juggernaut and every endorsement added to Michael's influence. Another benefit to associating with the Jordan brand was an element of escapism, because when you wore the shoes and stuck out your tongue to mimic one of his signature moves, you co-opted a bit of his swagger.

In terms of building Michael Jordan's personal brand, the Nike deal clearly stands above the rest. This is in part because Nike's advertising found unique ways to tap into culture. The primary example was Nike's clever use of the filmmaker and actor Spike Lee as Jordan's sidekick in a number of spots. However, Spike didn't play himself. Instead, he was always Mars Blackmon, a character from his breakout film *She's Gotta Have It*. Because Mars was a proud Brooklynite and New York Knicks fan, in a subtle way this gave everyone permission to wear Jordans, even if you rooted against his team, the Chicago Bulls.

This campaign connected Jordan with New York, one of the most important media markets in the world for branding and advertising. It was also an authentic connection as Jordan was born in Brooklyn, even thought his parents moved him to North Carolina as a toddler and that state is most associated with his upbringing.

> *"It's gotta be the shoes."*
>
> —Mars Blackmon

Jordan also starred in the animated/live-action film *Space Jam,* alongside many familiar cartoon characters. Not only did the film cross-promote a new pair of Nike Air Jordans, but the lead single for the movie soundtrack was performed by the other MJ—Michael Jackson. In the video, the two MJs square off in a game of one-on-one, a collaboration most never imagined. It's impossible to overstate the buzz and excitement that this generated at the time, especially since both were in their prime. It was a hit and once again millions of people around the world, myself included, were compelled to buy the shoes.

To this day, 20 years after Jordan's prime, every new Jordan sneaker release is a major event. A TED Talk by Josh Luber, "Why sneakers are a great investment," revealed some staggering statistics about the impact and popularity of the Jordan brand. In terms of sales, at the time of his talk in 2015, the secondary market of resale Nike shoes, which are primarily Jordans, were bringing in more money than any other brand selling directly at retail. That means for years, the number three best-selling sneaker brand in the world, adidas, sat behind Nike and Nike. As mentioned, adidas recently took over the number two spot, but you can bet the Nike team is working overtime to slow down their growth.

It's hard to believe that Michael built such a powerhouse brand without social media. He and his team have leveraged new channels over the years, but for most of his career he relied on traditional media coverage and endorsements to grow his personal brand.

Michael did understand the value of content. Beyond the games themselves, he participated in the NBA dunk contest and the Olympics. He was also the subject of a number of documentary films, which, other than *NBA Inside Stuff*, an occasional *Sportscenter* feature, or a *Sports Illustrated* story, were the only way to get a glimpse of Jordan off the court.

But contrast Michael's off-the-court exposure with today's greatest player, Lebron James, who we can follow directly on social media through his own athlete-driven media platform Uninterrupted, and indirectly as fans capture and share his every public move. We can learn a lot from Michael, but the rules of personal branding and collaboration have clearly evolved.

From Promotion to Products

Athletes and celebrities can use their fame to sell sneakers, and much more, but the savvy among them have always taken it further by leveraging their personal brands to create entertainment destinations (Dollywood), restaurants (Jimmy Buffett's Margaritaville), and even their own kitchen appliances (George Foreman Grill). Now a new breed of celebs are recognizing the opportunity to create their own properties on the back of digital media.

If you don't follow her closely, you may be surprised to hear that Gwyneth Paltrow was a pioneer in terms of the opportunity for celebrities to expand their influence when she created a branded platform that mixed content, commerce and collaboration. Years ago my friend Brett showed me Gwyneth Paltrow's email newsletter and the blog she calls goop. He keenly pointed out why this was different from anything we had seen before and the lessons marketers could learn from her example. Brett also introduced me to the work of my favorite marketer, Seth Godin, so when he shares a marketing insight, I'm all ears.

At the time Gwyneth was essentially sending a weekly email about her life, with tips and links related to her personal travel, food, fashion, music, arts and cultural experiences. What made it so unique was the first-person narrative and what seemed to be unfiltered access into the life of a globetrotting celeb.

While most fans seek out tabloids, TMZ, Twitter or Instagram to find out what their favorite actor, athlete or musician had for dinner, those curious about Gwyneth can find out where she shops, where she eats, and where she stays when visiting Nashville, for instance, through goop. She regularly shares her favorite recipes (often crafted by famous chefs who she introduces to her audience), books, boutiques and bands in a way that makes readers feel like trusted insiders. This all taps into some of the same emotional drivers that build the kind of reverence people have for the mavens, to steal a term from Gladwell, they actually know in real life. It also balances the aspirational nature of celebrity with accessibility.

After consistently posting these updates over a number of years, Gwyneth built a media platform that rivaled many boutique publishers and bloggers. In addition to the weekly updates, she began launching a series of paid mobile apps that organized her travel-related content by city (NYC, London, LA), a very clever way to monetize all the existing content.

Her platform continued evolving, and instead of simply talking about certain products and services she began featuring curated product collections—most likely receiving a commission for her ability to drive sales for these brands. However, the most impressive and bold phase of the platform is based on weekly collaborations between her original brand, goop, and other brands. For example, she offered a limited run of jeans from rag & bone, wingtips from Esquivel, greeting cards from Sugar Paper and a personally curated box of goodies from Birchbox. These are now offered through pop-up shops, summits, podcasts and a print publication. Her ability to marry content, great storytelling and commerce, while creatively merchandising with unique collaborations, has become a powerful formula that brands would be smart to engage with, mimic or remix in their own way.

Find Your Creator

While Gwyneth represents a modern example of the expanded influence of mainstream celebrity, and many others have used social media to build their brands, there are now an endless number of nontraditional celebrities who have built personal brands solely through new media. Yes, reality TV persists, but that's not what we're talking about. A new breed of celebrity has emerged and it's driven by creativity, talent and expertise. These creators are gaining influence by taking advantage of the democratization of content creation tools—like the cameras we all carry on our phones—and the distribution platforms that enable connection at scale. Audiences tune in, or follow and subscribe, to see what will be published next from their friends, family and from creators at every level.

This emerging class of creators is defining completely new rules for content creation, promotion and marketing from which brands can learn and benefit. As opposed to the traditional entertainment industry, which has been thriving on exclusivity and scarcity of talent and media, there are millions of successful creators and even more channels. These individuals and small teams also produce content at a pace that's difficult for brands and traditional media to keep up with. Not to mention the way they embrace audience interaction, collaboration and community building.

One Size Doesn't Fit All

Influential creators also now exist across every industry and represent every interest imaginable. This provides the perfect opportunity for partnerships, and points of entry into culture, if brands are proactive, thoughtful and willing to give up some control.

To illustrate this, let's juxtapose Kanye's influence with YouTuber Casey Neistat.

While Kanye's first big break came when he produced a song for Jay-Z, Casey's came from making a short film about the Apple iPod. Today Casey is one of the most influential creators on the planet, but long before he redefined daily "vlogging" and racked up hundreds of millions of views, he created one of the first viral videos ever. In 2003!

The project began when Casey's iPod battery died and he received a less than sympathetic response upon calling Apple customer service. The rep explained that the cost for replacing the device's battery was more than purchasing a new one, acknowledging that he was essentially out of luck. Casey recorded the conversation and turned it into a video. After hearing the recording of the conversation with the rep, viewers see

Casey spray painting a stencil that says "iPod's Unreplaceable Battery Lasts Only 18 Months." Casey goes on to spray paint this phrase over the iconic Apple iPod posters throughout New York City, with Public Enemy's "Fight The Power" playing in the background to reinforce the Robin Hood-esque nature of this effort. Titled "iPod's Dirty Secret," the video was initially posted in message boards, shared through email and passed along through pre-social media word of mouth, racking up over 6 million views in the first month, three years before YouTube.

This is a great example of the power that individuals have as a result of technology. Before the internet, Casey would have only been able to tell a few friends, or at best submit his film to festivals and hope someone would provide him a platform to share the message. Instead, his response to the brand's poor customer service reached millions without needing anyone's permission. It marked the end of an era for traditional media gatekeepers and sent a clear warning to brands.

Since then Casey has made award-winning films, turned his "handmade home movies" into a TV show that aired on HBO, and worked with a number of brands on groundbreaking campaigns. When he went rogue and ditched an approved video concept in favor of a completely different idea for a Nike campaign, it led to the one of brand's most viewed online videos. Nike was initially apprehensive about posting the video since it strayed from their original strategy. With this in mind, they allowed Casey to post the video on his own YouTube channel first. The video generated a ton of earned media attention, in part due to a debate about whether or not Casey had truly gone rogue or if the brand was in on it. Whether intentional or not, this drove up the number of viewers and subscribers for Casey. In my mind this was another major turning point in the relationship between brands and online creators. Rarely had individuals garnered so much attention through their own personal channels thanks to a brand collaboration.

It is now commonplace for brands to ask influencers to post branded content through their own channels, but at first this went against conventional wisdom. What Nike learned, and what we can all apply to our work as marketers, is that today it's best to truly empower creators once you've determined they are a good *fit*. This is inherently risky, but the potential upside is huge. These creators have built up trust and influence that can't be found elsewhere.

Influencer marketing is here to stay, but brands have to decide if they want to truly go on offense and change the way they operate, or hold onto old practices and play defense.

Not every brand has caught up, but the ones who are winning recognize this shift and the value of truly symbiotic relationships with consumers and creators.

It is also important to realize you don't need Michael, Gwyneth, Kanye or Casey to tap into the same phenomenon. Influencer marketing can scale up or down, and for some brands, the best value is in the emerging end of the spectrum. By that I mean you can find a number of individuals who have relatively small audiences to collaborate with and still make a huge impact. Start identifying the creators who already have the attention and respect of your target audience, and see if you can find the ones who truly *fit* just as you would do when approaching any brand collaboration.

MODERN MARKETERS: **Melissa Rifkin**

Let's think about just how far we've come in terms of individual influence and then use an everyday example to put the new media reality in perspective. Take food. When my grandmother wanted to try a new recipe she either pulled a cookbook off the shelf or called her friend who was known as an exceptional cook. She may have also referred to a recipe she found in a magazine or a small collection of recipes she received in the mail from a brand. Those were really the only options.

One thing that has not changed is that we all know someone who we consistently turn to for advice based on their specific interests and expertise. In addition to knowing a great cook, you probably know a film buff, fashionista, DIY designer and music junkie. However, for my grandmother, and most of my life, we had to reach out to these individuals directly, over the phone, or beginning in the 90s through email. That was until a few short years ago when blogs and social media emerged, giving these experts, artists and creators the ability to share their expertise broadly.

Today when I'm looking for a new recipe I start on Instagram. There are a few go-to individuals whose taste, literally and figuratively, I trust. One is Melissa Rifkin, who creates content under the moniker Confession of a Dietitian. She's always posting photos of great culinary creations and sharing recipes, short-cuts for meal planning and other food related tips.

Melissa made a deliberate choice to leverage her passion and professional expertise to build a personal brand that commands the attention of audiences across a variety of mediums. She could have continued practicing her craft by only working one-on-one with individuals at her day job, but instead she decided to share her expertise, interests, ideas and recommendations with the world through social media. It started slow, but her following grew and at the time of this writing she has over 207,000 followers on Instagram.

When Melissa posts ideas for meals she regularly features brands that she has partnered with. She uses her own criteria to determine which brands are a *fit* for her personal brand and her audience, and then she weaves them into the content. She often deploys the fashionable flat lay* style, creatively juxtaposing a number of dishes and products in a single post, which has become a very popular way for brands and individuals to execute brand collaborations in the form of cross-promotions that often involve contests and giveaways. People look to Melissa for advice and trust her opinion, so when she collaborates with a brand it makes a favorable impression.

....

* *Many connect the flat lay style, now popular on Instagram, with the idea of knolling, or arranging and organizing objects, traditionally in parallel or 90-degree angles. The term was first used in architect Frank Gehry's studio when he was designing the now iconic chairs for the brand Knoll. Tom Sachs, a prolific multimedia artist and creator, worked in the studio for a few years and made the term and style a central element of his own work. Check out the film* 10 Bullets, #8: "ALWAYS BE KNOLLING" *by Tom Sachs, where this style is explained. The video was created by Tom with Van Neistat, Casey's brother. Both worked for Tom early in their careers and his influence can be seen in their work, as well as Casey's studio which is a shrine to knolling. This creative lineage illustrates the value and importance of finding inspiration and mentorship and building upon it. I'm biased, as Casey has roots in my hometown in CT, but this also shows the widespread impact of the Neistat brothers and the influence modern creators can have on brands and culture. Next time you see the flat lay style on Instagram, remember Gehry, Knoll, knolling, Sachs, Neistat and connecting the seemingly unconnected.*

....

There's no shortage of brands creating and sharing recipes, but many of the ones that seem to resonate are created in collaboration with individuals like Melissa. If this seems simple and intuitive, it's meant to. That's why it's so powerful. I connected with Melissa to get her take on all of this:

What made you decide to focus on building your personal brand and sharing your expertise?

After years of being on Instagram, I realized that large accounts did not have credentials to back them up if they were posting about nutrition or health. Therefore, with my credentials, I felt that it was my time to share my wealth of knowledge with an engaging audience that needed to be led by someone who had years of education, experience and 12 years of practicing nutrition.

What makes collaborating with influencers a smart move for brands?

More than 70% of consumers are more likely to make a purchase after a social recommendation. 74% of consumers use social media to make purchasing decisions.

How should a brand identify the right individuals to partner with?

Seek out an individual that boasts qualities that your company represents or is striving to be. For example, a new company with a protein bar would reach out to an individual in the health industry whose Instagram handle speaks health, balance, nutrition and overall wellbeing. That influencer is representing a brand, therefore choosing the right voice, so to speak, is imperative in order to drive a positive message to the consumer and to represent a brand in a positive light.

How can a brand empower you to do your best work and make the biggest impact on their behalf?

Speaking from personal experience, when I am given an assignment, I am not only representing my page, I am representing a company as a whole. Therefore it is my duty to come up with not only a creative post, but a post that is meaningful and has impact, catches my followers eyes and engages.

Do you think influencer marketing will continue to be effective for a long time?

I know it will. We live in a fast paced world. If I can hold my phone, scroll, find a product I love and order it all from my palm of my hand, easy! I saved time and stress, and trust that this product is going to be great because an influencer I find to be a role model marketed it. Marketing has taken on a whole new meaning, Instagram is one giant shopping mall.

Any new trends in the space that brands should be aware of?

Choose the individual you want to market your product carefully. You want someone who represents your company. Just because an individual has a large following does not mean that they're someone you should choose.

Today, Instagram stories are a great way to market a product, as they run for 24 hours and can have a smaller price tag than a hard post on Instagram.

▼ ▼ ▼

Do I Need An Outside Creator?

While many brands have staffed up, and now employ teams of creators, most of the time content is not their company's core competency. They can hire agencies and freelance resources to help, but they are missing a huge opportunity if they are not also developing co-branded content in collaboration with creators who have their own personal brands and corresponding audiences. This generates a three-for-one value proposition: content (great recipes), distribution (if they publish through their own channels), and influence (over the audience that follows because they trust and respect their expertise). This same dynamic is driving the growth of native and branded content created by media brands and publishers who make similar claims in terms of understanding their audiences, commanding attention and wielding influence.

$$\left.\begin{array}{l} \textit{Fit} \times \text{Content} \\ + \text{Distribution} \\ + \text{Influence} \end{array}\right\} = \begin{array}{l} \text{24K} \\ \text{Collaboration} \\ \text{Gold} \end{array}$$

Put yourself in the consumer's Air Jordans and ask what you would rather see: a slick commercial with actors touting all the great benefits of a new gluten-free cake mix, a Facebook post with a faceless image of a cake and a brand logo, or a recipe posted by Melissa and branded Confession of a Dietitian (as featured in the Modern Marketers profile in this Chapter)? Remember, for hundreds of thousands of individuals, she's the modern equivalent of the health-conscious friend who always brings the best desserts—and apps, and entrees, and sides.

When a brand enlists a creator like Melissa they associate with all of her expertise, borrow a little attention and trade on the trust and respect she's built up. Their work together has a collaboration story built in that makes the content more nuanced and compelling.

UP AND DOWN THE FOOD CHAIN

The food world is filled a wide range of traditional and modern influencers like Melissa. It's easy to forget the food industry had very few TV stars before the relatively recent era of the celebrity chef (ushered in by marketing mastermind and legendary entertainment manager Shep Gordon*).

* *If you haven't seen the documentary* Supermensch *about Shep's career, add it to your Netflix queue.*

In many ways, the evolution of food culture is a perfect corollary for the proliferation of brands and collaboration. The opportunities to connect the unexpected across product, service, experience, personal and media brands in the food ecosystem are endless. Whether it's Martha Stewart and Snoop collaborating on a cooking show and then flipping that into a T-Mobile Super Bowl spot, Vice teaming up with Chef'd and renegade Instagram star chef Matty Matheson to deliver branded meal kits, or fellow Texans Whataburger and Yeti partnering on a co-branded tumbler, there will be an appetite for collaboration as long as there's *fit*.

Redefining Fame

According to a YouTube survey of teen and millennial subscribers, as outlined in the book *Streampunks* by YouTube's Chief Business Officer Robert Kyncl and Google's Communications Manager Maany Peyvan, 60% would follow their favorite creators' advice on what to buy and 40% said YouTubers understood them better than their friends or family. Perhaps even more impressive, 60% said a creator has changed their life or view of the world.

This is further proof that influencer marketing is powerful and much more than a trend. Collaborating with an individual who has earned attention, respect and trust from an audience lends credibility to a brand that is impossible to replicate through traditional advertising, even when campaigns feature well-known personalities.

In fact, when it comes to partnering with online creators vs. traditional celebrities, Robert and Maany referenced another astounding study in their book. According to a *Variety* survey of high school students in America asking who the most influential celebrities were, the top six spots were all YouTubers. That's right, YouTube creators come in above Selena, Beyoncé, Drake, Taylor, Bieber, the Ryans, Kyrie, Lebron and others you might expect to make up the top of this list.

Mainstream celebrities are beginning to recognize this trend and are getting on board. In late 2017, Will Smith* took to YouTube and began his own vlog, tracking his daily travel, introducing audiences to his family members and promoting his Netflix film *Bright*.

....

* *I was first introduced to Will in elementary school when he was part of the group DJ Jazzy Jeff and The Fresh Prince. Their song "Nightmare on My Street" was named after a familiar and popular movie,*

making it easy to relate to. Then he partnered with Quincy Jones—
who famously produced Michael Jackson's Thriller *and dozens of*
other iconic albums—to create The Fresh Prince of Bel-Air. *I memo-*
rized the show's theme song and emulated Will's style, especially his
love of Jordans, just like millions of other kids and teens. Then Will
became an action hero, and when he partnered with Ray Ban for the
Men in Black *special edition sunglasses I mimicked his style once*
again. Big Will's recent foray into YouTube is especially fascinating to
me because it builds upon his track record of career reinvention and
evolution at a time when we're clearly in uncharted territory in terms
of media.

The style and aesthetic of his videos are reminiscent of many popular YouTubers, but of course Will has the benefit of a built in global fan base so his subscriber base is growing rapidly. In most videos he's wearing a Nike shirt and a W hat, the latter presumably representing his own line of merchandise, another increasingly popular YouTuber move.

What's most inspiring about this to me is Will's genuine excitement about this form of creative expression. "YouTube has really given me an opportunity to flow a lot of the creative ideas that were dying, you know, on my creative interior vine…I'm able to come alive in away creatively that I thought was behind me. This is a massive creative explosion for me."

While YouTube certainly enjoys a lot of attention (it is often cited as the second most popular search engine to Google, its parent company), and that's a great place to launch a collaboration with a creator, it's important to think more broadly. Facebook, Twitter, Instagram, Snapchat, Twitch, Music.ly, Reddit, LinkedIn, Medium, and others are all worth exploring. Where should you play? It depends on your brand, your why, your audience and the story you're trying to tell.

Most of these channels offer the ability for your brand to build its own presence, distribute brand content, and even pay for promotion, all of which you should probably be experimenting with. But the beauty of influencer marketing, assuming it's based on *fit* and you've given the creator room to do their thing, is that it touches on all of the above, especially if you have a strong foundation of engaging content spread across all of your owned properties. When someone discovers you through an influencer—point of entry—they may want to get to know you more, so your own content and experiences need to be on point if you expect to hold their attention.

Playing in the Gray

I was visiting my parents recently and, as I always do when I'm at their house, I flipped through the local newspaper during breakfast. It was Sunday, so there was a huge pile of brand circulars and coupons. I don't have a newspaper subscription, and I rarely purchase the newspaper, so when I have one in front of me I dive in. It's fascinating to see who is advertising and how they are positioning themselves. I also like to think about how retailers feature and promote the products and services they offer from other brands.

Somewhere in the pile there's always a copy of *Parade* magazine. The target demo seems to be a bit older, which makes sense given the trajectory of the newspaper business. Safe to say, *Parade* is not the type of magazine that prides itself on being hyper targeted or cutting edge. They typically feature mainstream celebrities on the cover, so when I finally dug up *Parade* on this particular fall Sunday in 2017 I was surprised to find a podcast host on the cover.

Although they are still consumed by less than half the U.S. population, podcasts have been experiencing significant growth. They are in many ways a bridge between old and new media (the "father of podcasting" is the famous MTV VJ Adam Curry), which makes them a great place for brands to play. As you probably know, podcasts resemble radio broadcasts (interviews, stories and even music), but they are downloaded or streamed by the listener. The on-demand access makes it a perfect audio complement to the way our video consumption habits are changing—watching when we want and how we want.

Once again, it's easy to forget that binge viewing, or in this case listening, is still a relatively new phenomenon. Perhaps it's fitting then that *Serial,* a long-form narrative podcast that debuted in 2014, was considered the breakthrough moment for the medium. In the years since then the number of listeners, and content, has increased steadily.

The cover of *Parade* magazine I found at my parents house featured Marc Maron, a journeyman comedian and host of the podcast *WTF.* Marc has turned the interview show he records in the garage of his home in LA into a massive hit. His podcast is downloaded over six million times a month, and listeners tune in to hear Marc interview A-list celebrities, musicians and even President Obama, who made a visit to his garage to appear on the show in 2016.

Influential voices like Marc, and Bill Simmons who we covered in Chapter 2, are emerging in every corner of the podcast world and they present a powerful opportunity for brands. Because of the way people listen, often through earphones in a solitary state, podcasts often feel more personal than other forms of media. This makes the ads even more impactful and memorable, especially when they are more than just traditional radio spots.

The most successful podcast advertising gives hosts creative leeway. Brands send them the product or provide access to the service that's being marketed and encourage them to test it out. Assuming the host likes it, the resulting advertisement becomes more of a story where the host shares their personal experience with the offering. The ad then resembles more of a collaboration than an interruption.

These "live reads" are not new but they are part of an increasing shift to more native advertising. For example, when author and podcast host Tim Ferriss tells his audience about cricket flour protein bars, they sell. That's because Tim is known for his experimentation with nutrition and body hacking, thus making the association and collaboration a perfect *fit*. His loyal listeners and fans trust his opinion and they are there to learn about ways they too can experiment, so when Tim says it's a good idea to eat bugs, people chow down.

According to Kurt Kaufer, Partner and CMO of Ads Results Media, a firm that claims to place more than ⅓ of all paid podcast advertising, "endorsed" ads in podcasts are an average of 3.73 times more efficient than dynamically inserted pre-recorded ads from a cost per acquisition (CPA) standpoint.

While podcast advertising continues to grow in popularity, a number of brands are making a different kind of investment in the medium by publishing branded podcasts. Just like the wave of branded video content we talked about in Chapter 3, branded audio aims to deliver value to audiences in the form of entertainment, inspiration and education. By developing content that reinforces and complements brand values, audiences are introduced to brands in a favorable way.

But what happens when you combine the impact of podcasting with branded content and influencer marketing? That's exactly what Dell achieved when they launched *Trailblazers*, a podcast dedicated to telling stories of innovation and technology. In a brilliant move, they enlisted author and influencer

Walter Isaacson to host the show. By collaborating with Walter they benefit from his brand and his role as the author Steve Jobs personally selected to write his biography. When most people think of Walter they think of Steve and Apple. This association with him enables Dell to co-opt a little of that Cupertino magic.

Once again, you don't need Walter or a traditional celebrity of any kind to make this equation work. Just as we explored with Melissa, there are experts and creators in every category, in every city and town around the globe, willing to collaborate and put your brand in front of their audiences. Just remember to use your values, goals and audience as a filter to align with someone who has a complementary personal brand. Then consider ways to truly collaborate with that individual, or group, to influence your audience by delivering value.

Architects of Influence

Before looking outside for personal brands and creators to collaborate with, be sure to look to your own teammates. If you work for a company with an outspoken leader then you have built-in talent, and potentially reach and influence, that you can tap into. The same goes for team members at any level. Their personal stories can provide an honest and emotionally driven way for people to connect with the company.

John Legere, CEO of T-Mobile since 2012, has one of the most unique personal brands of any executive in the world. Under his leadership the company has completely turned around, doubled their customer base and exceeded Wall Street's expectations. What's unique is the unapologetic way he promotes the company and makes it his personal mission to be the living embodiment of the T-Mobile brand. He does this by wearing the company colors of magenta and black every day, fanatically engaging with employees and customers, making himself extremely accessible through social media and embracing collaboration with other brands.

In a sense he's built a presence on social media that resembles any other contemporary influencer. Brands including Vans, Converse and numerous others regularly send him T-Mobile co-branded branded gear. Twitter even created an emoji of his face that appears when someone uses the hashtag #TweetJohn. He also hosts his own weekly cooking show called "Slow Cooker Sunday." It's deliberately low budget, adding to his relatability in an era when CEOs are often criticized for being out of touch. Legere has certainly made some controversial moves but I share this story not to endorse or condemn him. It's just hard to argue with the fact that he understands personal branding and the influence one can create when leveraging modern technology.

Another vocal and somewhat polarizing business leader who has developed his own personal brand is Gary Vaynerchuk. Not only is he the CEO and voice of one of the hottest marketing agencies in the world, as well as a progressive athlete representation agency, he has personally started dabbling with brand collaborations.

Gary started his entrepreneurial career at a young age selling baseball cards. He was making thousands of dollars a week, but his father forced him to trade in card shows for a job at the family liquor store. He quickly noticed wine had many of the characteristics of baseball cards (some were rare, they changed in value over time and they both had people and stories attached to them) and over a number of years grew the business's revenue to over $60+ million dollars.

What's most interesting to me is the way Gary developed his personal brand alongside the business. In the early days of YouTube, he decided to create the first online video series about wine. He filmed shows daily and soon built up a huge following long before most of the YouTubers we know today. Gary made wine more accessible by educating consumers in a relaxed manner not typically seen in the category. He would swear, spit into a metal Jets bucket and reference everyday items like Big League Chew in his tasting notes.

What most people didn't know until Gary took to Twitter was that he had been an early adopter of internet marketing. Before his success on YouTube, he was the one of the first to focus on ecommerce in the wine space, took advantage of email marketing before spam was a thing, and exploited search engine marketing before the rest of the world caught up and started bidding on basic keywords.

In the early days of social media Gary also began proactively engaging consumers through Twitter. In doing this he accomplished three things: he sold more wine, he publicly demonstrated his marketing prowess, and he built true relationships with thousands of individuals. Eventually, Gary took to the speaking and conference circuit, published a book about entrepreneurship, invested in dozens of startups, and launched a social media consulting business that is now a well respected global agency.

Gary has long outgrown the wine-guy moniker, even though he still owns that business, and today he reaches millions of people through his own media channels. He also has a long line of personal, product and service brands waiting to collaborate with him. It's not a coincidence that the guy leading one of the fastest growing agencies in the world built a massive personal brand by leveraging content and social media before he got into the agency game. This absolutely plays a role in his ability to convince global brands to trust him with their marketing.

Recently I noticed that Gary was a featured influencer in a new campaign for K-Swiss sneakers, touting the brand's support for entrepreneurship. They aren't going to beat out Nike or adidas as a performance sports brand, but K-Swiss clearly decided they could build their brand by delivering value to those who value creativity and independence.

Gary narrates the campaign video, which also features startup leaders and artists, including fashion entrepreneurs Coco & Breezy. I had the honor of sitting on a panel with this dynamic duo to discuss artist and brand collaborations, and they are the real deal. I give K-Swiss a lot of credit for finding them. They don't have the largest brand in the world, but that's the point. They have an incredible story and they are doing things on their terms. They fill a niche, just like K-Swiss is trying to do.

Beyond on the campaign, the brand also released a specific collaborative shoe that's co-branded with Gary. Design details reflect Gary's personal brand, including the use of green because he aspires to buy the NY Jets, and cork material at the end of the laces, a nod to Gary's roots as an entrepreneur in the wine world. Like any sneaker collaboration they also relied on scarcity by promoting a limited quantity that sold out quickly, further proving the power of Gary's personal brand.

Let's break that down one more time. This is an example of a businessman and entrepreneur who has a strong enough personal brand to develop, launch and sell out a collaborative sneaker with a large footwear brand. It's one thing when athletes and rock stars pull it off, but the CEO of an agency? Things done changed.

While Gary may not be a likely candidate for a sneaker deal, or the most famous person to do a collaboration like this, the level of engagement he has with his community is off the charts. Whether you're a fan of his boisterous style or not, it's hard not to acknowledge his impact. Once again this demonstrates the opportunity that exists, given today's technology, to build, nurture and activate a passionate tribe of people. When individuals channel this power, smart marketers jump on board.

Creators Need Room

Hopefully by now you agree that publicly aligning with creative individuals inside and outside of your company is imperative. However, you can't hire someone and expect them to simply execute your strategy or creative idea. In the beginning brands should carefully and creatively evaluate which creators seem to *fit*, but once they've identified the right collaborators they should make sure to give them enough freedom to do what they do best. That's not to say they can't be a part of brainstorms or still work closely together during the process.

Some marketers and execs will be uncomfortable with this approach since brands are used to micromanaging every aspect of their business, and often dictate what they want internal teams or agencies to do when it comes to marketing. But everything we've explored in this book suggests it's time to step out of your comfort zone if you want to make an impact with your marketing.

It's easy to just accept the idea that individuals have an increasingly powerful influence on the way products and services are perceived, but I think the impact is still underestimated. The fact that smart brands are taking on personalities of their own, aligning with actual humans to reinforce their values and aggressively leveraging technology to tell stories and interact with consumers is a major threat to traditional brands that remain faceless. It's one reason you now see more storytelling on packaging, including the names of product founders and featured artists. Pepsi even went as far as launching an entire brand of water with the tagline "Thirst Inspiration" and the name of the respective artist who designed the label. According to the brand's website, "LIFEWTR believes inspiration is as essential to life as water, because it moves us forward by unleashing our creative potential. That's why we're excited to partner with artists and turn every LIFEWTR bottle into a canvas for new art."

This might sound opportunistic on Pepsi's behalf, and in some ways it is, but it shows that large brands understand the need to demonstrate their humanity, embrace values and add value for consumers beyond their core products. But fancy taglines are not enough. The reason this works is because it's backed up with substance. Each of the three series they've released have been themed. The first featured artists who worked on public art, the second highlighted female artists and the third, through a partnership with the esteemed Council For Fashion Designers, featured three emerging fashion designers. This collaboration layering empowered the artists and encouraged them to share the work with their own audiences.

The brand also invested in a high-profile advertising campaign to bring additional attention—featuring a performance by John Legend, yet another layer of collaboration with an influencer—and a series of activations tied to different cities (we'll talk more about geography as an ingredient for collaboration—just as it was for Jordan, Mars and Brooklyn—in the next chapter).

Last but not least, they launched a limited-edition product bundle in collaboration with Le Pen and visual artists Craig & Karl, who are known for their work with LVMH, Nike Air Jordan and Apple, among others. "In honor of our collaborative first year with our incredible emerging artists, we've created this limited edition holiday gift set with the help of visionary duo Craig & Karl. We welcome you to use the included journal as a blank canvas to fill with your creativity, and to help replenish your well of inspiration. Inspiration is as essential to life as water." I don't know how well the LIFEWTR brand is doing overall, or if this is simply a strategic use of scarcity, but as I'm writing this Amazon shows they only have 17 of the gift sets left in stock.

This example draws upon all of the influencer trends we've discussed and reinforces the importance of collaboration on many levels. The rise of personal branding by individuals, including traditional celebrities and modern creators of every kind, will only continue to force brands to stretch the ways they communicate, interact and collaborate. This will not only impact marketing and promotions, but also products and the way businesses operate.

CoLAB: *Personal Passion*

Let's think about influencer marketing and personal branding over our lifetimes.

In last chapter's CoLAB we looked at the leaders we've encountered in our lives and their unique skills. Now, let's think about the first person outside of those you actually knew in real life that you admired. Do you recall why and how you interacted with them, even if it was simply watching them on TV or raiding the local library for books about them?

Who filled this influencer role in your life when you were a bit older, like freshman year of high school? Were they they same as when you were a kid? How did the points of interaction change?

Now think about today and those who you follow closely. Did anyone make it from childhood all the way to the present day like Will Smith did for me? I won't even ask if the interactions have changed but I do want you to think about how much access you have to information about that individual, if not literal direct access to them.

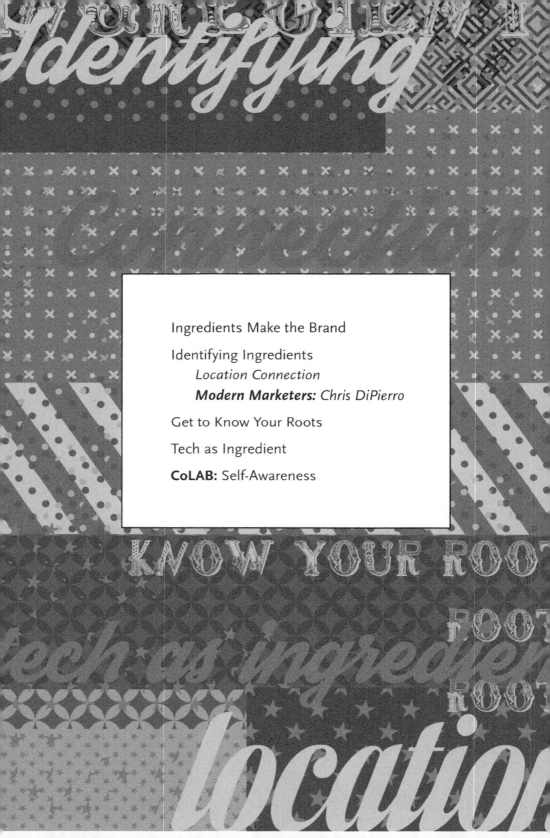

CHAPTER 6

Everything Is Connected

"There's really nothing made by any one single author anymore. Collaboration is the key."

—Marc Ecko

WHEN DR. DRE thought about diversifying his business interests and tapping into the power of his personal brand he considered the sneaker game. After all, many of his contemporaries had successfully developed collaborations in the space as we touched on in the last chapter.

He approached his friend, mentor and partner Jimmy Iovine, a legendary music exec and producer in his own right, with the idea and asked for his opinion. Iovine, being an extremely savvy marketer, pointed out that Dre could not add any value in the sneaker domain because it wasn't his area of expertise and he didn't explicitly rely on footwear to do his job. He wasn't even known for energetic live performances, which could create a direct link between a musician and a sneaker brand. This would have likely been a prosaic entrance into the space, not something particularly unexpected or uniquely credible.

When you picture Dre utilizing his talents, he's hanging out in a production studio, making beats and helping other artists find their voices. Iovine recognized this and proposed that Dre leverage his personal brand in a space that aligned directly with his skill set. "F*ck sneakers—let's make speakers," Iovine famously said. Shortly after that conversation, Beats by Dre Headphones were born and less than five years later the company sold to Apple for a reported $3 billion. Presumably he could have launched a successful sneaker collaboration, but sometimes saying no to one opportunity opens up another.

Prior to its acquisition the company built a strong fan base around the personal brand of Dr. Dre and his music. This could not have been a better *fit* for the product given Dre's track record, credibility and cultural relevance. He was a pioneer in the rap game, known for his accomplishments as an artist and producer, while also being credited with discovering some of the most iconic rappers in the music business as we touched on in the first chapter. The message was clear: these headphones and speakers were superior, especially for listening to the kind of music Dre produced. Commercials for Beats not only featured Dre, but also a myriad of artists and athletes.

As we've explored throughout the book, music and sports tap into "moments of collective joy," to steal a phrase from Brené Brown, and they provide fertile ground for collaboration. These two art forms crossover quite a bit and borrow from one another, so bringing them together to promote Beats played on a natural alignment. Not to mention, hip-hop, more than any other music genre, leverages team dynamics and competition just like sports. Artists like Dre form groups and label alliances that resemble teams, and they recruit individual players to join them in producing and recording. At the same time, a critical part of the hip-hop platform has been an ever evolving debate over talent that plays out in a variety of different ways, including artists competing and directly challenging one another.

Ingredients Make The Brand

When Hewlett Packard (HP) considered a partner to help them develop and market a laptop targeting music fans, Beats by Dre was a natural ally. HP, once a pioneering brand in the computer space, had in many ways lost its relevance, especially with young consumers. By working with Beats to co-brand laptops they harnessed the power of collaboration to shift their narrative. For fans of the Beats brand, this offering created a compelling point of entry to consider HP. Chrysler used a similar strategy when it worked with Beats to deliver better sound systems in a variety of models.

These product collaborations all rely on the branded ingredient approach, where a secondary brand is literally built into the primary product or service and then leveraged to amplify the value proposition.

A classic example in the technology space is Intel*. Very few people know what makes Intel's technology superior. After all, their primary business is producing microprocessors. Intel sales are mostly business-to-business (B2B), but television commercials promoting "Intel Inside" made them a household name. This also trained many of us to believe that they significantly impact the performance of our products and there's added value when their components are inside.

* *Intel is actually a portmanteau; a linguistic blending of words, in this case integrated and electronics. Once again we see that collaboration surrounds us!*

Bringing this otherwise behind-the-scenes brand to the forefront became a win for brands like Dell who heavily promoted their collaboration with Intel. Over time, these co-branding deals became more common as Intel provided a valuable point of reference that consumers recognized.

"We don't make the products you buy.
We make the products you buy better."

— BASF

Beginning in the early 90s and running for almost 15 years, this famous tagline from one of the largest chemical manufacturers in the world could be heard coming through TVs across America. The strategy behind the message, and the corresponding promotional effort, was yet another monumental example of the ingredient approach that Intel and others leveraged.

BASF primarily served the B2B market after discontinuing their magnetic tapes (remember cassettes?). Around the same time they launched this campaign and focused on creating the perception that they were more than a commodity chemical company. Instead, they positioned themselves as an indispensable partner in the eyes of businesses and consumers. Every brand that worked with BASF could count on this built-in partner to provide expertise, literal ingredients and marketing support. They also knew that including the BASF brand alongside theirs provided a familiar and credible reference.

While this kind of significant investment and ongoing commitment to collaboration as a marketing tool is rare, it's actually more common than we realize for brands to work together. We just don't think about it as a collaboration because most of the supporting brands are kept in the background and, unlike the ingredient partners we just covered, most remain anonymous to the buyer.

As I alluded to with Intel and BASF, in reality it takes a variety of ingredients to build most products. The same goes for delivering services. Over time it will become more popular to proactively reveal these partnerships and market them as collaborations. The primary driver? Transparency. People will find out who you work with one way or another, so it makes sense to be selective, proactive and to use this as a competitive advantage. If your company relies on a factory that has cruel working conditions your consumers will know. On the flip side, if you go out of your way to carefully select partners who are relevant because they align with your values, and improve the product or service, discerning consumers will reward you.

This kind of emphasis on ingredients and sourcing as collaboration is happening in every sector. Look at the package of any food product and, as mandated by the FDA, there's a list of ingredients. However, the vast majority of the time the list is generic. We don't know who made the sugar, the salt, the corn, or anything else. But we are beginning to see more qualifiers, like organic, non-GMO, fair trade and others. In these instances we are just one step away from knowing the actual brand names of the ingredients and suppliers.

In the grocery store we can see this play out with companies such as Amy's Organics. Their frozen vegan pizza is co-branded with Daiya Foods, a popular brand known for making lactose-free cheese that melts like the real thing and tastes incredibly similar. Rather than simply buying the cheese from Daiya and white-labeling it, or leaving out the Daiya brand and claiming it as their own creation, Amy's uses the awareness and brand equity of Daiya. Together, they make the product more appealing.

The same thing is happening in restaurants. Think back to when you were a kid, or even as recently as few years ago. It was extremely rare to see any messages about where the food came from. Today it's becoming common to walk into a restaurant or look at a menu and see a list of farms where the products are sourced. This shows the owners are thoughtful about their ingredients and buy local, reinforcing values of quality and community, while adding new characters to the brand story. As technology makes it even easier to access sourcing and other information, whether a brand proactively provides it or not, we're destined to see more brands getting ahead by taking this approach.

Identifying Ingredients

As we explored with influencer marketing and personal brands, there are often existing resources within your company you can leverage to harness the power of collaboration. This goes for ingredients as well. Begin by examining your roots and your origin story. For most brands, this typically lives in the footer of a press release and in the "about us" section of the website, but that tends to be only a small piece of a much bigger story. If you manage a mature brand you may have a lot of history to dig through. If you're a startup or an emerging brand your story might be short. Either way, ask yourself a few key questions:

- Did the company rely on outside experts to help come up with the original product or solution?

- Has anyone on the team worked with, or for, another brand that might complement the current offering or campaign?

- Is there a collaboration already built into the production process like an ingredient or an existing affiliation with a brand we could bring to the forefront or shine a spotlight on?

- Would it make sense to tap into the story of the city or the environment where the company launched or where the products are made?

Geography is often overlooked but it is an ingredient that's often worth mining for stories and collaborations. As an example, over the past few years the city of Detroit has developed a brand narrative that appeals to a number of businesses and consumers. By aligning closely with the city, brands like Shinola have seen massive growth. If that name sounds like one you've known all your life it's probably because the original brand was created in 1877. For decades Shinola manufactured shoe polish until they went out of business in 1960. After that, the brand lived on in pop culture thanks to the phrase "you don't know shit from Shinola."

The same phrase kept the Shinola brand top-of-mind for Tom Kartsotis, the founder of Fossil Watches. Tom believed there was still equity in the Shinola name and decided to purchase the rights. He and his team at Bedrock Brands re-launched the brand as a line of watches and other goods with a timely and compelling narrative. Prior to launch, market research showed that consumers were willing to pay a premium for products made in Detroit, in part because they felt their purchases were helping the city's revitalization effort. While critics have called out Shinola, claiming they are taking advantage by exploiting the real problems faced by the community, it hasn't stopped the brand from going all-in on the city and adopting the tagline "Built in Detroit."

Shinola is directly investing in the city by creating jobs, training workers, redeveloping buildings and city parks, and promoting Detroit as a place where businesses can thrive. They have also launched a series of products in collaboration with other local businesses to help further grow the regional economy. One of their most high-profile collaborations to date is with General Electric, once known as a U.S. manufacturing giant, though today most of their goods are produced overseas.

GE receives their fair share of negative press and detractors challenge their corporate values. This is one reason why it makes sense for them to not only evaluate their practices, but also to align with companies that can help counter these claims. Enter Shinola and their ability to lend GE a new "made in America" story. Together the two created vintage clocks, similar to those once found in U.S. factories and classrooms, and a corresponding campaign with the tagline "Powered By Imagination, Crafted By Hand." Without making a judgement about business practices of either company, the partnership itself is based on genuine *fit* and that's why it works.

GE also has a track record of investing in content marketing—with projects like *Short Films, Big Ideas* that capture stories of "innovators" to reinforce the brand's history of invention—so it made sense for the Shinola and GE collaboration to rely on a similar idea. Campaign videos featured stories of Detroit factory workers who literally "make time" in terms of the product, but also stressed the importance of making time for friends and family. Each feature attempted to inspire by ending with an invitation and challenge to consumers that asked what they would do with the time.

Location Connections

When GE announced that Boston would be the home of their new corporate headquarters in early 2016, city officials celebrated. Not only was this expected to boost to the economy, it added to the evolving story that Boston was a great place to do business. This kind of economic development is critical, and just like every marketing effort it revolves around a brand.

Beyond its rich history, the city is perhaps best known for sports. That's one reason GE opted to sponsor the Boston Celtics jerseys in the first year this high-profile sponsorship was ever offered. Unlike NASCAR and soccer, up until 2017 NBA jerseys were off limits to brand sponsors. Now the GE logo patch sits on the jersey alongside Nike (who won the bid to be the official uniform provider), the team name, the player name and the NBA logo.

Supporting the hometown team is a great way to show you're proud of your new digs. But that surface level branding speaks to just one piece of the collaboration. GE will provide technology to the Celtics in the form of data analytics to drive on- and off-court decision making, as well as energy-efficient lighting for the team's practice facility and medical equipment to help take care of players. The team also benefits from the perception created by aligning with an innovative company, which is important in the "moneyball" era where data and tech directly impact wins and losses. In this sense GE has become not only a sponsor, but a marketable ingredient partner for Celtics.

Although I won't root for the Red Sox, when the NY football Giants and the Knicks are out of contention I'll support the Patriots and Celtics. If nothing else, it's also a lot more pleasant to collaborate in Boston when these teams are winning. But regardless of where my allegiances lie, when it comes to marketing I have a healthy respect for all Boston teams. Just as GE and the Celtics demonstrated, sponsorships must go beyond surface-level signage to add value for everyone involved, including the fans. And that's exactly what the Red Sox demonstrated when they teamed up with L.L.Bean in 2012.

Before planning their collaborative future, the organizations started by looking back for clues. Beyond their shared geography in New England, they realized L.L.Bean was founded the same year that Fenway Park opened. While this did lead to traditional signage for the brand in the ballpark, the L.L.Bean logo was also placed on the Red Sox rain tarp which is used to protect the field and keep it dry. This was a perfect way to demonstrate the utility of the actual L.L.Bean brand while providing exposure to a passionate fan base. However, the two brands took things one step further by literally weaving this collaboration into L.L.Bean products.

Rather than throwing away the tarp at the end of the season, L.L.Bean cleaned it and used the material to make commemorative tote bags. The limited offering sold out and raised the profile of the partnership. It also empowered fans of both brands to become walking billboards, by arming them with not only a product but a story. It would have been easy to stop with just the logo on the tarp, or the Green Monster, but instead the brands built a winning collaboration around shared geography, history and culture.

MODERN MARKETERS: Chris DiPierro

I learned about ingredient partners and the ability to form creative partnerships during the years I spent working in the sports industry. I worked with a minor league team, so our staff was small and we all wore a lot of hats, as the cliche goes. It was a great training ground early in my career and I had a chance to get deeply involved in all aspects of the business. One of my favorites was sponsorship sales, fulfillment and activation. We had standard inventory like arena signage, but we also challenged ourselves to creatively customize the exposure we could offer brands, especially during game days.

Internally we called the fan experience "the show," something we will explore more in Chapter 11, and it was actually something we scripted down to the minute. We tried to think through every point of the fan journey from the moment they walk through the door of the arena to when they leave. Our script outlined the music, public address announcements, video board programing, when to fly the blimp, pregame festivities, timeout promotions, half-time and postgame. Virtually everything was branded by a sponsor and their activations were key ingredients that supported the fan experience and the brand of entertainment we were trying to create.

While some of my colleagues went on to work at the highest levels in professional sports, I decided to take my chances in the agency business. I quickly realized that many of the skills I had learned with the team, especially the art of creative collaboration and marketing partnerships, would become even more relevant as technology infiltrated the traditional advertising world.

I caught up with my friend Chris DiPierro, Director of Marketing for the Boston Bruins, to dig a bit deeper into the power of partnerships and how sports can be a vehicle for collaboration in today's environment.

Why do you think collaborations are powerful?

Brand collaborations are an incredible marketing tool because when done well, they can be extremely versatile and provide much more impact than your standard impression metric. Collaborations can allow a brand to show a different side of themselves, gain credibility in a new marketplace and reach greater and potentially more engaged audiences. In sports marketing specifically, partnerships allow brand marketers to join a very passionate conversation that is constantly taking place among hyper-interested groups of people across different demographics.

Do you have a favorite endorsement deal you've been a part of or simply observed where a brand and player collaborated in way that made their partnership more impactful?

I'm a big fan of everything Dunkin' Donuts does in the sports marketing space. They have used the power of regional sports brands (both in their home base of New England and beyond) to build incredible brand consideration. In recent years, while their competitors were taking ad dollars out of local sports and putting greater emphasis on national TV buys, Dunkin' doubled down on their tie to local communities through team partnerships and player endorsements engendering even more brand affinity in a very competitive QSR landscape.

In New England, Dunkin' is a cultural phenomenon similar to the teams and athletes themselves and they've done an incredible job leveraging that to their audience using sports. Programs such as free coffee after Patriots wins to drive app usage and great sports-centered creative (Sox slugger David Ortiz and Patriots Tight End Rob Gronkowski singing in commercials and Bruins ads that featured fans, players and team personalities drinking Dunkin' Iced Coffee come to mind) have allowed the brand to tap into the passion that New Englanders have for their teams and favorite athletes while driving their own brand objectives.

Any advice for marketers to help make the most of their sponsorships with a team or endorsements of a player so

that it's truly a collaboration? How should they approach these discussions?

The biggest mistake I see is when marketers approach a sponsorship like they would any other piece of advertising. When you partner with a property, I think the first thing to realize is the audience you're reaching is engaging with the team, league or player first. That's why they are there in the stadium or engaging within the digital environment. The key to unlocking the incredible potential of your partnership is to build an integrated program that is in line with your brand's KPIs while authentically tapping directly into the passion and loyalty the audience feels for their favorite teams and athletes. That is the sweet spot.

What do you do when you are looking for creative inspiration?

I watch a lot of sports (all the North American major sports, golf, horse racing, the top European soccer leagues, NASCAR, college sports, minor leagues—really anything and everything!) but my primary focus is rarely on the game being played. I love to see what other teams, leagues and athletes are doing with brands and how fans react to those activations for inspiration (social media is an incredible way to instantly gauge interest and engagement.) Plus, when I'm able to get out-of-market to attend events at other stadiums and arenas, I find that it opens my mind and my creative approach to activation ideas. I rarely find that I'm interested in ripping an idea directly, rather in using elements and nuances that I see in different partnerships to build great integrated promotions for the brands we're working with at the Bruins.

▼ ▼ ▼

Get To Know Your Roots

Just as Amy's Organics discovered by sourcing and co-branding with Daiya Cheese, and the Red Sox demonstrated in their partnership with L.L.Bean, there's a good chance the efforts of your partners can strengthen and differentiate your brand.

Even if your brand is not inextricably tied to a city or geography that has a strong story, you should still dig into where the products or services come from. By that I mean the literal ingredients, resources and production partners you work with. Ask yourself:

- Are you relying on branded technologies, tools or uniquely skilled individuals to create your products?

- Was the product development inspired by something or someone?

- What are their stories, their goals and their unique values?

Imogene + Willie, an apparel retailer from Nashville, TN, has a fascinating origin story rooted in unique ingredients. The brand is based on a legacy of denim making in the founders' family and while that's interesting, and provides some credibility for denim connoisseurs, it's more impactful because the company relies on many of the same heritage manufacturing practices today that were popular in previous generations.

Even more specifically, they sourced denim from Cone Mills*, one of the only factories in the country that used old-school sewing machines to make traditional selvedge denim. Selvedge comes from the "self edge" that's created by these vintage machines. Most of the machines were sold off to Japan as U.S. companies opted for faster and cheaper manufacturing practices, but Cone Mills stuck with tradition. It's fair to say that Cone became the "Intel Inside" of modern denim. Everyone from J.Crew to Levi's to independent brands like Imogene + Willie all marketed the fact that they collaborated with Cone, and discerning consumers looked for their logo.

* *If you're the manufacturing brand, be sure to constantly reinvent and ensure you're relevant to your collaborators. High-priced denim is not for everyone and unfortunately Cone Mills closed in the fall of 2017. With it went 200+ jobs and a great American manufacturing story. I don't know why they shut down, but it goes to show that every brand is vulnerable and must be hypersensitive to the needs of the market.*

*"Two things remain irretrievable:
time and a first impression."*

—Cynthia Ozick

Even if you have a great material sourcing and production story, your brand must be equally discerning about your distribution strategy. Where products are offered says a lot about your brand and impacts sales. Bodega, a Boston-based fashion brand and boutique, is known worldwide as a respected curator of sneakers and culture. But what makes this brand a standout is their creative and unique retail experience.

To enter into Bodega you walk through a run-down convenience store and come face-to-face with a vending machine, before a door automatically opens to reveal the actual shop. It's a truly remarkable experience that you can't help but talk about. Whenever friends come to town, it's on the list of places I take them and it's fun to watch them fumble around the storefront as they try to find the secret entrance. This creates a sense of exclusivity and discovery that reinforces the value of all products they sell.

If your product is in Bodega, you're in good company. It's being associated with an overarching brand and a number of other brands that you're predisposed to liking. The context, and these adjacencies are a reflection of your brand. There are millions of retailers and potential partners around the world, but as we've observed, it's up to you to take an otherwise straightforward association and turn it into a meaningful collaboration.

Tech as Ingredient

When it comes to certain industries, you are only as good as the partners who help you deliver upon your promise and fulfill your value proposition. The most common of these industries is technology, where companies tend to be inextricably linked to one another.

While technology is now an ingredient in almost every industry and business, the tech sector itself is layered with unique examples of collaboration that we can all learn from.

Let's start with application programming interfaces (APIs), the code that allows software programs to talk to one another. These are rules and tools built solely to foster collaboration.

"Technology is the subtext of everything—
it is woven into nearly every creative expression.
It's the oxygen that our creative culture breathes."

— Marc Ecko

In tech we also have the open-source movement. Here individuals and companies contribute code and encourage others to build upon, evolve and share their creations. The leading site for this kind of collaboration, GitHub, has a thriving community of over 28 million users. Among other things, the platform provides tools specifically built to make it easy for a wide range of individuals to contribute to the same code base or project from anywhere in the world. In June 2018, Microsoft announced it was acquiring GitHub for $7.5 billion in Microsoft stock.

In addition to free and open-source solutions in the tech world, there are many collaborations built deliberately to drive sales. These include channel partnerships and value-added resellers (VARs) who take on the responsibility of selling products or services on behalf of another company.

Alliances like this are formed to make business more effective and efficient in every industry, but the tech sector has built an exceptionally strong collaboration ecosystem. Hardware and software companies are interdependent, and both rely on help from internal and external service providers to make their offerings work. An entire subset of the industry is built around customer support, including IT consulting, integration, customization, hosting, training and maintenance companies. Without all of these entities working together, the entire infrastructure falls down.

Just like we explored in the business-to-consumer (B2C) setting, collaborations in tech can also be bolstered by content, experiences and the power of personal brands. This often takes shape when companies hire or designate experts to evangelize their solutions. Thought leadership in the form of content creation can also come from outside the company in a manner that resembles the B2C influencer trend. In tech, influencers often help by authoring blog content, hosting webinars, organizing meetups and speaking at events on behalf of a brand.

"If you're trying to create a company it's like baking a cake. You have to have all the ingredients in the right proportion."

— Elon Musk

Whether there's a brand story in your heritage, geography, manufacturing process, distribution, retail strategy or technology partner, remember that context implies an association, and just like the five people you spend the most time with, these relationships impact perception. I believe every type of ingredient we have touched on will increasingly go from the background to the forefront as consumers and businesses look to make their interactions more deliberate and meaningful. This will be exacerbated by the fact that technology will continue removing barriers to entry, allowing competition to grow in every category and giving consumers increasing visibility into corporate practices. If your brand ignores the opportunity to develop and nurture these stories, you can be sure your competitors will take advantage.

CoLAB: *Self-Awareness*

In Chapter 2's CoLAB I asked you to audit the brands in your life to see who and what you surround yourself with. Now it's time to revisit that list of brands to see if any prominently layer in collaboration by featuring ingredient partners. You're looking for products that have one primary brand and a subsequent or supporting brand also visible.

A great place to start is your kitchen cabinet. Do the products list all generic ingredients or do any use brand names?

If yes, did this factor into why you purchased the items? Is the product's story more impactful, or are the claims more believable?

Check your closet for clothing and footwear examples too. Are you finding relatively hidden brands like the YKK on your zipper or deliberate co-branding like the Gore-Tex in your boots?

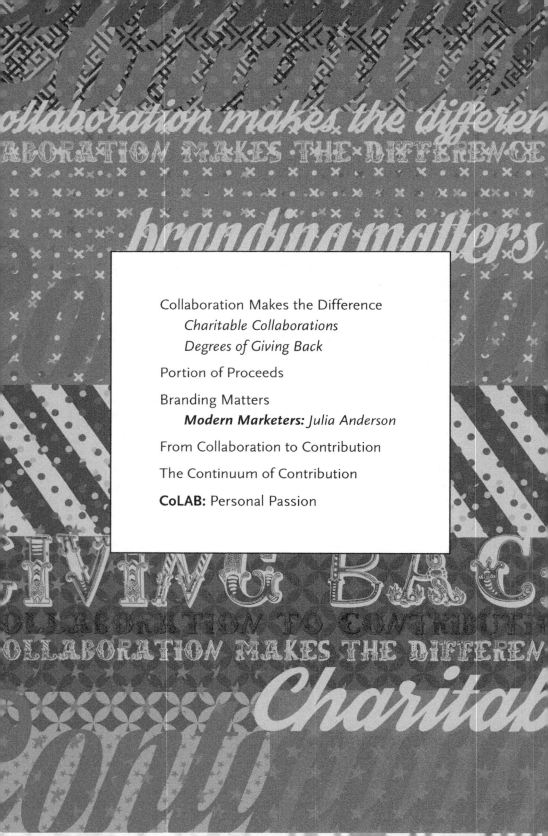

CHAPTER 7

Collaborate for Good

"I don't care what happened to your profits. Have you improved your share of the customer's mind and heart this year?"

— Philip Kotler, author, professor, distinguished marketer

I'M TEMPTED TO say brand collaboration is a shortcut to improve marketing and to increase sales, but that wouldn't be fair. It actually requires a lot of work and a commitment to leadership and creativity. Yet it can feel like a <u>hack</u>, to use another term borrowed from the tech world, due to its ability to break through the cluttered media landscape and generate interest.

In addition to demonstrating how collaboration is a unique and timely tool for business success, my other objective is to inspire individuals to learn how it can help them achieve personal goals. The idea of using collaboration as conduit for empowerment, calculated risk-taking, creative expression, networking and career development is a not-so-subtle thread I'm hoping you've picked up on.

We'll talk more about personal habits and activities you may want to try in Chapter 9, but if this strikes a nerve, know that collaboration is not only a business driver and outlet for your creativity, but also a way to make a positive impact on the world. You can use this approach to help companies assert their values and reinforce your own at the same time. But just like any productive brand collaboration, this assumes a strong *fit*.

Collaboration Makes the Difference

Whether you are promoting the type of ingredient partner we explored in Chapter 6, reframing an existing collaboration or launching a completely new one, your efforts should always come back to adding value for the customer. By cultivating empathy and understanding their needs, as well as your own goals, expertise, resources and values, you can uncover insights that lead to valuable new products, services and experiences.

I've said this a few dozen times throughout the book, because it's easy to forget when a business is evolving and dealing with pressing internal challenges. Unfortunately your customers don't care much about your operational issues and won't give you a pass because of them. They have endless choices and higher expectations. This is why corporate America and the media are focused on innovation. As we see with the decline of traditional retail, the market demands that businesses evolve or fail—not only from a product and service standpoint, but in terms of entire business models.

One result of this focus on disruption and reinvention has been a movement of companies working to make a positive impact on the world, while simultaneously delivering value to employees, shareholders and customers. That may sound altruistic, but it's a reality that's taking shape in a variety of different ways. From social impact businesses to conscious capitalism (also the title of a book by Whole Foods co-founder John

Mackey), regardless of what you call it there is clearly a slow but steady movement in this direction.

Demonstrating how you make a difference in people's lives, and a positive impact on the world, allows your business and brand to connect emotionally and go beyond surface-level transactions. In doing so your goal is not only the altruistic impact, overall awareness and and the additional revenue, but also ongoing attention from customers who share your values and want to join your efforts (not to mention the employees you attract for similar reasons). Fortunately the technology now exists to create and help nurture these genuine connections that are created between brands and consumers. When executed well, the resulting attention, and in some instances loyalty, can help drive the mission, sustain the business and provide a platform to solicit and test new ideas. These customers also tend to become strong advocates, making marketing more efficient and effective.

Charitable Collaborations

When it comes to embracing social impact as a marketer and brand, one way to dip your toe in the water, or completely dive in, is to collaborate with nonprofits. For those in large or established businesses, it's likely this is already happening in some capacity and you just need to apply a little leadership and creativity.

Many companies have established corporate social responsibility (CSR) programs or mandated bylaws that govern community donations. Countless others engage with nonprofits simply as a matter of principle. In doing so, these efforts often go under the radar and do not become part of the brand's public narrative. While it is admirable to give without hoping for reciprocity, in most instances the nonprofits would also benefit from more overt partner promotion.

When these collaborations are well executed, and the impact is communicated in a creative way, brands can count on them as a point of entry for consumers, who then use this as a reference to determine how their personal values might align. This connects once again to our thesis: you are the average of the other brands that you are most associated with.

Proactively aligning with nonprofits provides an opportunity to guide the perception of your brand in a deliberate and emotional way. Specific partnerships can also play a key role in the development of products, services or campaigns. But just like any collaboration, there must be a real connection with the nonprofit or cause, as opposed to one that feels opportunistic. The good news is your internal and external audiences have already rallied around a common set of values, interests and beliefs, even if you haven't clearly developed collaborations to support them.

As Simon (Sinek) says, start with your why and what you believe in. Then consider nonprofit partners that share these values, just as you would do with any collaboration. If you already have nonprofit partners, do an audit and evaluate whether or not they *fit*.

Similar to the ingredients that make up your supply chain and other aspects of your business, there's a good chance your company has a few great partners and programs ready for deeper collaboration and the customer spotlight. This may be challenging as nonprofit activity is often handled by resources outside of marketing, and cross-departmental collaboration is not a given. To be effective the two need to be in lock step, informing one another of all activities and recognizing their mutual contributions to brand building.

While it may be politically charged, in reality this internal collaboration is relatively simple to initiate. Invite cross-functional teams to join in creative jam sessions where you share ideas in an open and judgment-free environment. This is especially important in the early stages of a new campaign, product launch or other major development. In the discussion, keep coming back to the shared values, goals and audiences of the business. In doing so be sure you consider how any nonprofit activity will reinforce why consumers buy into your brand. Then try to identify opportunities to connect the seemingly unconnected, and find a balance between what's good for business and for the soul.

Don't forget to survey your employees to see what they are supporting. You may have someone on your team who is deeply engaged with a nonprofit that aligns extremely well with your brand. Just as we discussed in the last two chapters, collaborating with internal audiences, influencers and creators within your company presents opportunity.

Another key distinction here is not just why you engage or who you collaborate with, but how. Although you can start small, you must do more than just make a donation. For a nonprofit collaboration to be effective, you have to literally take action.

Degrees of Giving Back

Over the past decade, nonprofit innovation has been increasingly coming from for-profit brands. Many have created new models that focus on giving back as a core tenet of their businesses, even though their end products and services compete with brands in traditional categories.

TOMS Shoes has been one of the most high-profile examples given the unique way they give back with their "One for

One" model. As you probably know thanks to the strength of their marketing, with every pair of shoes they sell, a pair is donated.

What consumers appreciate about this is the "free prize inside" as Seth Godin would say. This speaks to the added benefit, like the feeling of goodwill, that comes from a purchase one would theoretically make anyway. But would they? If not for the alliance with a cause, the values-based rationale, the emotion it evokes and the personal badge that says "I support a brand that supports people in need," would TOMS have caught on the way it did?

TOMS also relied on collaborations with well-known brands in the for-profit and nonprofit space to market the company. Their first retail partnership was with Nordstrom, who committed to carrying the shoes with the condition that TOMS's founder, Blake Mycoskie, agreed to personally stand with the product every Saturday and share the brand's story with customers. In this example, we see a new product, a clear cause, a brand collaboration and personal branding at work.

TOMS also launched in the early days of YouTube, and Blake credits their commitment to digital storytelling—creating videos people could easily share to help their peers understand the significance of a purchase—with a lot of their success. People were proud to be a part of the story, which was an ongoing journey they could impact.

TOMS also created a smart and effective campaign and collaboration platform called "One Day Without Shoes," where they encourage people to ditch their kicks for one day a year to spread awareness. In return, TOMS agrees to donate a pair for every picture posted on social media with the hashtag #withoutshoes. A variety of large corporate partners and celebrities collaborate in support of the effort, creating additional buzz for the campaign and the brand.

Since Blake proved the "One for One" model could work at TOMS, a number of companies have followed in his footsteps (couldn't resist). Perhaps most notable are eyeglass company Warby Parker, which donates a pair of glasses for every pair that someone purchases, and Bombas, a company that gives a pair of socks to those in need every time they sell a pair. Turns out socks are the number one requested item at homeless shelters.

Bombas, which leads with their mission to "Stand for Something Good," has also layered in unexpected partnerships with popular restaurant chain Shake Shack and *Shark Tank*'s Daymond John (who backed the company when they appeared on the show). Prior to his investment, the company ran a very successful crowdfunding campaign on Indiegogo where they teamed up with individuals to help grow. The campaign secured $140,000 worth of commitments.

Not only does the company have over 250 "giving partners" in the form of nonprofits and other organizations who distribute socks on their behalf, they also encourage employees to hand out socks personally. In fact, every new team member receives ten pairs on their first day and are expected to give them away immediately. This helps employees see and feel the impact the company is making and gives meaning to the work they are about to embark upon.

Portion of Proceeds

Yet another model is to donate a portion of the proceeds from the purchase of a given product or service to a specific cause. This works in every industry, and it is now a very popular tactic, but those who approach this as a true collaboration have been most impactful.

ALEX AND ANI, a made-in-America jewelry company from Rhode Island, is a great example of a company that has made collaboration a critical part of their business. They are best known for their bracelets, each of which comes with a specific charm that carries a message. There are generic designs like animals and musical instruments, but also a series of charms that are co-branded with the likes of Disney, Life is Good, Major League Baseball and others.

In 2011 they decided to launch a line of these bracelets dedicated to charities, with each charm representing a cause and a portion of the proceeds allocated to a related nonprofit. In this case the products are created from scratch and directly align with the partners. To date they have worked with over 55 charities.

"CHARITY BY DESIGN is the heart and soul of ALEX AND ANI and our goal is to impact as many lives as we possibly can by co-creating with our partners meaningful pieces that deeply resonate with those touched by these causes or who want to support them."

—Carolyn Rafaelian, Founder, Creative Director
and CEO of ALEX AND ANI, in a press release
announcing that the effort had eclipsed $20 million
in donations less than five years after launching.

Nicki Maher, Vice President of ALEX AND ANI | CHARITY BY DESIGN Division, explained the multi-layered benefit the program creates in the same announcement, stating, "CHARITY BY DESIGN is truly a three-way relationship between our company, our partners and our customers all working together to make a positive impact on the lives of others."

Food company Deep River Snacks employs a similar model, promoting a different nonprofit on every one of their products. How do they choose the organizations they support? Each featured charity has personal connection to an employee. The effort is captured in their "We Give a Chip™" tagline and results in a minimum donation of 10% of profits to charity every year. Then, after years of focusing exclusively on employee-selected nonprofits, Deep River launched the #PutACauseOnIt campaign to solicit recommendations from consumers for a charity to feature on their new Black Truffle Kettle Chips.

Although the products now enjoy widespread distribution, in the early days when the brand had less awareness I first learned about them through my sister Marla, who worked at the American Liver Foundation. Their organization was featured on a Deep River product, so she was both proud and motivated to spread the word to supporters, friends and family. You can see how that enthusiasm compounds when you consider the passion and reach of the almost 20 different nonprofits with which Deep River partners. That's not why they do it, and the quality of the product stands on its own (NY Spicy Dill Pickle, yes please), but it does differentiate them and create a base of vocal advocates.

What all of these companies have in common is a commitment to push their philanthropic efforts and integrate cause-based collaborations into their businesses. This deep values-driven approach provides a point of entry and a distinct reference for consumers to decide if the brand aligns with their personal beliefs. When offered the choice between a product or service with this added benefit, it's easy to see why one has a clear advantage.

Branding Matters

When exploring partnerships, charities and nonprofits need to be just as proactive, discerning and creative as for-profit companies.

While nonprofits do not have the marketing budgets of most other brands, they also don't get a pass if they lack marketing sophistication. They must adhere to a standard that results in a clear articulation of what they stand for and a corresponding marketing program to tell their story in a way that fits with modern communication. They must also have their own criteria to establish *fit,* and offer ideas and resources to help brands activate their participation in mutually beneficial way.

charity: water is a nonprofit that was built to feel like a consumer brand. In fact, it was created with a deliberate commitment to branding because founder Scott Harrison saw how many other causes missed the mark in that department. He felt people would find it more appealing to align with a nonprofit that had a strong brand, and he was right.

Scott's background was in club promoting in NYC where he was often paid by liquor brands to rep their products. He understood the fundamentals of marketing and eventually decided to apply his knowledge to a cause he felt passionate about.

One reason many nonprofits don't present themselves in a way that resembles consumer brands is because they are simply comparing themselves to their peers. This is a classic mistake, as looking only to your direct competitors and industry limits your worldview and cultural connections. Try comparing yourself to other brands in other categories, then narrowing to those with direct relevance to your audience. That will help expand your thinking and the scope of what you can achieve.

In an effort to take on this common mistake, Scott and his charity: water team created a different kind of nonprofit brand, both visually and in practice. They have a contemporary logo, a remarkably consistent design style, and a conversational tone that reveals an approachable, yet inspiring personality. They also use social media channels in the same way, adding to their reach and approachability.

As we've explored, companies need to back up their messages with action, so Scott set out to develop a business model that deliberately addressed the number one complaint about nonprofits—money.

Research shows that most people believe only a small portion of their donation actually ends up where they intended, which creates a larger trust issue. With that information Scott organized charity: water so he could honestly say 100% of all donations would directly impact the cause. He funded the administrative side of the business through separate corporate partnerships, and consumer donations exclusively fund new wells to provide clean water around the world.

When it comes to collaboration, Julia Anderson, Senior Manager of Brand Partnerships at charity: water, told me their team thinks of themselves like an advertising agency in terms of their ability to work closely with brands. They also invest in annual summits for their partners, providing an in-person forum where brands in their ecosystem meet one another and form ancillary collaborations.

MODERN MARKETERS: Julia Anderson

It's common for nonprofits and charities to work with a variety of brands, but those who look at this through the lens of marketing and collaboration take a decidedly different approach. I connected with Julia to hear more about the way brand partnerships help drive charity: water and what they offer in return:

Philosophically, does charity: water try to make their corporate partnerships feel like true collaborations more than just donations?

Yes, the last thing we want is for a partnership to feel like a transaction. It's about building human relationships and trust. Our corporate partners are a community of amazing brands and organizations that are fundraising for clean water, getting their customers to round-up at check-out, hosting events to raise awareness, and lending their creative brainpower. They are true collaborations.

Is there an example of a specific brand collaboration you're particularly proud of and why was this unique?

We kicked off an awesome partnership with WeWork last year. The message from WeWork to their community members is "we don't take clean water for granted." The company is donating $30 (the average cost to bring one person clean and safe drinking water) for every fruit water dispenser across NYC WeWork locations. WeWork and charity: water share so many values around community, transparency and innovation so the partnership felt very organic.

How does the fact that charity: water has a modern and desirable brand impact your partnerships strategy and success?

We've been in a fortunate position where most of our partnerships to date have been inbound, brands that love charity: water's mission and want to get involved. The brand partnerships team has now grown where we're able to be strategic and identify the companies across the fashion, tech and lifestyle landscape that are doing incredible, innovative things and pro-actively try to seek out new partnership opportunities. I think this will greatly increase the level of impact we're able to have in helping even more communities around the world get clean and safe drinking water.

You mentioned that charity: water resembles an ad agency in some ways. How so?

charity: water focuses on inspirational story-telling. Our mar-keting team is brimming with brilliant, creative minds that get to dream up new ways to engage our community of supporters, fundraisers, donors and brand partners and bring them closer to the work that we do. We're launching campaigns throughout the year—whether it's for World Water Day or Back to School—to share the amazing stories of people whose lives have been transformed because they now have access to clean water.

The partner summit is fascinating. Are there any specific activities from the event you'd recommend others replicate?

I think what was most valuable was giving our brand partners time to network, get to know each other and share learnings. Things like how have they gotten their employees or customers involved, what are the challenges in working with a non-profit and what has proven successful.

When you are pitching or beginning to implement a new partnership, do you have any internal processes for brain-

storming with your team and/or with partners that seems to yield creative ideas?

We always try and do our homework, but there isn't a universal formula. Sometimes brands come to us with an idea fully baked and other times we're building something from the ground up. If we're crafting a bespoke concept, we'll pull in our brand content lead, social media strategist, designers, Scott, and ask ourselves: *What problem are we trying to solve? How can we maximize the impact given the brand's objectives? How can we approach this from a holistic lens?*

You've worked in for-profit and nonprofit, what is the most unique thing about how collaborations work in the nonprofit world?

I was surprised by the sheer number of brands and organizations that are fueled by pure generosity.

Any advice for nonprofits who are trying to tap into the power of personal branding or celebrity?

Transparency in your mission and hire good talent.

Where do you personally find creative inspiration? Are there any habits you've formed or go-to activities that help you come up with new ideas and stay relevant?

I find a lot of inspiration from my friends. One of the many blessings of living in New York City is that you get the opportunity to meet such diverse people. I have friends who are graphic designers, photographers, writers, chefs, hustling entrepreneurs—all of whom are incredibly passionate about their craft. Aside from that, reading online publications (Fast Co, Inc,

Refinery29), listening to podcasts, and talking to my husband who is a spark plug of creative energy.

▼ ▼ ▼

From Collaboration To Contribution

As we've covered, there are many ways to develop partnerships with nonprofits. But some organizations have taken this even further by building platforms that rely on collaboration at every stage. What these unique entities all have in common is an emphasis on branding. By making this a priority, they become a clear and appealing option for partnering brands that want to demonstrate their commitment to a cause in a creative way.

One of the best examples is Product (RED), a nonprofit launched by Bono to raise awareness and funds to fight AIDS. In addition to having a strong brand that's visually appealing and memorable, (RED) was built to promote a variety of partnerships.

This organization has been around for a while, so it's easy to overlook just how unique it is. But there are very few examples of long-standing collaboration platforms that rely on a consistent formula to drive their efforts. In the case of (RED), each partner creates a co-branded limited-edition product or service. The offering always adopts the (RED) color palette and incorporates the parentheses that surround the logo as a design element on their packaging and marketing materials. For example, Belvedere Vodka turned their otherwise clear bottle completely red for their (RED) collaboration, and Apple released a red iPod back in the day. Each partner benefits from the exponential awareness, and the association with the others who have participated, not to mention Bono and the long list of celebrities who have supported the effort.

I remember my first (RED) purchase: a t-shirt that came from their collaboration with GAP that had the word "Desi(RED)" across the chest. This was a little corny, but the decision to adapt the brand's logo to create new words was clever. This was also a great example of combining functional and emotional utility. It allowed me to literally make a donation to a charitable cause and provided a brand badge that in my mind said I was both socially conscious and fashionable.

"To do good you have to do something."

—Yvon Chouinard, Co-founder, Patagonia

Partnering with a nonprofit is a great way to explore collaboration and do good at the same time. But just like any marketing campaign, you must clearly articulate why the effort provides value to your audience, even if it's just an emotional connection that makes them feel proud to associate with your brand. Furthermore, we see that nonprofits need to increasingly rely on the kind of marketing typically reserved for consumer brands. This creates a perfect environment for mutually beneficial collaboration.

The Continuum of Contribution

All of these examples illustrate the range of commitments companies make to acting in accordance with their values. Certain companies are building philanthropic endeavors into their business models while others have made it a byproduct of their success. In the middle of this continuum there is yet another opportunity to leverage collaboration and give back—this time directly to your customers.

In the wake of the great recession, American Express decided to launch a new campaign that supported their customers. While most of the marketing we traditionally see from this brand promotes the advantages of carrying an AMEX card, this campaign was aimed at helping a different customer segment: small businesses.

The effort centered around the idea of promoting these customers at a time when they really needed the help. Today small businesses are often overlooked due to the tech-enabled convenience that comes when shopping with big brands, not to mention the ability for large brands to outspend and overshadow small businesses. Even when it comes to B2B sales, as we saw with the demise of Cone Mills, it can be difficult for specialized businesses to thrive. AMEX recognized this and turned it into an opportunity by creating "Small Business Saturday," a campaign that increased awareness and sales for small businesses by encouraging people to go out and "shop small" on the Saturday after Thanksgiving.

The multifaceted collaboration platform enlisted the help of the businesses themselves, in addition to consumers and organizations known as "Neighborhood Champions." Together with these advocates the effort grew year after year, and by 2016 there were more than 6,700 Neighborhood Champions, covering all 50 states. In addition to advertising and promotional support, AMEX provided small businesses with marketing education and materials to raise awareness for the effort.

As a result, the "Shop Small Movement" not only created positive awareness for AMEX, but it also provided an opportunity to add value for multiple audiences at the same time. Sure,

AMEX works with the largest brands in the world, but they also know the vast number of businesses in America are small. The campaign website included data on the small business climate in every state and tools that helped consumers discover local shops. When I searched Massachusetts I learned there are approximately 640,000 small businesses in the state, making up over 95% of all businesses there.

What's most impressive to me is the way in which AMEX has directly reinforced their value proposition—enabling transactions—for multiple audiences while rallying individuals to become vocal advocates on their behalf. They also found a way to scale the number of unique collaborations in which they are participating. The literal real estate, and corresponding awareness, generated by the Shop Small signage (which includes AMEX branding), combined with the earned media they generate, is astounding. It's hard to imagine what it would cost to generate that kind of exposure through paid advertising, let alone the goodwill, which is even more difficult to put a price on. And they accomplished all of this while creating a program that promotes their B2B and B2C offering at the same time.

An overlying theme of this book has been the opportunity for brands to complement paid advertising with activities that generate earned media in the form of news coverage, social media mentions and word-of-mouth exchanges. This kind of exposure is often the result of an investment in a new initiative, new product or a special promotion, but the ensuing coverage feels more organic. That's because it takes advantage of the fact that third-party endorsements are always viewed more favorably, and seen as more believable, than direct brand messages.

What the AMEX example also demonstrates is the opportunity for brands to identify insights, often tied to consumer challenges, that they are uniquely suited to address. When they do so and take action, they can show up in an empathic way that reinforces the overall impact they hope to make beyond sales. There are social enterprises explicitly built to make a positive impact on the world, but today every company is at risk if they ignore the need to be a good corporate citizen. This is driven by the fact that so many companies are embracing the opportunity and offering alternatives to those who fail to demonstrate a virtuous reason for being.

CoLAB: *Personal Passion*

Go to the homepage of your favorite cause. How long does it takes you to find one of their corporate partners? Do any jump out in terms of their unique involvement with the organization?

Now go to the homepage of one of your favorite brands. How long does it takes to find information about their charitable efforts? Does this meet your expectations, impress or disappoint you?

Lastly, other than Bono, can you name a celebrity you admire and a cause they publicly champion? If not, check out their social media profiles and see how prominently they talk about giving back.

Now that you've taken stock, do the nonprofit "friends" in your brand ecosystem seem to align with you and your values?

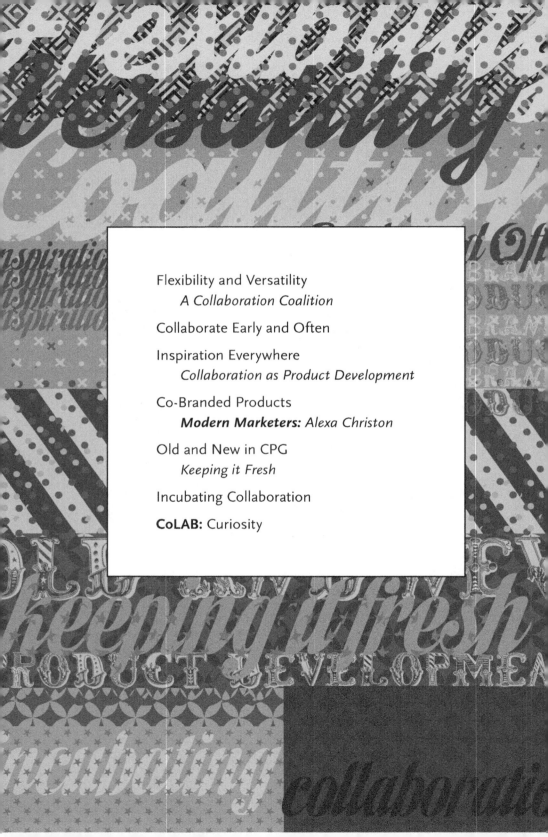

CHAPTER 8

Mastering Brand Collaboration

"Setting customer expectations at a level that is designed with consistently deliverable levels of customer service requires that your whole staff, from product development to marketing, works in harmony with your brand image."

—Richard Branson

TODAY BRANDS NEED a wide range of touchpoints to engage new and existing consumers. Regularly launching collaborations under an umbrella promotion, campaign theme or sub-brand can help support these demands on the modern marketer.

Both (RED) and ALEX AND ANI's CHARITY BY DESIGN, which we explored in the last chapter, are examples of collaboration platforms in the nonprofit space that invite a variety of brands to participate. In doing so they extend the reach, frequency and quality of the interactions they have with consumers.

Flexibility and Versatility

One of my favorite brands to watch in the collaboration space is Target. Like Ikea in the furniture industry and H&M and Uniqlo in fashion, Target's brand has become synonymous with affordable design. But they have also developed a strong track record for launching collaborations with brands including Victoria Beckham, Kate Spade, Joanna Gaines, Lilly Pulitzer and over 200 others. While their one-off partnerships are typically strong, and tend to generate a lot of buzz, their collaboration platforms are equally intriguing from a marketing standpoint.

When the great recession hit in 2007 it became challenging for some large brands to separate themselves from the negative consumer sentiments developing around corporate interests. This argument framed a huge divide between Wall Street and Main Street, with the latter representing small businesses and entrepreneurship. The entire debate called into question the values of large corporations like Target and some of that skepticism remains today.

In early 2012 Target announced the "Shops" program, which aimed to help the brand combat some of the lingering negative Wall Street attention by supporting small businesses. Target teamed up with the owners of five different specialty stores and boutiques to "co-create affordable, limited-edition collections for its guests." The partnerships resulted in 400 co-branded products that came to life at each Target store. Dedicated signage and product displays identified the items in departments including home, beauty, fashion and pets. To promote the campaign Target produced short videos introducing each Shop owner and their brand. Not only did these entrepreneurs explain what inspired them, but they also spoke highly of their relationship with Target and what it meant for their business.

By teaming up with these brands Target seemed more re-latable and aware of the challenges many were facing due to the economic downturn, while simultaneously bringing a fun and spirited campaign to life. My favorite collaboration from the Shops platform was with The Webster, a boutique based in Miami, Florida. Together with Target they produced a variety of items including men's clothing that featured palm trees and flamingos. Even though I was shopping in New England, the collaboration provided a sense of discovery and made me feel like I had a little piece of Miami style.

More recently Target has been focused on Made to Matter, another collaboration platform that relies on curation rather than co-branding. Just as they did with Shops, Target formed a series of partnerships to amplify certain aspects of their own brand and personality—in this case, their interest in wellness and the environment. Made to Matter became an ongoing cam-paign platform and labeling system highlighting a portfolio of brands that made better-for-you products.

"Guests love the Made to Matter collection because it offers them a way to easily discover new products that are better for them, their families and the world around them," said Target's CMO at the time, Jeff Jones, in a press release announcing the most recent iteration of the program.

The platform kicked off with a relatively broad description of why certain brands were featured, but over the course of a few years Target outlined more specific criteria. This includ-ed reduced waste and packaging, closed-loop production sys-tems, clean label products, dietary and allergen restrictions and less sugar.

"In our third year, we wanted to make an even more mean-ingful impact, so we moved from curator to catalyst and chal-lenged our partners to innovate with five important criteria in mind," said Jones. "The refined approach ensures that our guests can continue to count on Made to Matter to offer a wide variety of new products that truly make a difference."

"Designing a product is designing a relationship."

—Steve Rogers, Director UX, Google

While this is an example of Target using their size and power to dictate the way smaller brands do business, the criteria was only applied to partners of the Made to Matter program, which was voluntary. It's an interesting example of collaboration driving innovation as the brands were certainly incentivized to implement the changes. It also provides a platform for Target to demonstrate what's important to their culture, and create the same kind of values-based emotional connection we talked about with nonprofits like Alex and Ani and AMEX, with their Shop Small initiative.

As a result of programs like Shops and Made to Matter, Target has become a magnet for a variety of potential partners. For example, when Harry's, a shaving startup that set out to disrupt the men's grooming category, decided to go after physical retail, they aligned with Target as their exclusive partner. They could have stayed focused solely on their direct-to-consumer model, or launched with widespread retail distribution, but instead they made a strategic decision to collaborate with one specific brand: Target. They know Target understands the value of truly partnering rather than just stocking a product, and the right way to promote collaborations with brands of every size. Target is now poised to be the go-to for other emerging and digitally native brands looking to cross the chasm and show up on retail store shelves.

Target always seems to be on top of trends, and their partnerships clearly consider the broader cultural context. They are also a pioneer in high-low collaborations, where otherwise exclusive and expensive brands create more accessible offerings through partnerships. H&M and Uniqlo are the other retailers best known for this, although many brands have emulated the strategy. In a way, the Supreme x Louis Vuitton collaboration we talked about in Chapter 4 plays on a similar high-low approach, connecting seemingly unconnected brands.

Music is another creative layer and conduit of collaboration that Target has been committed to. Even as CD sales plummet, they continue offering exclusive albums and bundles (packaging music with other merchandise like t-shirts and posters) for the likes of Taylor Swift, Katy Perry, Pentatonix and Prince. Like many brands, Target also relies on music to drive the emotion in their traditional advertising, but during a recent Grammy telecast they aired a particularly timely and progressive commercial with layers of music-driven collaboration.

While the Grammys always pay homage to late musical icons, 2016 was different as the industry had lost two relatively young legends, Prince and George Michael. The entire night of the Awards show seemed to focus on nostalgia, including kicking things off with Michael Jackson's daughter, Paris, as the first presenter. Culturally, the show also aired at a time when 80s and 90s nostalgia was hot, and a number of brands were making attempts to get in on the action.

In my mind Target stole the throwback spotlight that evening, while demonstrating their marketing savvy, by mixing old and new. The result was a full video remix of the 80s hit "It Takes Two" by Rob Base and DJ Easy Rock during a commercial break. Rather than relying on the original artists, the song was remixed by two young pop stars, Lil Yachty and Carly Rae

Jepsen. Target teased the video in the early part of the evening on TV and social media, where both artists also posted about the campaign to help build buzz.

When it eventually ran, turning an otherwise traditional commercial break into one long music video, the spot promoted a variety of different brands and leveraged Target's unique formula for showcasing products in a fun visual manner. This all added up to a demonstration of their commitment to collaboration, cultural savvy and their understanding of modern media, especially since the entire effort hinged upon one of the only television products that still has a significant live viewing audience—awards shows. In doing so they entertained the audience and held their attention for a few minutes, rather than using a traditional commercial to briefly interrupt them.

A Collaboration Coalition

After graduating from college on the east coast, my high school friend Justin and I headed west. Way west. We ended up running a bar and restaurant together in Hawaii for a short stint before helping to launch a startup scuba business. During our six months or so at the restaurant we had a crash course in entrepreneurship and gained an appreciation for grassroots marketing.

I made my way into sports marketing and the agency business, but Justin stayed close to the hospitality industry by going to work for Anheuser Busch (now AB InBev). One time I decided to join him for a trip to Chicago where we linked up with his teammates who were responsible for activating their brands on the Dave Matthews Band tour. After a great show at Wrigley Field, we headed to the after-party. I fully expected we'd be in a bar or restaurant, but instead we were directed to a Burton retail store. I later learned that the Band's bass player Stefan

Lessard was an avid snowboarder and had established a strong relationship with brand.

I had worked in retail for a few years but I had never been to a party in a store, let alone after hours with live music. Everyone at the event was granted a special discount that could be used storewide, which made the experience feel even more exclusive and valuable. That evening opened my eyes to what is possible in retail and it inspires me to this day. Since then I've helped a number of brands put their spin on this concept by bringing artists into different retail environments for performances and product collaborations. This work also helped me see just how complementary the two could be. Brands need artists to help tell stories, create content and energize experiences, while artists need brands to help reach people and make money.

I recently went back to the same Burton store for the first time in about six years and was happy to see they continue to innovate around artist partnerships. When I approached one of the sales reps, she told me they not only still host events in the store, but they have established a much larger collaboration strategy.

On the second floor I found Burton's collaboration with L.A.M.B., the fashion brand created by Gwen Stefani. Not only was the collection fun and unique, the merchandising was on point. Displays highlighted the two brands side by side, and a painted wooden block on the shelf explained why they teamed up:

"L.A.M.B. and Burton are mixing up the newest round of winter's most wanted designs in a collection that combines punk rocker edge and elegance with Gwen Stefani's always-original style."

This kind of merchandising is often overlooked and brands forget to tell the story, but that's a mistake. You can't assume people know why you're collaborating even if there's a strong *fit*.

On the third floor I found another music-inspired collaboration, this time a line of snowboards and gear co-branded with Led Zeppelin. The sign read:

"'Mellow is the man who knows what he's been missing.' Toss some classic rock mysticism into your all-terrain shredding with the Led Zeppelin adorned Easy Living series."

This is a lyric from their song "Over the Hills and Far Away," which is an apt title for an outdoor brand. It also reinforces the company's current marketing campaign which celebrates their 40th anniversary, the journey, and the idea of always moving forward. This works well on the surface and even better when you dig a bit deeper. Needless to say, I was impressed by the intention with which Burton forms and promotes their collaborations.

On my way out, I thanked Burton's staff for indulging my curiosity and picked up its most recent catalogue. It was rich with storytelling about the brand and the individual products, including the collaborations. But what I found most impressive was the two-page spread at the back of the catalogue that framed up their commitment to collaboration. The section was called "The Burton Coalition," and under all of their partner logos it read, "The Burton Coalition taps into the creative force of brands that carry the same attitude, influence, and dedication to progression. A collaborative spirit of creating new takes on instant classics—that's the Burton Coalition."

Go ahead and read that last line a second or third time. It's a gem.

Now let's break it down. First, they've given their collaborations a home, a platform and a name that tells the consumer this is something they care about. Next, they lay out the criteria so it's clear these partnerships are not conveniently created solely to drive commerce. Instead they are built on creativity and shared values. Then they merchandise the collaborations in the store and online with additional storytelling. That doesn't even take into consideration the various events and promotions they layer on top.

Burton's collaboration and co-branding strategy feels thoughtful, cohesive, fun and functional. In doing so they create a clear value proposition for consumers and also provide a platform that allows them to set expectations with brands for future partnerships. This is a blueprint we can all steal and build upon in our own way.

Collaborate Early and Often

The U.S. eyewear market is dominated by one company. Even when you see branded eyewear from well-known fashion brands, most are the result of licensing deals with that one industry behemoth. Even the popular chains of eye doctors and sunglass purveyors are owned by this giant corporation. However, the consolidation in this space was not known to most consumers until Warby Parker, an upstart prescription glasses company, decided to poke the bear.

The founders of Warby Parker launched their eyewear company with a focus on functional and emotional benefits, including high-quality, stylish frames, a thoughtful customer experience—built around an innovative "home try-on" program that addressed the challenge of buying eyewear online—and a give-back component that donated a pair of glasses to a child in need for every pair purchased. They also leveraged a number of collaborations to provide the ideal environment and context for early adopters to discover the brand.

I first encountered Warby Parker in the lobby of The Standard Hotel in downtown Los Angeles, a result of their partnership with the boutique hotel chain. Although Warby's core business at the time was direct-to-consumer e-commerce, they knew that some semblance of an offline presence was necessary to build trust with a core audience. Rather than investing in expensive stand-alone retail stores, they developed a number of collaborations with offline brands that attracted the same target audiences—primarily young people who appreciated smart style and value. In this instance Warby branded the lobby activation and collaboration as The Readery, a physical booth structure that housed the products and resembled a classic newsstand. It was hosted by a representative from the brand and featured a mix of periodicals alongside the glasses. This was a win-win, giving The Standard a new unique way to monetize their lobby and add to the guest experience, while Warby built awareness among their target demo alongside a revered brand.

Around the same time, the Warby Parker team began investing in a variety of other carefully selected sponsorships, including *Austin City Limits* and Art Basel in Miami. Each activation was chosen based on cultural relevance and an environment that would help reinforce the company's values. They also showed up in clever ways like turning pedal bikes into mobile showrooms, bringing the product to the people, just like their online service did.

The second time I ran into Warby Parker was in Nashville at Imogene + Willie. As mentioned in the last chapter, the store has become a popular destination and the brand is known for their premium denim. Imogene + Willie is housed in an old gas station on the outskirts of downtown Nashville, and the location means you have to veer away from the increasingly crowded tourist destinations and famous honky tonks. This makes the experience feel like even more of a discovery and plays into the thrill of the hunt that motivates so many of us.

In addition to the branded jeans and tees they produced, Imogene + Willie also featured a small collection of curated goods from other brands, including the heritage boot company Red Wing and sneaker company P.F. Flyers. Both were a strong *fit* and spoke to the same throwback craftsmanship the brand was built on. I distinctly remember walking to the back of the store to discover a branded glasses case from none other than Warby Parker. They weren't a heritage brand, or a product that was a made in America, but sitting alongside the other brands in Imogene + Willie spoke volumes about who they were and who they would become. This shop-in-a-shop retail model provided a platform for Warby Parker to associate directly and indirectly with a variety of other fashion brands that all had their own unique stories and lent credibility.

My most recent interaction with the brand highlighted their investment in personal brand collaborations. I tried on a pair of sunglasses in their Boston showroom and found the following inscribed on the inside of one arm: "Tyler Oakley × Warby Parker." Oakley is known primarily as a YouTube personality (over 8 million subscribers) who advocates for teens and LGBTQ rights. Beyond the glasses, each purchase came with a lens cloth that doubled as a pocket square and designs for both were inspired by Tyler's style and mood boards.*

---

* *Interestingly Tyler has also teamed up with another brand we've covered for their commitment to collaboration: Taco Bell. In this instance Tyler was the spokesperson for a campaign that was launched in partnership with the non-profit Get Schooled. Together with Taco Bell, they provide middle – and high-school kids the resources they need to graduate, find jobs and go to college, as well as incentives and scholarships.*

Today the Warby Parker brand has more than 50 stand-alone retail stores in some of the most popular shopping districts in this country, including Newbury Street in Boston, South Congress in Austin and Abbot Kinney in Venice Beach. The same attention to detail and creativity that made their collaborations successful have been applied throughout their business, including the in-store experience.

In Boston their company history is mapped out in the form of a timeline on the table at the center of the store where orders are taken. It includes all the important phases of the brand's evolution and the partnering brands they collaborated with along the way, including those mentioned above. Today their reach goes far beyond the early adopters, but the visual story displayed in the shop allows people to quickly catch up and feel like they are in the know. Interestingly, the brand is also expanding their physical footprint while most other brands are closing stores at an alarming rate.

> *"I don't think retail is dead. Mediocre retail experiences are dead."*

— Neil Blumenthal, co-founder, Warby Parker

Remember, consumers will automatically associate you with many things, especially other brands, based on the various interactions they have with you. As we saw with Warby Parker, being deliberate about the brands you align with becomes a tool that helps you impact the way you are perceived. Collaborations also expand the points of entry to your brand and reveal aspects of your values, personality, and the "jobs" you are most qualified to do.

Target, Burton, Warby Parker and the other brands we've explored throughout the book reinforce our thesis: your brand is the average of the other brands it is associated with. That is why you can't leave it up to happenstance. The best marketers, artists and entrepreneurs strategically and proactively align with other brands on a regular basis to drive their business forward.

While it's common to hear pundits say consumers are now in control, and they do have more power than ever before, there are very few instances where a completely choose-your-own-adventure brand presence works. Instead, marketers can launch deliberately crafted tools—a story, content, experiences, products, services, collaborations, and most importantly a clear value proposition—that consumers then use to shape their personal opinion of, and experiences with, a brand. By doing this, the overarching perception of a brand is led by brands and marketers, even if we don't fully dictate how it is interpreted.

Inspiration Everywhere

I'm energized by being around people who are making things happen and following their passions, so in addition to carefully selecting the five people I spend the most time with, I attend key events where I can meet and learn from industry leaders. Networking can happen through social media, but until virtual reality advances quite a bit more, nothing comes closer to the value of connecting with someone face-to-face. If you picked up this book I'm sure you already know the importance of networking and doing so in a genuine way.

One event I enjoy attending is the annual Nosh Live food and beverage conference, where established and emerging brands connect, trade notes and initiate partnerships. Large companies such as Hershey share the stage with emerging brands like Arctic Zero, all with an eye towards creating products that consumers will find appealing and valuable.

One of my favorite talks came from Phil Anson, the founder of EVOL, a frozen foods company that makes an incredible burrito, among other things. He spoke about building his brand and the fact that he looked at the entire business as a creative outlet. That was refreshing to hear. Then Phil described his lifestyle, and how it helps him develop ideas. He seeks out new experiences, constantly travels, pays close attention to his surroundings and takes pictures everywhere he goes. He then groups these photos into books that he shares with friends and colleagues.

During the presentation he shared a collage of photos from his experience in New York in the days leading up to the conference. He had been to a variety of restaurants, bars, food halls, markets and music venues, and as a result he identified a series of trends. Next, Phil explained that this approach was exactly how he came up with the best-selling product in EVOL's history: truffle mac and cheese.

I can vividly remember learning to boil water and making pasta as a kid. It was a big deal to graduate to the stove after years of being relegated to the microwave. (Safety first!) I also remember getting toaster oven privileges somewhere in between the two, and I made a killer pizza bagel. But my go-to stovetop meal became mac and cheese, rotating between Kraft and Velveeta. The only innovation I recall happening in the category back then was the color and consistency of the cheese. Contrast that with EVOL's truffle mac and it's clear we've come a long way.

But where did Phil come up with this combination? Years ago as he chronicled his travels he noticed a trend. Truffle fries were showing up everywhere. He thought about other ways to deliver truffles as an ingredient and eventually married them with a tried-and-true winner: mac and cheese. This was not easy from a logistics standpoint, but innovation never is.

Although truffles, often referred to as the diamond of the kitchen, don't have a corporate brand attached to them, they have many of the same characteristics. They are perceived a certain way, have cultural and geographic connotations and appeal to those who appreciate distinct and rich flavors. As we explored earlier, literal ingredients are a great place to look for a potential collaboration that might be hiding in plain sight. When Phil combined truffles with mac and cheese, and offered the combination as a frozen food item, he created something completely new and unexpected.

Collaboration as Product Development

A few years ago I had the privilege of meeting my favorite marketer and longtime virtual mentor, Seth Godin, and I asked him what he thought the future of the marketing agency business would be. Although we only had a few moments together, he very succinctly described an opportunity for agencies to go beyond marketing products and instead play a key role in developing products. His rationale? An agency's job is to understand people. What they like, what they want, what they need, what they purchase, how they spend time with media and, most importantly, why.

If the core business of an agency is to be really good at understanding what motivates people, then agencies are perfectly equipped to help develop products and services to satisfy their wants and needs. This got me thinking about the ways marketers at agencies and in-house at brands could expand their roles and bridge the gap between marketing and product. As Phil Anson demonstrated, inspiration for new products can come from anywhere.

At the same time, I understand why professional product development teams might be protective of their domain. A related challenge is that many large brands have design and production rules in place that actually limit experimentation. Despite these roadblocks, if you're a marketer, and you recognize the opportunity to play in the product development space, a great way to start is collaborating with another brand.

A benefit of collaboration is that it allows companies to explore new things without making huge bets or committing permanent resources. Instead you can rely on the expertise and resources of another brand to share in the development of something that goes beyond your current infrastructure or core capabilities. It also gives everyone a reason to break from tradition and a chance to push the boundaries of the brand without completely rewriting the brand story or the way core products or services are delivered.

There's a good chance you're collaborating with this team already, but if the folks running product are reluctant to go down this path, start by setting up a jam session with your co-workers in the nonprofit or community engagement departments. The goal is similar: to understand more about the people on this team, what they are dealing with and the way they think so you can connect the dots.

When it comes to the product team, you need to understand how they view the current product mix, what's in the pipeline and their interest in developing completely new ideas. Be sure to send them some information ahead of time, and in the meeting ask where major roadblocks (literal and political) are. Next consider how these can be solved or tested through collaboration. When possible, try to bring data that supports any ideas you put forth, or take a deeper look at the numbers once the product team points you in a direction.

Don't forget to consider an existing ingredient partner that warrants more overt promotion. If you can't find one, you may be able to build upon or remix an existing product with a new ingredient from an outside brand. This could be a distinct name brand like we saw from Cinnabon in their collaborations with Pinnacle Vodka, Airwick and others, or you could take a cue from Phil Anson and work with a more generic ingredient that has the essence and built-in story of a brand, like truffles.

As always, the partners you identify must be a *fit* with your brand—in terms of shared values, shared goals and a common target audience—to ensure the story is authentic and the value proposition is easy to understand from a consumer standpoint.

Your process can certainly deviate from this, but either way begin building relationships with the product team so you can uncover opportunities for future efforts earlier in the process. Soon you'll uncover the personal passions and sources of inspiration that not only drive these team members to develop products, but more importantly that motivate them personally.

Companies that have these strong alignments between product, marketing, customer service and philanthropy tend to create more overt and effective product collaborations.

Taco Bell is one of my favorite examples. Earlier we talked about their collaboration with Lyft, which was based on an insight the two companies uncovered by mining social media for customer feedback, as well as their effort to help kids in partnership with Tyler Oakley. But those were just two unique partnerships created by the fast-food giant.

Perhaps the most fun, and the most profitable, was Taco Bell's collaboration with the Frito-Lay brand Doritos, where they tapped into product development and ingredients. Together they created a platform and a series of new menu items branded as Doritos Locos Tacos. The first in the series became the most successful product launch in Taco Bell history, and in just over one year they sold more than 600 million units.

In a press release announcing the Fiery Doritos Locos Taco, the third iteration of the product which was preceded by Nacho Cheese and Cool Ranch, Taco Bell's chief marketing officer at the time, Chris Brandt said, "The partnership continues to prove the power of two mega brands working together to create firsts in restaurants and on the grocery aisle."

The last part of his comment speaks to the fact that the collaboration was actually a two-way street. In addition to Doritos flavored products showing up in Taco Bell, bags of chips were branded with both entities and sold in retail stores.

This was a smart move, as they not only played off each other's brand equity and expertise, but also their collective distribution channels.

MODERN MARKETERS: **Alexa Christon**

In order to be productive and proactive marketers as well as great collaborators, we need to build our creative muscles. In fact, it is essential. We will get into this in more detail in the next chapter, but for now I'd like to get you thinking in this direction.

A great way to build our creative muscles, is, you guessed it—simply create and put yourself out there, or as one of my favorite visual artists and skilled brand collaborator Shantell

Martin says, "make, share, make, share." To complement this, we also need a diverse range of influences and perspectives that we can learn from.

Fortunately we live in an amazing time when so many people are creating and sharing their thoughts and their work through different channels. This can feel overwhelming if you don't carefully monitor your media diet, but when you find your own balance and mix of resources it can be extremely energizing. One of the relatively new additions to my feed is *ADLANDIA*, a podcast about the world of advertising, branding and marketing. Not only are the guests top notch—a mix of CMOs, entrepreneurs and media execs—the hosts are too. They present their ideas in a casual, unfiltered and strategic manner that's always thought-provoking. With that in mind, I caught up with one half of this dynamic duo, Alexa Christon, to get her take on the collaboration space and the evolution of marketing:

Why do you feel collaborations are especially timely for marketers right now?

With some exceptions, brand partnerships and collaborations have been historically campaign-driven and established for a specific time period, seeking to associate a brand with another brand's audience and grow market share around their existing products and services. While I'm generally a fan of "pop-up" partnerships and collaborations, there is a bigger opportunity for brands to engage in more transformative partnerships that focus on developing new and co-owned intellectual property where both brands focus on their current audiences, while also finding new audiences through new products and services developed with partners.

More now than ever, I think we'll see brands establishing more "unlikely" collaborations that accelerate new product development and open up new market potential. These types of partnerships can leapfrog brands into new verticals that weren't previously imagined—i.e. like an apparel retailer turning into a travel company that becomes a competitor to say an Airbnb or a QSR company bridging into alcoholic beverages. At the end of the day, any collaboration and partnership has to be true to both brands' beliefs, ethos and most paramount, focused on driving value for the consumer.

There's a lot of chatter about the role of CMO/CTO merging, and you've championed the idea that marketers should be more than storytellers. Can you elaborate on why you specifically believe the role should involve, or at least influence, product development?

We are close to reaching a critical place where if a CMO doesn't understand technology and communication networks, they're not effective marketers. Ideally the marketers are the people in an organization that understand the voice of their customer best. They're constantly seeking new opportunities for the brand message and marrying it with context and culture. If they're doing that and focused on building business for their companies, they should be leading how the brand evolves and grows into new areas of business opportunity—this includes new products, services and potentially entrance into new verticals. This doesn't mean marketers should take the job of engineers and designers, but they need to have an intimate knowledge and perspective that bridges marketing and technology.

You helped create a number of award-winning branded, or native, content initiatives on behalf of GE, a brand that pioneered this practice with the radio and television program, *General Electric Theater*. What have you learned about the space and what should marketers keep in mind as the world of branded content evolves and becomes more competitive?

I've always felt that good branded content is just good content and consumers tend not to differentiate between the two unless the content doesn't pay off on a need, provide valuable experience or the brand (logos, logos, logos) gets too much in the way of the message. I think most marketers today understand that content > advertising is typically the way to a more meaningfully relationship with the audience.

Perspective is one of the most important pieces as a brand develops content—asking and answering with honesty pretty basic questions: who is this serving, what do they want, how can we provide them this experience in a new and interesting way, and is it true to who we are, how do we come through vs take over—these are some of the most important questions brand marketers should be asking themselves as they go through the planning and execution process. If it ends up that the content is only serving the brand, the content won't be successful. With a constantly increasing flood of content, if brands miss the mark on their content, the risk can be big—consumers just turn you off, scroll past you and continue to a more valuable experience, potentially from your competitor.

You co-host your own podcast, *ADLANDIA*, and you led a marketing effort that resulted in one of the first break-out podcasts from a brand with *The Message* by GE Podcast Theater. What have those experiences taught you about the medium and the opportunity for brands in podcasting?

Well, I'm a huge fan of podcasting and I think it's a new way for brands to tell their story that takes the imagination of the listener with them—you can create whole new universes, characters and realities that engage in a totally different way then the visual medium. My co-host Laura Correnti and I have long talked about how podcasting is an entrance, for many brands, to the larger world of audio. Podcasting for many brands is a way to get their foot in the door and start testing the waters of audio and audio interaction. I think brands that are slow to experimenting and adopting the medium could get left behind when auto interaction becomes more mainstream with further adoption of home assistants like Amazon Echo and Google Home.

It's tempting to focus solely on conversions given the tools and metrics we now have, but you've also worked on a number of campaigns that test new platforms and appeal to niche audiences. Can you share your perspective on short-term vs. long-term marketing efforts and the pressure marketers are under to justify investments?

There's always a place (as I mentioned earlier) for pop-up experiences and I like the concept of ephemeral offers, advertising and limited-time experiences as they typically drive volume and action. However, I'm always one for longer-term vision and building from the inception of an idea towards a horizon line that a brand works towards. This doesn't mean that everything has to be methodically planned, but it does mean brands have to create frameworks of growth with purpose. As some of our guests on the podcast have said in one way or another, you can't fool people to trust you and you can't build a brand or loyal audience overnight. I think so many marketing organizations are challenged to prove their worth in a generally short-term minded economy—which is scary to think about, but I do think we're coming to a time that if the market continues to dictate such rapid growth, more often than not, brands will come into existence and fade away just as quickly.

Are there any brands or specific campaigns that you've admired for their unique approach to collaboration?

Not surprisingly, I think one of the best examples to date is Red Bull. They listened and understood their audience and quickly evolved from partnerships with athletes and risk takers, to becoming the support and infrastructure from which these athletes do some of their best work—and evolving the brand into a media company. I also was a big fan of what Mondelez was doing a few years ago—going into original games development and building relationships with consumers outside of purchase—it was ahead of the times.

Has your art history degree informed the way you look at marketing or brand collaboration today?

At the time that I decided to study art history (and that's a funny, but long story), I had no idea that it would be the backbone and place where many of my ideas are sourced. I spent most of my time studying the DADA movement. I was obsessed with communication and representations of "truths" starting from WWI to WWII. I remember a paper I wrote questioning if revolutions came from this "alt" minority population or if they were actually a manifestation of the mass majority to drive change. I also spent time studying other contemporary art and artists like Adrian Piper—who's a huge hero of mine. Piper's work centered around xenophobia and identity. I think more now than ever, these topics are not only relevant, they are still contemporary issues and ideas that inevitably brands have to address in one way or another (think Pepsi's Kendall Jenner ad)—and even in less dramatic day-to-day ways, understanding communication and communication tools of a community is so important in how brands interact, engage and are ultimately successful and gaining positive constituency with consumers.

▼ ▼ ▼

Old and New in CPG

Remaining curious and open-minded will protect against some of the common traps marketers and brands fall into at different stages. Nobody wants to water down their brand, but being overprotective can be equally damaging. One of the most common ways this plays out is the dance between legacy and emerging companies. If you or your organization are unwilling to align with other brands because you're afraid you'll lose control, you're missing a huge opportunity. In the modern marketing world, isolation is unsustainable.

The good news is, established and emerging brands can add value to one another in a variety of mutually beneficial ways if they are proactive. As we discussed earlier with Ball and Buck x New Balance, from the established brand standpoint, collaborating with an emerging brand gives you instant freshness, a source of innovation, introduces you to new and likely younger audiences, and shows a commitment to evolution. On the other hand, collaborating with an established brand can provide credibility and reach, or a point of entry, for an emerging brand, in addition to being a familiar reference for consumers. It can also make a statement to investors, partners, retailers, distributors and the other businesses you may eventually want to bring on board.

Keeping it Fresh

This struggle between old and new is currently playing out in the consumer packaged goods (CPG) industry, mostly driven by the fact that grocery, club and mass market stores are filled with brands that have enjoyed a long shelf life without being challenged. As dietary trends shift and the tools needed to build a new brand become more accessible, upstart brands are increasingly disrupting conventional wisdom in every category.

Most of the established players in CPG are owned by holding companies that manage portfolios of brands. These are big ships that turn slowly. Many established brand execs and marketers don't feel they can innovate quickly enough, so they acquire brands to keep up with consumer demand, or to get ahead of it. Unfortunately that has not been a silver bullet as the young brands often lose their mojo when they are sucked up into the bureaucracy of the big guys. After a few high profile failures, the industry has developed new models to deal with this. Among other things, almost every major food and beverage brand now has an investment arm or incubator dedicated to collaboration with emerging brands.

After watching others accidentally crush the DNA of many brands, General Mills became one of the companies that took a different route. After acquiring the natural foods favorite Annie's Organic, they decided to let the company maintain most of its autonomy. They have also made subsequent acquisitions in the natural food space "under" that brand.

Although it's unclear what such acquisitions really look like inside the company from an operations standpoint, in the eyes of partners and informed consumers, it creates a natural collaboration platform and a buffer between General Mills corporate and the emerging brands they are acquiring. Campbell's soup has made a similar move, acquiring natural food companies under its Bolthouse brand. This represents a shift to more of a collaborative culture that values the relationships people have with brands and the notion that compromising an existing consumer relationship, even with good intent, can be detrimental.

It may sound obvious, but the idea of allowing acquired companies to maintain some autonomy is relatively new and not necessarily in the DNA of legacy brands, especially in CPG. So far the shift has worked out well for General Mills, at least on paper. According to an interview on the *Food Navigator* news website in the fall of 2017, Annie's marketing director, Dan Stangler, said the brand is growing household penetration, a key metric in the industry, faster than any food brand in the U.S. According to the same article, that number has gone from 10 million households at the time of the acquisition in 2014, to almost 25 million.

> *"Annie's is performing really well, across the total brand, but what we're really excited about is that we're connecting with more people..."*
>
> —Dan Stangler, Annie's marketing director in *Food Navigator* article "Annie's enjoys explosive growth in household penetration, unveils new snacks campaign."

General Mills also launched 301 Ventures, an investment arm dedicated to funding and nurturing brands by not only providing cash, but also resources like market research, ingredient sourcing, buying power and distribution. These B2B collaborations happen at an arm's length from the traditional business, which allows early stage brands to get help when it makes sense while maintaining their independence.

In some ways this commitment to investing in emerging brands also allows General Mills to avoid the Innovator's Dilemma, a concept from a book of the same name by Clayton Christensen, who we originally talked about in Chapter 4. Clayton explained that innovation is extremely difficult because it often cannibalizes a company's existing business. He uses the example of Netflix. The company housed a new team building their streaming service in a separate building because they were directly competing with their colleagues who were focused on the legacy business (mailing DVD's). The new streaming service team that's trying to reinvent the business would be held back if they were too close to those tasked with trying to keep the legacy products and process humming. It's easy to see the comparisons in CPG, as corporations work to maximize profits from existing brands when they know they eventually need to drastically change or replace them.

Nestlé, the largest food and beverage company in the world, has also recognized the pressing need to innovate through an aggressive acquisition strategy. However, just like General Mills, their approach sounds more like collaboration. In an October 2017 LinkedIn post titled "We're putting our money where your mouth is," Nestlé chairman and CEO Paul Grimwood wrote, "You can learn a lot about Nestlé by seeing where we put our money."

After explaining more about Nestlé's forward-looking strategy, and outlining three recent investments, including Freshly meal delivery, Sweet Earth healthy frozen foods and Blue Bottle Coffee, Grimwood went on to explain how these brands provide more than just revenue by impacting corporate philosophy, operations and external perception. "Our new partners will give us fresh eyes and new ways of thinking about the way we go about the business of enhancing quality of life and contributing to a healthier future," he said. "Each new investment Nestlé makes in the years ahead will indeed say something about us."

These investments and behind-the-scenes collaborations seem to be working well. But as large CPG brands continue to evolve, they should also consider publicly creating and co-branding existing products with emerging brands. By leveraging brands that are more relevant today, big CPG will show consumers they are listening and changing.

It's common to see established brands teaming up, and the same for emerging, but it's rare to see old and new ones side-by-side, especially in this space. Imagine if Ritz crackers used Justin's nut butter? That would be unexpected. I'm sure experts in pricing, sourcing and supply chain will come up with reasons why that wouldn't work, but that's Clayton's point. There's a natural pull not to innovate in the short term when you have a lot to lose. But as we've seen, it's becoming clear in food and other industries that if you don't commit to experimentation and tangible evolution, your company can't win the long game. Fortunately, collaboration is a great way to accomplish this, whether it leads to a full acquisition, ongoing partnership or just a well-executed promotion.

Because I'm genuinely passionate about marketing, I always find it fascinating when conventional brands do show up in an unexpectedly relevant way. That's how I felt when I read that in 2018, TGI Friday planned to roll out a collaboration with Beyond Meat. As a result, the plant-based brand that counts Tyson Foods, Leonardo DiCaprio and the former CEO of Mc-Donald's as investors, will be featured in the chain's revamped Burger Bar. Unexpected indeed, but also a sign of the times and one to watch from a marketing standpoint.

Incubating Collaboration

Yet another path to collaboration is creating or sponsoring a startup incubator or accelerator that provides tangible resources and expertise to companies in their early days.

Chobani, a CPG brand known for innovation and fast growth, launched their own incubator where emerging companies receive money, space, tools, informational programming and access to leadership and mentoring.

According to the Chobani Food Incubator website, "We're here to help small companies with big hearts and ideas challenge the food industry, improve broken systems, and make a difference." They make it clear that there are "no strings attached," so why would a company like Chobani spend all of this time and money on companies they aren't literally invested in? Just look at why they exist: "Our company's mission is to provide better food for more people. We want to extend our mission beyond our own products and into the communities we live in by helping socially responsible food entrepreneurs make their products available to all. We believe that together, we can challenge the food industry, improve broken systems and make a difference."

Apparently the Incubator was dreamt up by the company's founder, Hamdi Ulukaya, who seems like someone who genuinely believes in that mission statement. However, it doesn't diminish the program to acknowledge the value Chobani receives in return. In addition to the goodwill and satisfaction that comes from knowing they are giving back, Chobani executives build relationships with dynamic entrepreneurs, learn about their innovations and observe the consumer and business trends impacting their respective brands.

Should Chobani want to follow in the footsteps of others in their industry and begin acquiring companies, they have a pool of prospective brands they know intimately well. Either way, they have created a community of young leaders within their own industry who are likely huge brand advocates. That is extremely valuable, especially at a time when food, just like so many sectors, is changing rapidly. Most of the companies also share their experiences through social media, so while this is a B2B program it generates goodwill with consumers.

As we explored earlier, it's now common for brands to have investment programs and divisions where they develop relationships with emerging companies. What's unique about Chobani is they do this without taking an ownership stake.

Outside of company-owned incubators and investment arms, there are networks of branded entities that operate in a similar way. The most popular and diverse example I see in the market is Techstars. Companies apply to participate in this program, and if accepted they agree to give up equity in their company in exchange for a cash investment, a formal training program, access to mentors and the opportunity to pitch their startup to outside investors on "demo day." Beyond their industry-agnostic division that welcomes companies from different sectors, Techstars has also launched a series of focused and branded programs including Techstars Disney Accelerator, which is focused on new media and entertainment, and the Techstars Alexa Accelerator in collaboration with Amazon.

In the future we'll see more brands investing in collaborative opportunities like these because they clearly provide access to talent, a pipeline of innovation, industry influence and community building.

CoLAB: *Curiosity*

For this one you'll need at least one buddy but it also works well with a small team.

Have you ever been part of a gift exchange game during the holidays? This is a take on that, combined with Phil's approach to finding ideas through pictures outlined above.

Over two weeks everyone participating promises to take at least one picture everywhere they go. More specifically, you are all on the lookout for two things: brands of any kind that grab your attention, even if it's just a split second, and anything that inspires you creatively. By that I mean you recognize the thoughtfulness, attention to detail or purposefulness of the way something was created. This could be a certain type of architecture, a plate of food, the outfit someone is wearing, a menu or list of specials at a restaurant, a window display or anything else that catches your eye.

At the end of the two weeks each person selects 20–30 of these photos and organizes them in an album. If you want to go old-school, print them out and put them in a traditional album, more power to you. Otherwise find one of the many online photo book sites and have it shipped. Don't worry about the quality of the book or the design, but do take a little time to group the photos in a deliberate way.

Now swap books with your buddy or the individual in the group that you were paired up with. If you want to add another layer and you are doing this as a group everyone can draw a number privately that correlates to a secret partner, all books can be distributed anonymously and then everyone can try to guess who created the book they received.

Either way, take some time to analyze the images and ask yourself a few questions:

- Why did these capture this person's attention?

- Are there themes that show up?

- Is there anything that inspires you to change the way you're designing your next campaign or product?

- Is there a brand featured that complements your brand in a way that seems like a *fit*?

If this was an anonymous swap, try try to guess who created the book. If it was a group exercise, get everyone together, huddle around each book and quickly flip through while sharing your key observations. Allow a moment for others to call out anything they find interesting and then move on to the next one.

Now that your creative juices are flowing, switch gears and dive into a jam session to address a current business challenge or your next project. Do the ideas seem to flow more easily? Are you hearing fresh perspectives?

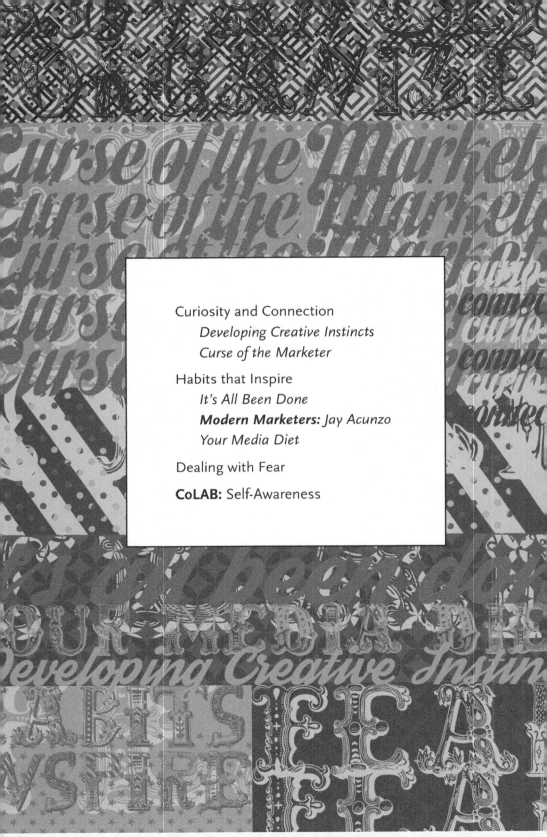

CHAPTER 9

Getting Personal with Collaboration & Creativity

"Ultimately it comes down to taste. It comes down to trying to expose yourself to the best things that humans have done and then try to bring those things into what you're doing."

—Steve Jobs

AS WE'VE EXPLORED, businesses of every size are being forced to adapt as technological innovation disrupts one industry after another. Some are getting ahead and thriving while others are falling behind and beginning to look (and act) like they are out of touch. Fortunately it's up to each of us, as individuals, to decide how we want to spend our time and whether or not we're happy with the way our careers are developing.

We also have to be honest about whether we are playing offense or defense. This can be incredibly difficult, and everyone has their own financial realities, but if you're not where you want to be, don't settle. Try developing a series of career experiments to help identify a new path, launch a side hustle or find a core gig that's more fulfilling. In reality your solution may be a combination of these things. There's nothing wrong with having different jobs, hobbies and creative outlets, as long as you're being honest with yourself and sharing your talents.

> *"There's no such thing as creative people and non-creative people. There are only people who use their creativity and people who don't. Unused creativity lives within us until it's expressed, neglected to death, or suffocated by resentment and fear."*
>
> —Brené Brown, *The Gifts of Imperfection: Let Go of Who You Think You're Supposed to Be and Embrace Who You Are*

In the Netflix documentary *Jim & Andy*, about the making of the movie *Man on the Moon*, Jim Carrey explains the heartbreak he witnessed when his father was fired from what he deemed to be a safe job. This was especially painful because his father had chosen this path over pursuing creative interests and ambitions. As Jim explained, this taught him an important lesson, "When you compromise and fail it hurts even more than failing at what you love."

Just like everything in this book, or any advice you receive, it has to be applied to your circumstances before you can determine how or if it's personally relevant. The most important thing is to take responsibility and empower yourself.

Curiosity and Connection

Whether you are looking to make a career move or not, investing in your personal growth is always worthwhile. We've heard some version of this advice since kindergarten, but it was often coupled with the promise of predictability that Jim's father embraced. This was dictated by our modern education system, which initially set out to produce factory workers who could follow directions and repeat tasks.

I grew up with two parents who were lifelong educators, and I spent a few years in my early 20s substitute teaching at the elementary level, so I've been privy to many debates about the state of education in America. Fortunately there's a growing movement to change education at every level and I'm proud of my parents for the years of passionate work they contributed.

One core principle behind the shift in our approach to education that I find particularly relevant to the work of marketing is deprioritizing memorization and investing more time in metacognition, or thinking about how to think. While careers in engineering and data science are often promoted as the most promising, according to a survey from Burning Glass Technologies, which relies on technology to study job trends, the "soft skills" of communication and writing are actually the most in-demand across nearly every industry.

Developing Creative Instincts

Collaboration challenges us to develop new relationships, acquire new skills, indulge our own curiosity and embrace a willingness to experiment. It is also a tool we can use to advance our careers and rally against the faulty assumption that creativity is relegated to certain types of individuals or to specific departments. This is an idea often perpetuated by the structure we use to build businesses and teams. For example, most agencies have a "creative department" and many brands have "creative services" teams.

In today's business setting, everyone must constantly work to build their creative muscles, but this is especially true for marketers. I find many of us went into the field to be right in the middle of the creative action, but have been held back from crossing the chasm by conventions of traditional business.

I am also well aware of the Chief Marketing Officer meets Chief Technology Officer convergence, and I agree that modern marketers must embrace technology and constantly evaluate data. However, when looked at in a vacuum, these data points often focus on the bottom-line performance or utilitarian traits of a product or service, which is a limiting proposition that overlooks more nuanced insights and opportunities.

Great leaders and companies balance data with investments in creativity and storytelling to build empathy, trust and connection. These lead to the experiences and emotions brands want and need to create if they expect to differentiate themselves, attract consumers, establish long-term relationships, build community and inspire advocacy.

Curse of the Marketer

For those of you who proudly own the artist or creator moniker already, I hope this book will inspire and empower you to seek out unexpected partners, have more productive conversations and create more impactful collaborations. For those squarely focused on more traditional business, or afraid to embrace their own creativity, hopefully this book helps you feel more connected to whatever you are passionate about, reminds you why that matters and helps you grow.

In order to really own this way of life, marketers, artists, creators and entrepreneurs need an endless flow of new ideas, data and a willingness to experiment. We must also nurture our own curiosity, yet another soft skill. For those of us lucky enough to embrace this, it eventually turns into what I call the *Curse of the Marketer.*

The word "curse," like the word "cut" discussed in Chapter 2, typically has a negative connotation, but I believe this interpretation of the word can be a marketer's best friend. You know you have been cursed when you cannot help yourself from instinctively noticing and critiquing marketing messages as you encounter them in everyday life. Product placements can steal your attention away from a great movie. Billboards compel you to stop the car. Times Square is Valhalla.

* *Curse of the Marketer: A note of caution, and sympathy, if you've experienced this phenomenon. While this is not contagious, friends and loved ones tend to get annoyed when you are cursed and constantly vocalize your observations. Go easy on them.*

Earlier I talked about the insatiable curiosity that manifests if you are passionate about something, and this is yet another way to look at the *Curse of the Marketer.* But what is really happening when you feel you have succumbed to the *Curse?* In reality, you are fine-tuning your observation muscles, directly related to your creative muscles, and seeing things that are not as obvious to others. This activity results in the constant observation and evaluation of the overt and subtle brand messages we encounter, and it adds up to a collection of endless references we can draw upon when doing our own creative work.

By constantly seeking out new information and experiences, we also build empathy and generate a better understanding of people and culture. From a personal standpoint these practices and experiences can help us develop critical thinking, the ability to recognize cognitive biases, self-awareness, the willingness to take risks and the ability to be decisive when it comes to our lives and our businesses. What we're really talking about is building habits.

Habits that Inspire

So far we've looked at our collaboration thesis primarily through the lens of how the perception of you and your brand changes based on whom and what you associate with. However, a key reason Jim Rohn proclaimed that "you are the average of the five people you spend the most time with" is because you'll develop similar beliefs and habits to those around you. In fact, we all have built up a number of habits that have become so ingrained in our routines we don't even realize we've adopted them. Some people only think about the negative connotation of the word "habit," but just like the *Curse of the Marketer*, developing positive habits can set you up for success in your personal and professional lives.

Throughout the book I've challenged you with a series of experiments (CoLABs) aimed at taking on these universal challenges and developing a creative approach to brand collaboration. Beyond exercising, eating well and getting enough sleep, here are a few more key ideas and activities that will help you personally and professionally develop the habits we all need to succeed.

> *"We are what we repeatedly do. Excellence,*
> *then, is not an act but a habit."*
>
> —Aristotle

One way to ensure constant learning and growth is to follow a routine. That's why I like author and podcast host James Altucher's "Daily Practice." Among other things, his advice is to list out ideas under a certain theme, making sure you get to at least ten. After you write down a few it gets difficult and your brain starts to "sweat," as James would say. That's how you know you're exercising your idea muscle, so keep pushing until you finish and then repeat the process often. While we're on James, he's also fond of what he calls "idea sex." This involves simply combining disparate ideas to move past the obvious and onto something unique.

Another exercise I find valuable is journaling. More specifically, a practice developed by author Julia Cameron in her book *The Artist's Way*, which she calls "Morning Pages." It basically involves hand-writing three pages of free-form thoughts every morning, combined with a weekly "artist's date" where you take a solo trip to "receive." This is meant to be fun and initiate play, so it could be a trip to a gallery, a performance, a game, people watching or any other activity that feels right to you. When I make time to consistently do these two things, journaling and artist dates, the process creates a bit of give and take that can lead to profound breakthroughs.

A vast majority of the authors and creators who inspire me also recommend some kind of meditation practice. Choose your own adventure in terms of what styles you try, but in my experience sitting quietly and simply focusing on your breath for as little as a few minutes a day makes a huge difference.

One last exercise I've found extremely liberating, and directly linked to collaboration, is improv comedy. You've probably seen *Whose Line Is It Anyway?* or maybe you've been to an improv show, but did you know there's really one main rule that governs the entire discipline? It's called "yes and." The idea is that no matter what another person says, your answer must always agree with them and then build on what they presented to you. There's an element of respect and collaboration built in when you approach a conversation, brainstorm or partnership this way.

This is by no means an exhaustive list, and fortunately there are endless resources online that you can use to discover, experiment and shape your own habits. The point is, when you consistently engage in exercises like these, and combine them with specific goals, the dots start to connect, also known as synchronicity. To understand this, think about when you're looking for a new car and then decide on a certain model. All of the sudden you start seeing that same model on the road, right? It seems like there are actually more of them than there were before, but it's just your consciousness recognizing something you weren't registering before.

This idea of synchronicity can get a little woo-woo from some people, but don't let that stop you from experiencing it. In my estimation the phenomenon is similar to a heuristic and cognitive bias, but a helpful one. As a result of focusing on what you want, and having a more deliberate filter, you become more observant and make empowering decisions. Ultimately, carving your own path and worrying less about what other people think might be the most important and challenging practice of all.

I encourage you to seek out your own tools and build your own habits. But to give you a few more ideas, I asked a number of friends and marketers I admire what they do to stoke their own creativity. You can find their answers in the Modern Marketers section in Chapters 2–12.

It's All Been Done

As noted above, most marketers I speak with originally entered the field because they want to embrace and express their own creativity. The good news is we now have endless opportunities to creatively market a brand. The bad news is that it's becoming increasingly difficult to stand out in this environment and that creates added pressure to be original and do things that are perceived to be novel.

As we've established, humans use existing references and look for things that confirm our existing beliefs in an effort to efficiently process information. But we are also hardwired to seek out new. This is rooted in the idea that knowledge is power and that growth fuels our survival. However, in the context of creativity, if you feel like you have to come up with something nobody has ever done before, you may never do anything.

It's likely you will also feel like you're late to the party and just copying others when you lean into your own creativity, but this is actually quite common. At points during every creative endeavor you'll ask yourself why anyone would give you their attention. You'll see others doing similar things and feel like you're ripping them off. You'll become convinced you are not good enough, you are being egotistical, overconfident, or maybe just seeking attention. This is called Impostor Syndrome. It's a real thing and we all feel it at times. It comes and goes, but it's especially strong if you take action and gain even the slightest bit of momentum. I certainly felt it at points creating this book.

The best way I've found to combat this is to think about Austin Kleon's philosophy of "steal like an artist," which is also the title of his first book. This idea borrows from a phrase uttered by Picasso, Steve Jobs and most recently Kleon, who is a self-proclaimed "writer who draws." His thesis states that very little is truly original and attempting to achieve this is an excuse that stifles creativity and holds back creators. Instead this theory suggests that artists overtly take something and build upon it. They should always give credit to their influences, but steal nonetheless. This is similar to what the art world refers to as pastiche: creating in a style that overtly imitates. The key is to not only copy that style, but to advance it by adding something of your own.

Another corollary would be remixing in music, as we explored in Chapter 1, and more broadly to the concept of collaboration. In collaboration, and creativity in general, we are not obsessed with completely new ideas. Instead, we take existing ideas and then evolve, expand, reinterpret, reapply, or combine them. This brings us full circle back to the definition of creativity from William Plomer we outlined in Chapter 2 and the power behind collaboration: "Creativity is the ability to connect the seemingly unconnected."

From my own experiences, and what I've observed, another thing that holds people back from creative endeavors is waiting too long to start. We habitually procrastinate and this goes for anything that feels risky. It's much easier to plan, obsessively weigh options and continue collecting data. Author Steven Pressfield dubbed this natural inertia that shows up "resistance." It comes in all shapes and sizes, so the key is to develop habits and creative muscles that allow you to do your work in spite of these feelings.

Over time, with a positive attitude and productive habits, you'll begin creating more freely, connecting things and people more frequently and mastering collaboration.

MODERN MARKETERS: **Jay Acunzo**

A quick note on originality, which is directly related to Impostor Syndrome and the pressure to develop new ideas. According to Jay Acunzo, content marketing expert, host of the *Unthinkable* podcast and former content director for Google and Hubspot, your unfair advantage is you. That is the truly original thing that will make your work and your collaborations succeed. I connected with Jay and asked him to unpack this idea and the current state of marketing:

You have been studying unique examples of how organizations and individuals work differently and rally against conventional wisdom in your podcast *Unthinkable*. Why has intuition become a focal point of this exploration?

It has never been easier to be average than it is right now. If we don't have an idea or an answer, we can instantly find and follow everyone else's thanks to the ubiquity of information. And while the Information Age is largely something to celebrate, it has created a dark side: Advice Overload. What's getting lost is the ability to find your own answers, tailored to your situation specifically, rather than an expert's answer, which at best has been tailored to the average and at worst serves to promote their own agenda.

When I first started the show, it was an exploration to create better content, because I came out of the marketing world. But from talking to listeners. I quickly realized that there were far more than just marketers listening—and listening with passion and excitement. For context, I schedule 6–10 video calls per month with listeners, one-on-one, and I found myself talking to CTOs and CEOs, software engineers, graphic designers, musicians, professors, you name it. So I realized right away that "creativity in content" was a symptom of an illness that I hadn't identified yet.

Over time, we moved from talking about creativity to talking about craft (i.e. focusing your work on the process instead of the results, which so often yields better results too). More listener calls revealed a variety of professionals you wouldn't associate with craft, like accountants and lawyers and recruiters, and other people who don't "make stuff" in the obvious sense. I was still addressing a symptom.

In the last three months of 2017, I believe I've found the actual illness: We just keep following best practices and producing commodity work and average results. So today, the show centers on the idea of intuition at work. As a word, "intuition" comes from the Latin "intuir" which means "knowledge from within." So that's the treatment I now explore to the illness I think I've finally identified: How can we find our own answers in our specific context, rather than continually glom onto the next trend, tactic, or tool shilled by an expert?

In the end, intuition is the process of thinking for yourself. In a world where having "the" answer in some generalized way has never been easier, exceptional work comes from those who know how to find their own.

You've talked about the need for brands to now hold the attention of their customers and audiences. What do you mean by this and why is it increasingly important for brands and marketers to consider?

The reality that underscores all of marketing today is that the consumer has all the power. (And at this point, we've had the power for a number of years.) If we don't want to hear a brand's message, we don't have to put up with it—we can use technology and capitalize on all the infinite choice out there to navigate around it. Even when we can't escape an ad (e.g. while watching live TV), we can simply pull out another device to find something we want to consume without so much as moving our lazy butts.

So in the past, before this reality took hold, a marketer's job was to simply acquire your attention. The goal was to appear in front of the right consumer with the right message, and that consumer had far less choice and little control to navigate around it. But today, when the consumer has all the power, that's insufficient. Marketers need to go beyond simply acquiring attention to genuinely holding. Things like awareness, consideration, purchase, trust, loyalty, advocacy—all the things marketers want can only really come from holding attention. Today's great marketers care about subscribers, not clicks. They measure time spent with the brand in minutes or even hours, not seconds.

In the end, this is Humans 101: People spend time with, remember, and take action based on things that resonate, not just "reach" them. Just because you go to work as a marketer and have access to technology and strategy documents doesn't change how people act. Understand that and start there, and your purview in the Information Age becomes a lot clearer: Don't just seek to acquire attention, learn how to hold it.

When it comes to influencer marketing, where do you think marketers tend to fall short and how can they begin to think differently about the opportunity to collaborate with individuals?

When a marketer abuses a tactic or channel, you can typically point to the effects of mass media marketing that echo through time and across channels. Marketers think in total reach in an era where precision is possible. They think in media buys and campaigns instead of earning and owning attention over time. And the latter is really where influencers excel.

Most brands fall flat on their face when working with influencers because they're essentially performing micro media buys, treating influencers as small media publishers that offer audience access. But just look at the name: INFLUENCER marketing. Shouldn't the goal to be influenced, not reach? Influence means persuasion. Influence means resonating deeply enough with an audience to trigger an action. Influence does not mean total impressions or likes.

So a great partnership between brand and influencer must start with that first principle of the matter: Influence is something earned, not purchased. From there, seek to work shoulder-to-shoulder and build unassailable assets together. The wave of brands paying influencers to simply promote their products is sure to crash, thanks to both increased FCC regulation and increased audience fatigue. Like any trend or technique, once that wave crashes and the tide goes back out, the ones washed away will be the short-term thinkers—in this case, those treating influencers as media companies. The brands that remain and find true success will be those doing it right: working in-step with influencers to earn influence over time.

What do you do when you're looking for creative inspiration? Any particular habits, certain places you visit or things you do?

Whenever I hear the word "inspiration," I hear the artist Chuck Close in my head, delivering his now-infamous quote: "Amateurs look for inspiration; the rest of us just get up and go to work."

It's not that inspiration isn't real—it very much is. However, it's entirely too easy to externalize your creative abilities to this notion of "inspiration." If you can't come up with an idea or if you didn't do the work, it's not your fault: You just couldn't find the inspiration. But, of course, it IS your fault, and great ideas aren't found, they're built.

In my line of work, with podcasting and keynote speaking, I try to swap out the idea of inspiration for the idea of excitement. Am I excited to do this thing? Why not? Then it becomes incredibly tangible to get excited again. Do I need to put on a playlist? Do I need to watch a speech to fire me up? Do I need to walk down the street to a coffee shop instead of work from home?

In every case, it comes back to the same issue: When we need inspiration, it's because we're not being sensitive enough to the world around us. We're caught in a routine, and we need to break from that. This is why travel or really emotional songs can be inspiring—they're unusual. They shatter the routine, and they enable us to sense the world in new and distinct ways. But we can get that from simply crossing the road on our normal route to work or sitting in a new spot while working. The goal shouldn't be to "get inspired." The goal should be to get excited, to avoid feeling dull to the world so you can invest your time with vigor into the work. But make no mistake: It's not "out there." It's on you.

▼ ▼ ▼

"The future belongs to a different kind of person with a different kind of mind: designers, inventors, teachers, storytellers—creative and emphatic "right-brain" thinkers whose abilities mark the fault-line between who gets ahead and who doesn't."

—Daniel Pink, *A Whole New Mind*

Your Media Diet

When we take our thesis literally it's all about the people we spend the most time with, but it's also about the brands we regularly engage with and the corresponding media we consume. This is yet another major influence on the development of self-awareness, as well as the ability to come up with and execute creative ideas.

It's easy to get caught in an echo chamber today because we can curate our own lives, especially when it comes to the media. We also arrange our social networks to determine who shows up, and who doesn't, in our respective feeds. This means we can create a system that tells us what we already know or want to hear. And that has the opposite of the effect that we're looking for if we want to build our creative muscles.

Instead we need to expand our worldview and our own references. This is not about politics, it's about maximizing our impact. Before ruling something out or writing anything off—whether underground, mainstream pop culture or somewhere in between—we need to make sure we give it a real look (or listen). Then we can understand why it's relevant to some, even if it doesn't resonate with us. The more of that we do, the more likely we begin connecting the seemingly unconnected.

Inviting in enough content and experiences to be open-minded, while filtering out the noise and avoiding constant distraction so we can do the work, is a tricky balancing act. We all know what it feels like to go down the rabbit hole on a web search or social media binge. However, we can't let this avoidance of distraction make us too rigid or close-minded. One way around this is to regularly schedule time explicitly for research, experimentation and play, just like Julia's "artist dates" suggest. By doing so, and using this as a positive restraint, it's more likely you'll make this kind of consumption a productive exercise.

Dealing with Fear

The ability to embrace creativity, to push for collaboration, and to advocate for new ideas in general, has been challenging at different points in my career. I've struggled with every creative insecurity we covered in this chapter and more. When it comes to business there's always an urgent matter or project competing for attention, a short-term sales goal, the perceived need for new or different technology and a host of other factors that make it seem like creativity and collaboration can wait. It is far too easy to rationalize decisions, more often leading to indecision, when these pressures and fears take hold. Unfortunately, we can fool ourselves into thinking that we're doing the right thing by putting off a creative venture, or giving up on it too early. By now I hope you see through that and realize it's a fallacy.

When I unpack the times I did break through, it wasn't that the fear didn't exist or the competing interests went away. I just found the resilience, mental strength and agility to compartmentalize things and move forward. I also found key allies who I partnered with and others I turned to for moral support and guidance.

If you believe in something enough, you have to take a bit of the improv comedy approach we talked about earlier in this chapter and say, "yes, and…" That means you accept the reality of all the things competing for your time, put your ego in check *and* you do the new, different or scary thing. If you decide it's really important, you'll make the time and find the chutzpah.

> *"Don't worry about failures, worry about the chances you miss when you don't even try."*
>
> —Jack Canfield

CoLAB: *Self-Awareness*

One of the most satisfying aspects of my career has been the opportunity to mentor people. In some instances this took on a formal structure, but there were far more occasions when the interactions were contained to a single lunch, coffee or informational interview. I was always surprised that copywriters, graphic designers, developers, editors and photographers seemed to be the only ones with portfolios, while "marketers" never had them. Of course this was the result of simply following tradition, not a lack of things to share.

Here's the unfortunate reality. Upon first glance, the only thing that really stands out is where you've worked or interned. We live in a visual world, and we're all in the business of storytelling. You're doing yourself a disservice by not leveraging the tools you would use to market a brand, regardless of what career stage you're in.

I understand that many businesses still request traditional resumes, but if they aren't willing to receive and review something a bit more creative is it really a place you want to be? Furthermore, this isn't the kind of thing you do just to land a formal gig, it's something that helps you connect with potential collaborators on every level.

For this CoLAB, let's think about what your portfolio might look like, especially if you're not in a field or role that typically calls for one. As we've talked about throughout the book, demonstrating the ability to think creatively will be increasingly important for all of us in the future.

Don't think you have enough worthwhile experience to create one? Let's challenge that assumption. This process can evoke a daunting feeling at first, but I find most people have compelling and relevant stories worth sharing. They just need to frame up the experiences they have and consider adding non-traditional examples.

And if you already have a portfolio, you may still find this to be a fun thought experiment and an opportunity to evolve the way you present your experiences.

Here's a stab at how one might go about this:

Step 1—Take Inventory
What valuable creative or marketing experience did you gain in your previous jobs, even if it wasn't obvious at the time or directly tied to marketing? Try to pull out a few specific initiatives that demonstrate your creativity, technology prowess, business savvy and willingness to take action.

Step 2—Old School
Did you do any in-depth research or take part in any group projects that generated tangible results at work or in school? If you're early in your career, what about extracurricular activities? Did you join a fraternity or sorority? Maybe you were in a club? Perhaps you managed your school paper or hosted a campus podcast? Did you book bands or help plan fundraisers? Maybe you were in the military or perhaps you took some time away from your career to travel? Volunteer in your community or serve on a nonprofit board? Do not discount any of this. It may very well lead to something that makes you uniquely qualified.

Step 3—Pick Your Passion
What are you most interested in? Music, painting, fashion, film, photography, working out, beauty products, playing sports,

travel, architecture, cars, bikes, video games, meditation, mentoring, philanthropy, vintage t-shirts, gambling or sneakers? Ok, now that you have something in mind, ask yourself a few more questions:

- Have you had any experiences on the business side of this passion?

- Could you be considered a subject matter expert in any aspect of this?

- Do you know any experts in this space that you could interview to create content for your portfolio?

As stated in the first chapter, I truly believe that you have a higher likelihood of succeeding if you find a role that reinforces your passions as an individual, so be loud and proud about them.

Step 4—Audit Your Assets
Look at everything you identified in steps 1–3 and figure out if you have any supporting assets that help illuminate these stories. We're in the digital age, and pretty much everything is documented in some way. So, by assets, I mean written content, photos, videos, audio recordings, social media posts, articles or any other artifacts that represent your experiences.

Step 5—Make Your Case (Study)
Pick 3, 5, 7 or more experiences to focus on and write a quick overview of each one, paired with the supporting assets. Remember, this can be as simple as a paragraph describing what you learned and a photo of the experience. Think of each one as mini-case study that reveals something about you and reinforces the idea that you would be a thoughtful and productive team player. It's simply meant to give someone a glimpse into who you are, what you've done, how you think and hopefully prompt a conversation where you can tell a story about the experience.

Step 6—Go To Your Home
Pick a user-friendly platform like Squarespace, Wordpress or any of the other content management system and begin developing a simple website where your portfolio can live. If there's a domain available for your exact name, grab it. If not, just come up with something creative, fun and short. Now, let's build out your new home.

Front Door—This is the landing page where you welcome your audience, prospective employers or collaborators. Include a statement about yourself, what you're working on and what you're pursuing.

Living Room—Also known as the "about" section, this is where people get to know you a bit more through all of the stories (case studies) and supporting assets you collect.

Dining Room—This is where guests have more in-depth conversations with you. Provide a variety of options including direct contact information and links to your relevant social media accounts.

Remember, this is just a starter home and there's more than one way to build it. I encourage you to architect your own plan and include anything you think guests will find interesting.

Step 7—Keep Cooking
If you decide to expand your site, consider a blog. This is a great way to keep things fresh and showcase your critical thinking skills. Maybe you create a series of posts about one of your passions (interviews are great here too). If audio is more your bag, try out Anchor, an app that takes the friction out of recording and publishing podcasts. While you're at it, check out my audio journal on Anchor or Apple Podcasts, *Curse of the Marketer.*

Step 8—Go Live

Now you're ready to share. Link to this new portfolio in your email signature (personal account if work doesn't allow or make sense) and to all of your other accounts, especially LinkedIn. Also, be sure to share this with prospective employers, collaborators and clients.

This is also a great way to learn more about your teammates. Challenge a few co-workers to create a portfolio and set a date to reveal them to one another or collaborate along the way. You're bound to learn something about the other person that makes your time together, and the work you produce, more impactful.

Last but not least, what is the one project you've been putting off or an idea you can't get out of your head? What's holding you back? Be honest with yourself. Now, look at your portfolio and all of the things you've accomplished, even if it's just a written list. Hopefully this serves as a reminder that you're more than capable. Now it's time to take action. And when this new project is live, don't forget to add it to your portfolio.

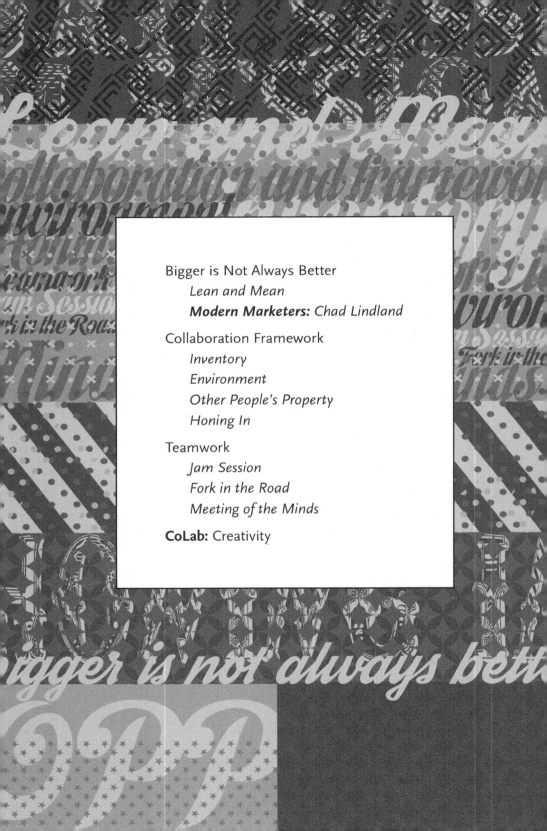

CHAPTER 10

Developing a Culture of Collaboration

*"Change is hard at first, messy in the
middle and gorgeous at the end."*

—Robin Sharma

I WANT TO acknowledge that brand collaborations are not
easy. It is hard enough to gain internal consensus, develop and
manage your own marketing efforts. Adding outside partners
may complicate things, which can be a demotivating factor. I
recall a time when I suggested the idea of adding a collaboration platform into a campaign and the response was, "That
gets messy."

Yes, collaborations require more effort and coordination
than a traditional promotion, but doesn't this hold true for
the development of anything new? Similarly, if the early stages
of a collaboration process are too focused on details, and not
enough on an overarching insight and vision, it's easy to frame
the extra work as too complex or costly. This is why it's important to take your own circumstances and context into consideration, work with the right people and establish a framework
that allows time for big thinking and ideation. You don't want

to kill a great idea simply because the clock runs out or because it requires more work.

Bigger is Not Always Better

To get in the brand collaboration game or take your existing partnership approach to the next level, start by picking your spot. In other words, where are you going to focus your precious time, energy and resources?

Only you can decide how aggressive you want to be with your initial efforts. Remember, many of the examples we've explored unfolded over years, gaining momentum and building upon each experience to improve the next. Hopefully you've been doing some of the creative exercises we talked about in the last chapter and those recommended by the Modern Marketers featured in the book. This will put you in the right mindset to make things happen.

As you narrow down your focus, anticipate the questions and potential objections you'll get from your teammates or client. This can be tricky because unless this is part of an existing platform, you won't be able to accurately predict the immediate impact of a collaboration. Your gut tells you it's the right thing to do, but in most organizations you won't be able to win over anyone on gut alone. That's actually a good thing as it keeps you accountable and forces you to be strategic. After all, you're not throwing your existing brand strategy away, you're building upon it. That said, if an initial branding or repositioning project is really what you need, it's a good idea to take that on first. You want to get your own house in order before you enter someone else's.

When you do share your initial rationale with your team or client, focus on the overarching strategy and top-line organizational goals that your approach will address. Go through the exercise of documenting those items and be sure to set appropriate expectations. It's a cliche,* but under-promising and over-delivering is probably the best way to begin.

....

* *It's okay to roll your eyes when you hear cliches, but it's also worth a few seconds of contemplation. Oddly there's a lot to learn from cliches and conventional wisdom. I find they are frequently used because they are often true. This also reminds me of the way the last chapter's Modern Marketer Jay Acunzo challenges the idea of best practices. They are fine to consider, but they have to be put in context and questioned because following anything too closely ignores your unique situation.*

....

Let's think about this in a different context like creative writing, since it's something you do in one way or another every day—those Tweets, emails and text messages count—and because it's top-of-mind for me as I make my way through the process of creating this book. Even if you have a very clear sense of what you want to do or say, it's important to write a draft of your initial thoughts. Only then can you go back and edit your draft. If you try to both create and edit or revise at once you are tapping into different parts of your brain. As Brené Brown says, you need to get your "shitty first draft" done first. If you are too analytical in the early stages it will be even harder to overcome the natural resistance we all face when we do something creative.

As I alluded to earlier, another common hurdle you may need to overcome when you begin championing collaboration is a hyperfocus on revenue. Meaning, if you can't align your

effort with immediate sales it may be a non-starter in the eyes
of your team or leadership. We touched on this phenomenon
earlier, as our society tends to promote the idea that businesses
should always be expanding. In doing so, sometimes we fail to
evaluate why we want growth or what it really looks like. This
logic is flawed because it fails to distinguish between growth
and evolution.

An example of evolution would be offering fewer items but
selling more because you focus time, energy and artistry into
creating a best-in-class product or service. In the hospitality industry, this might mean having a lower occupancy rate, but a
higher spend-per-stay because you've attracted guests who are
likely to take advantage of certain amenities or activities. In the
sneaker game, this could mean offering fewer pairs of a hot release, but garnering a ton of earned media that generates a halo
effect and impacts sales the following quarter.

The fixation on volume is often applied to metrics like event
attendance as well. But if you have the right strategy, and set
the right expectations, a small crowd might be exactly what you
 need. Conventional wisdom makes us want to pack the room
when we host anything, and more feels better on the surface,
but a small group of influencers, for example, can now reach
millions and create valuable content in the process. Think
about how this applies to everything you do in your business,
especially your marketing and media efforts.

Lean and Mean

As we explored in Chapter 6, the technology industry has its
own ecosystem that thrives on collaboration at every level.
Many of these companies have also adopted a process for developing new products and services that can be helpful when
considering how to initiate collaborations.

The lean startup methodology was created by Eric Ries, a technology entrepreneur who wrote the best-selling book *The Lean Startup*. After achieving mixed results with a few companies, Eric began applying lessons he learned from studying Japanese manufacturing processes and as a result found more success.

> *"Don't be in a rush to get big. Be in a rush to have a great product."*
>
> —Eric Ries

The core tenet of what he uncovered revolved around the idea of a <u>minimum viable product</u> or MVP. This approach attempts to test a hypothesis by getting a product or service into the hands of customers as quickly as possible. At the same time, it involves soliciting their feedback, measuring the results and iterating accordingly, rather than unnecessarily investing before you know whether your solution will be valuable. According to Eric, "lean thinking defines value as providing value to the customer, anything else is waste."

If we apply this to our work, and some of the challenges we will inevitably face, we can consider what I like to call the <u>minimum viable collaboration</u>. This can exist within the context of our overall effort to develop more collaborations for our brand, or to the way we approach working with a specific partner. As long as there's *fit,* and a clear way to measure the impact, getting a small win under your belt may provide exactly the kind of creative and political capital you need to rally your teammates, organizational leadership or other brands you aspire to jam with.

Furthermore, as I suggested in Chapter 6, there may be a variety of collaborations already built into your business that you can take an MVC approach to marketing. What if you invested in promoting a current supplier or partner to make your efforts more impactful? That could be a powerful story, bringing to the forefront the fact that this otherwise hidden brand provides key ingredients that make the end product more valuable to customers.

MODERN MARKETERS: **Chris Lindland**

When Bill Murray and his team decided to explore the idea of bringing back bell bottoms* with their brand, William Murray Golf, they didn't just produce and sell them. They started by telling a story and asking consumers to weigh in through a unique platform called Betabrand.

....

* *This collaboration included a clever launch plan as Bill actually wore a prototype of the pants at the AT&T Pebble Beach Pro-Am, giving his new product, and Betabrand collaboration, a national audience.*

....

The Betabrand website and process combines creative design, storytelling, community building, audience engagement and e-commerce in one cohesive offering, or as their founder Chris Lindland calls it, "an R&D lab for testing new designs online." Instead of making product decisions in a vacuum, they rely on digital rendering and 3-D modeling, public voting and crowdsourcing to determine what to sell.

When an idea for a product is first conceived—either by a Betabrand designer, community member or an outside brand—it is presented to the public on their site, along with background information about the designer, their inspiration, the product utility and more. If a certain number of people vote on the item—incentivized by a future discount and the opportunity to help co-create the product by providing feedback—then it becomes available for crowdfunding. If it passes this next stage, and enough people commit to purchasing it, not only do they personally receive the product but it also becomes part of the Betabrand e-commerce offering.

At this point there's an ever-evolving and diverse portfolio of products, including the now iconic executive hoodie, disco pants (think Burning Man) and cordarounds, to name a few. When they team up with other brands, they help designers break from traditional industry norms and provide a safe place to test ideas that typically get cut well before consumers have a chance to weigh in. This distinct approach to collaboration— brand-to-brand and brand-to-consumer—is rarely present in the world of apparel and footwear. However, as fashion shows become more consumer-focused, and fast fashion pushes ev- eryone to close the gap between the runway and retail, we'll likely see more companies looking for ways to break from tra- dition. In a sense they will be tapping into the same philosophy as the lean startup ethos championed by the tech communi- ty. Perhaps it's fitting then that Betabrand is not based in New York, London or Paris, but instead San Francisco.

I connected with Betabrand's founder and CEO Chris Lindland to dig into his platform and their unique take on col- laboration:

Can you explain Betabrand's approach to collaboration and crowdfunding?

Betabrand is an R&D community for designers and brands—a place to socialize new ideas and see what sticks. They post design concepts (usually in sketch or illustrator form) and fans provide feedback on what's hot or not. The most popular ideas are rapidly prototyped and launched as crowdfunding concepts where consumers ultimately decide if these ideas are ready for market.

Why is this useful for designers, brands...and ultimately consumers?

Designers and brands ultimately have to make investments in inventory, which is always a risky decision. Risky decisions often lead to conservative bets. So Betabrand's platform gives designers and brands a risk-free place to test out ideas on the edge of their collections. By inviting consumers into their design departments, they get a better read on what people want, and consumers have the opportunity to bring braver ideas to life.

Can you expand on what you mean by creative theater?

It's an exciting new experience for consumers to be invited into the design departments of brands like Timberland, The North Face, Vivobarefoot or Smartwool. That's where you find the freshest, boldest ideas—stuff that rarely makes it to market. The same is true of all the creative designers who post concepts on Betabrand. Now you can connect with their ideas as soon as they can sketch them.

The theater: We welcome people into the design process, asking fans to influence creative direction. They watch as products evolve before their eyes. It's our job at Betabrand to make the experience as immersive and interesting as possible.

Do you think more brands should explore this kind of crowdfunding?

It's safe to say that any brand can benefit from it—because EVERY brand generates designs that can't clear all the hurdles that the industry puts in front of them. Consumers miss out on the creative talents of a brand as a result.

Each time we work with a large company, consumers often take them in an unexpected direction. These ideas have gone on to gain wider adoption from their retail partners.

It sounds like the root of what you're doing is helping brands build relationships with consumers.

Yes. It's not so much the magic of crowdsourcing or crowdfunding, it's about connecting consumers to the creative engines at brands. Nowadays brands are looking for ways to connect with fans on a more regular basis. Today's social consumer demands it. They'll find no shortage of engaging content in their design departments.

What has your work at Betabrand taught you about the shift from traditional retail to e-commerce?

Clothing brands have traditionally relied on malls or retail stores to connect with consumers. In addition to this, they've used a seasonal release calendar. All told, that adds up to only a handful of interactions a year. Successful internet businesses do so on a daily, if not hourly basis, and that's something many traditional brands still have to wrap their heads around.

What drew Cheetos, a consumer packaged goods company, to Betabrand and what is the underlying lesson for marketers?

Margaret Johnson is a friend who heads up creative at Goodby Silverstein. She's known for creating campaigns that generate far more noise than they pay for. She saw Betabrand as a new storytelling medium for Chester the Cheetah—one that gets a considerable amount of press attention.

We give designers and brands the opportunity to present ideas at such a low cost—simple sketches will do—so Cheetos was able to present a set of fun concepts for the internet to talk about. And indeed they did.

You seem to personally have a knack for storytelling that also helps drive the company. What does your personal creative process look like?

I guess I start by asking, is this an idea people will talk about? And is it more interesting, to anyone, than the latest cat GIF or Trump tweet? That's a high bar. But it's necessary for Betabrand to create "fashion forwardable" content. Otherwise, the cost of getting traffic from ads alone is too much.

We bat around loads of ideas. Now and then one comes along that's worth promoting. Some work. Some don't. But we've had our share of hits over the years.

What does that say about the attitude that's required to be relevant today as a brand marketer or leader?

You need to know a good story when you see it—something folks would actually want to talk about online. Then have a plan of how to get folks talking about it. Above all, you have to be comfortable with lots of experimentation and able to generate lots of ideas and angles for you and your team to chew on.

▼ ▼ ▼

Collaboration Framework

The following is a framework you can use to deliberately explore collaboration, big or small, in your own company. It's not meant to be a step-by-step process because every situation is different. It does however provide a guide that you can adapt to *fit* within your organization and use to begin developing a culture that leverages collaboration more consistently and effectively.

Every worthwhile business endeavor starts with a strategy, and developing a collaboration is no different. But as outlined above, before you embark on the collaboration path, make sure you understand your environment. This includes the stage of your business, your overall brand strategy, your competition, your target audiences and the way your brand currently *fits* into culture.

Ask and answer these questions to help set the stage for you to appropriately plan and measure your approach:

- Where does the business stand today in terms of the evolution of the company?

- Are you a new brand or a heritage brand? In the middle of an overt shift or brand refresh?

- Are you in need of a brand evolution or revolution?

- Are you working to reinforce the current view of your brand or change perceptions?

For the purposes of this exercise, we'll build on your current brand strategy, assume you have a differentiated position in the market, have a well-defined set of values and a clear sense of your existing or aspirational audiences. As we've explored throughout, collaboration is a great way to make people think about your brand, so if your goal is to evolve the way you are perceived, this approach can be part of the solution. Just be clear about who you are as a brand, and ensure the collaboration reinforces and clarifies those values, otherwise the effort will confuse people.

Inventory

Once you've identified your focus within the broader range of company goals and personal responsibilities, it's time to check your inventory. When I worked in retail—for both mom-and-pop stores and large chains—we held dedicated inventory nights where we analyzed what we had and then made decisions about what we really needed to be successful moving forward. You can do the same with your brand. Begin by looking at all of the current partners that surround the business. Are there any nonprofit partners that might be prime for a more thoughtful engagement like we covered in Chapter 7? Do you have any ingredient partners in your supply chain or manufacturing process that might be worth a more consumer-facing treatment? Other brands you've teamed up with in the past?

If you find one or more that you think are worthwhile, begin excavating. Dig into what these partners do and whether or not they seem like a true *fit*. Do they appear to have the same values and goals as your brand? Do they reveal anything advantageous about your company, help you evolve your story or provide something that adds value for your customers? Ask colleagues or the partner what they think. You may be surprised what you find, and the fact that these brands are already in your orbit lowers the barrier to entry.

If you've identified a partner that you're bullish on, jump ahead to the next chapter. If not, let's keep working on our approach.

Environment

As more companies tap into the power of collaboration, brands must also be sure what they are doing is actually unique. In some ways, collaborations are inherently novel because the resulting product or service can only be created by a partnership between the participating brands. However, many collaborations feel similar. This is why it's important to do some research early in the process and ask yourself:

- Has anyone in your category developed a collaboration like the one you're considering?

- What brands do you admire in other categories and how are they leveraging collaboration?

- How about the brands that are adjacent to you in the lives of your customers?

- If you're selling staplers*, who are the other brands sitting on the physical or virtual shelf next to you?

- What about the other products that sit on your customers' desks?

There's a good chance these brands have many of the same goals, values and retail partners as you do. It's not the sexiest category of product, but that's the point. Every brand can leverage collaboration.

....

* *Does this word make you think of the movie* Office Space? *Isn't it incredible that a random object and a film can forever be linked? It's a small reminder that great storytelling is powerful.*

....

Other People's Property

And now it's time for the most important factor: your target customers. What kind of data do you already have about them? Can your retail partners provide you with any data related to their purchase behavior or media consumption?

If you are looking at your own customer data, that of a partner, or industry research, remember that conventional audience segmentation models are inherently broad. This information may be useful for guidance around a television buy, but today we have the ability to get much more granular. I encourage you to build out a number of different audience segments that can inform all of your marketing efforts, including collaboration.

I have always enjoyed the exercise of bringing existing and potential customer segments to life by developing audience archetypes. If you decide to try it out, have fun and conduct these exercises with others you trust and respect. Make it a judgment-free space to play where all ideas are heard. The output should include a series of individuals (give them actual names) who represent large groups that you can market to. Fill in their demographics, add their buying behaviors and then their psychographics (attitudes, values and media preferences). Last but not least, list out the other brands these individuals associate with. These are some of the brands you probably want to align with.

In addition to outside data, this work can be developed by mining your own customer data and social media presence, by conducting custom research, by tapping an industry expert or a combination of these. Keep in mind, this audience development work is similar to your brand positioning. The market will give you clues, but you must have a vision and take the lead in explaining why the world needs your product or service. This is especially true if you are in the early stages of developing or expanding your brand. It may also be true if you are an established brand looking to reinvent yourself.

Let's think back to the Natural Products Expo we talked about in Chapter 4 where Sir Kensington's showcased a number of collaborations in the context of audience segments. Expo is a massive show (~80,000+ people attend), but it broadly appeals to an audience known as LOHAS—Lifestyle of Health and Sustainability. While this audience shares a number of values, it has many different factions. Smart brands take note of this, and realize that their why can be an attractive differentiator that helps create brand advocacy. As long as the story is authentic, brands can choose to lead with certain practices or product benefits that align with environmental issues, humane animal practices, dietary benefits, exercise, cognitive function, convenience, food allergies and more. It wasn't always this way, but great taste is now table stakes for LOHAS customers (I still remember how bad some of the snacks were that my mom brought home from the "health food store" when I was a kid), so brands need to think deeply about what else they deliver both functionally and emotionally.

Once a decision is made regarding who to appeal to, it's easier to narrow down the attributes that are worth dialing up in a brand story. Clear communication and storytelling around this helps build deep connections with consumers, focuses overall marketing and informs a collaboration strategy. This clarity will also result in proactive outreach from potential partners since they can make a clear evaluation and see if there's *fit*. Think about to the lesson from Zig Zigler and be sure to stand for something rather than everything (aka, nothing).

I want to reinforce the importance of looking closely at social media when conducting audience analysis. As we saw in the example with Lyft and Taco Bell in Chapter 4, customers may be sharing who else they naturally think of when they are experiencing a product or service. Also consider a survey or focus groups as resources for specific ideas or inspiration. Remember, as simple as it sounds, adding value for customers will become a critical driver of your success, so get to know them and what they want you and your partners to deliver.

All of this work can inform another exercise that may be helpful: mapping the customer journey. You're probably familiar with this process, which involves documenting all of the experiences a customer could have with a specific brand, beginning with their first discovery. The value comes from asking questions like what takes place during each interaction and how can the experience be improved? Look at the time people spend evaluating a brand in the same way, followed by the purchase experience and what happens after they buy. It's likely there are already direct and indirect collaborations happening at every stage, along with opportunities to introduce new collaborations that will improve the interactions and experiences.

Honing In

Although it may not have mass appeal, targeting a niche can often compound collaboration novelty and the resulting exposure. Think about this in terms of your product or service:

- Is there a new offering that might be exciting to a specific segment of your audience?

- Can you work with another brand to tweak anything about the customer experience of your existing products or services to further differentiate?

- Perhaps you launch a collaboration for a limited time only, or promote a limited quantity—building buzz for both brands and demand for your next project?

Now take everything you've uncovered and create a wish list. Who do you want to collaborate with and why? Make sure they all *fit,* and document this for your team (even if it seems obvious to you).

Teamwork

Thus far you've primarily been working on your own, but now it's time to add some additional brainpower into the mix.

Convene a small group of open-minded individuals from your team, and maybe one or more people from another department, especially if they play a complementary role to marketing like product, corporate social responsibility or retailer relations. Gaining an outside perspective can also be helpful at this stage. If you have one or more agencies you can tag them in. You might consider inviting a friend from another brand. This is a great way to network and get a fresh perspective. The latter is potentially more impactful if they come from a completely different industry. Finally, you can call in one or more power users who already love your brand, in keeping with the theme of prioritizing the consumer.

Make sure you have an agenda, even if it's high-level, and circulate it ahead of time with your initial collaboration rationale and wish list (one page max). Consider giving the participants a simple homework assignment, like asking them to get familiar with some of the brands you have on your list and a few campaigns from other brands you may want to steal from.

*"Collaboration is not about gluing together
existing egos. It is about the ideas that never
existed until after everyone entered the room."*

—Unknown

Jam Session

When you get together, begin by reviewing the agenda and
your goals for the meeting. If everyone is one the same page,
move to your first item: the company goals you're planning
to address. Explain why you believe collaboration can make a
positive impact and do a quick temperature check to see if everyone follows your logic.

Next, quickly walk through your initial rationale, strategic
findings and your wish list, before opening up the dialogue
so others can share what they think and any ideas or examples they find relevant. Keep this first discussion light, fun and
short. Be sure to start and end on time as a sign of respect.
Try to create an environment where everyone feels comfortable sharing their ideas and knows they won't be judged. Make
it clear you want constructive feedback and real challenges to
your initial ideas and list.

In this first meeting you're really looking for input on
whether you're focused on the right company goals—in terms
of how to make an impact with collaboration—and more specifically, the brands with whom you might collaborate. If the
team feels you missed the mark strategically, did you collectively uncover another place to focus your efforts? Did the ideation
about specific brand partners move you in a different direction?
That's okay too. Sometimes the idea to partner with a specific
brand that *fits* might lead in terms of how you approach collaboration. Remember that collaborations can also form organi-

cally. You might meet someone who's repping another brand at an event or get introduced by a mutual contact. This kind of organic collaboration can definitely be successful and saves you the next step: outreach.

Fork In The Road

If your meeting adjourns with a clear sense of the company goals you're working to support, and a wish list of at least a few brand partners you and your team want to enlist, you now have two paths you can follow:

1. You can further develop the ways to activate collaborations independent of any one partner—deciding if you want to pursue a one-off initiative, a campaign or a platform that supports a variety of ongoing partnerships; or

2. You can simply reach out to one or more of the brands on your wish list and attempt to set up a meeting.

This decision is in some ways driven by who you're surrounded with, whether or not you have teammates to jam with, and how much time they are willing to invest at this stage. It's perfectly fine to connect with potential partners without having a full plan in place, but experiment with both approaches. This is another instance where you have to choose your own adventure and make decisions based on your situation.

If you select number one, put some meat on the bone and begin to think through the points of entry and the experiences you want to create for customers. In other words, even though you don't have committed partners, where might this collaboration live (online or offline), and what are some of the assets (existing resources or partners) you might leverage.

Meeting of the Minds

Now you're ready to reach out to the other brands you identified. Begin your effort by relying on existing relationships. It's likely the first meeting we described earlier in the strategy phase will bubble up some friendly connections. If not, keep searching within your company and touch base with those in the departments that might be impacted in any way by your collaboration. Let them know what you're up to, as both a heads-up and to see if they have any connections, ideas or resources that might be helpful. If they have objections, politely take them into consideration and circle back with them later in the process. Communication is key, so these initial discussions will help you see where you'll need to provide a little more time as the project moves forward.

When reaching out to brands, warm introductions are always preferred, but don't be afraid of cold outreach either. If you can articulate a strong *fit,* there's a good chance your fellow marketers will hear you out. If your company is small, or if you have a leadership team that's particularly engaged with marketing, it can be beneficial to enlist an owner or senior exec to make the initial contact. This demonstrates the importance of the initiative and the hands-on nature of your leadership. If not, reaching out personally, marketer-to-marketer, can be just as successful.

If the potential partner is receptive to the initial idea, schedule a time for a proper jam session with them. Always push for an in-person meeting when possible, but if it's going to be remote do everything you can to rely on video. I realize we're getting <u>tactical</u>, but you're proposing a collaboration that will require teamwork, so you want to get a read on your counterparts and vice versa. Too much gets lost in translation without literally seeing one another. Just like your internal session, send a brief agenda ahead of time so they know what to expect. Everyone appreciates this and it begins to establish your ability to responsibly manage and coordinate.

Start the meeting in a similar fashion, providing some context including the overall *fit* (shared values, shared goals and target audiences) you see. Next clearly define the area of your business you're aiming to impact with the collaboration, and then explain the specific approach to working together you have in mind if you chose that path. If not, ask for their initial thoughts on how you might be able to partner. Odds are you will both come to the table with ideas that can get things moving, but if there's an awkward silence ask about their previous collaboration experience, plans or examples they admire from other brands. You can also ask if they have been observing any customer trends or challenges that you can help them address.

It should become clear if you approached a brand at the right time, if you're talking to decision-makers, and if there's actually the *fit* you hoped for. It may take a few meetings before you feel confident that you've found the right partner because you not only need the brand collaboration fundamentals to be in place, you need to see a glimmer of rapport that you can collectively build upon. If it's not there, politely suggest you revisit this in the future (when the team, priorities, product or service will inevitably be different) and continue working down your wish list until you find a partner.

CoLAB: *Creativity*

The success of a collaboration often relies on the internal team and the resources invested in the effort. This means you need to be a leader and rally your teammates. But the idea of changing things up might be a bit overwhelming, especially if you don't know where to start. No worries, though, that's where this experiment comes in.

Well before you even suggest a collaboration, you can establish yourself as someone who is proactive and thoughtful. Start by sharing some examples with your colleagues of brands doing interesting things, even if they are not overt collaborations. The point is to begin a dialogue, and to establish a culture that invites everyone to participate by sharing ideas.

Next, search Instagram for points of inspiration, drop links to at least four different posts into an email and write 2–3 sentences next to each one describing:

- why this caught your attention,

- what you find interesting, and

- why it's relevant to your brand or business.

Send this email to at least two members of your team, mentors, clients or customers and ask them to add a comment next to each one. Let them know this is a safe, judgment-free exercise that's just between the two of you.

Encourage them to challenge your thinking and either agree or disagree and give you their reasons why as well.

Review the feedback and always reply, ensuring everyone knows you are really interested in their perspective and that you value their contributions. Additionally, this dialogue will give them insight into your thinking and reinforce the notion that you are someone they can count on when it comes to watching trends, being proactive and introducing new ideas. It doesn't need to result in any one project or deliverable, but I promise this practice will provide a foundation that spills into everything you do.

CHAPTER 11

Establishing a Partnership

"Coming together is a beginning; keeping together is progress; working together is success."

—Henry Ford

WHEN YOU HAVE a willing partner it's time to begin planning the details of the work you'll do together. The complexity of the initial discussions will depend on how clear or developed your concept already is. Even if it seems like a plug-and-play scenario where you've lined up a brand to fill a very specific spot, give that partner a chance to suggest opportunities to improve your approach and ensure you're aligned on the vision. In a sense, you can think about this like the scientific method. You want to develop a hypothesis that says, by working together, committing these resources, and taking these actions we believe we can collectively achieve a set of outcomes.

Great players double down on their strengths, so be sure to do the same in the hypothesis and development of your collaborative product, service, experience or content. This also ties back to the novelty we touched on earlier in terms of the ability to be different in a world that's increasingly competitive. If you and your partner both rely on your respective areas of expertise and differentiators, the cross section of these should result in a unique and valuable offering because no other brands can create this exact combination.

When you collaborate you also have exponential resources at your disposal. It is likely one or more partners has institutional knowledge, access to raw materials, proprietary manufacturing processes or production facilities that could be helpful. This applies to the work you do together to create something, as well as your opportunity to promote it. Each partner inevitably enjoys some level of awareness and has some semblance of a customer base. This was probably part of your strategy when you first decided to partner, but now it's time to get specific as this will directly inform the go-to-market plan we cover in the next chapter. You want to determine if either party has an email database, snail mail list, a strong social media presence or other ways to efficiently reach people who are likely predisposed to appreciating your collaboration efforts, assuming there's *fit*.

Beyond tapping into your collective customer base, consider each brand's existing partners. One or both brands may have relationships with influencers, artists, journalists, agencies, production resources, tech firms or nonprofits. Beginning with a clear look at these resources and relationships, and determining what each partner is willing to provide access to, will help reveal where you can focus your efforts and make the most impact.

During this stage of your collaboration it's also fun and advantageous to capture photos and videos of internal conversations, early brainstorms and prototypes. You could even begin interviewing key players to see how their ideas and perspectives change throughout the experience. Eventually you'll want to go back and reference this content as it will help ensure your narrative is consistent with your initial inspiration and vision.

You may also want to share the content, but don't get too hung up on that at this stage unless it's an overt part of your strategy to create in public and invite early consumer input.

Collaboration Playbook

After a few meetings it will be clear who is leading the charge, and that person (likely you) should take the initiative to begin consolidating the information related to your partnership in a Collaboration Playbook. For some of you this will resemble the kind of project brief often used by marketers to drive an initiative. I encourage you to customize this document based on your circumstances, relationships and previous experiences, but here are a few things you can consider including:

- **Players**—a brief overview of you and your partners, including high-level responsibilities and contact info

- **Collective Why**—the challenge and opportunity you identified together

- **Audience**—who you are targeting (customer segments or archetypes) and how your work will add value for them

- **Hypothesis**—what you are hoping to achieve together and any relevant research that backs it up

- **Inspiration**—a series of links, images, videos or mood boards that provide context and inform the vision for your work together

- **Resources**—what each partner has committed in terms

of expertise, time, physical space, key contacts, personnel and budget

- **Tertiary Partners**—any other collaborators you have lined
  up or want to consider

- **Output**—overview of the core product, service, experience or content you plan to develop together

- **Timing**—approximately when you will launch and any
  other key dates that are known at this stage

This Playbook can be outlined in any format, but the more visual the better. Remember this is an internal guide you'll share
with your team and close partners, not end consumers. It's
meant to help everyone stay organized and informed, to keep
the execution in line with the strategy, and to ensure you effectively and respectfully exploit the synergy between organizations.

Kick it back and forth with your core teammates and partners, and try to make it as thorough as possible before circulat-
ing it broadly to all the relevant players. It's also important to
treat this like a living document and not be too rigid. Update it
periodically and don't be afraid to shift gears if everyone agrees
that changes are necessary.

Now that you're on your way with a partner, and you have
a clearly defined foundation for your work together in the
Playbook, it's time to begin executing your collaboration and
thinking about how you will engage consumers.

First Impressions

Every night at the Comedy Cellar in New York City, audiences
pack the room. And while the up-and-coming performers are

great, that's not why this venue typically sells out multiple shows on a nightly basis. They come because this is where veteran comedians like Jerry Seinfeld, and numerous others, randomly drop in to do a set and test out new material in front of a live audience. The venue holds less than 100 people, so when this happens, everyone feels like they are seeing something special.

Typically, if a performer doesn't nail the timing or memorize every bit of their material at a comedy show, they lose the audience. But in this context it is the exact opposite. People love it. I've even seen comics bring a pad and paper on stage at the Comedy Cellar, further acknowledging that they are simply in test mode. As a result, people feel more excited about the experience and they leave with a deeper sense of connection to the comic. Everyone can see the finished product in a comedy special, or on the official tour, but very few get to hear and help impact the raw material as it's developed. The other benefit for a comedian building in public is that they know when material is ready for prime time.

When we connect this to the marketing world we can see why transparency is so buzzworthy and how inviting customers into an otherwise unfinished experience can help build or strengthen a relationship. This same thinking can be applied to collaboration once you and your partner have a few ideas brewing. I'm not suggesting you fully launch something that's incomplete. After all, you and your partner have existing reputations to uphold and promises you have made about how you will show up in the world. That said, consumers now expect a deeper level of interaction with brands and appreciate knowing what happens behind the scenes. Just like Jerry at the Comedy Cellar, creating an early opportunity to engage with a new product, service, experience or piece of content can be turned into a unique brand-building exercise. This is especially true if you're asking for feedback and then using it to shape your final offering.

If you go down this path and attempt to co-create with your customers, it can be helpful to have a sense of what you want to develop, along with guidelines that narrow down the input you're requesting. For example, you and your partner may already know you're creating a co-branded recipe that will be available for a limited time. In this case you can steer the consumer feedback by providing a distinct set of ingredients or combinations for people to vote on.

If you do have specific products or services defined, you and your partner can still take advantage of early audience engagement by creating prototypes and asking a group of customers to weigh in before going into full production. Maybe these individuals get a chance to beta test new technology or they get invited to an event where they have a chance to interact with designers and engineers.

This approach is similar to the minimum viable collaboration philosophy and the work of Betabrand covered in the last chapter. It can help you prove that an initiative will interest consumers and clearly deliver value. If this is the first collaboration you're pursuing for your company, and you anticipate some resistance, remember that the primary goal is simply to get a win under your belt. It's far too easy to let competing priorities or fear get in the way, so if customer engagement or some other creative spin on the early stage of the collaboration process helps you rally support, take that route.

At the same time, it's quite possible you were brought together or introduced with a defined output in mind. Based on your core competencies, it may be obvious to both of you how to put something valuable into the market. After all, you have existing experiences with consumers to draw from and hopefully you know exactly why they favor your brands. If this is the case and you and your partner are committed to a specific project, there's nothing wrong with jumping right into production. Still, it behooves you to get out in front of the launch from a marketing standpoint.

Creating in public, explicitly soliciting input or simply teasing out what has gone into the development process can be a great way to generate intrigue, awareness, demand and momentum for your collaboration. Even if someone never makes a purchase, this early effort introduces what you stand for and begins creating, or strengthening, relationships. More broadly, what this speaks to is the fact that you and your partner must expand upon the story that's inherently built into your collaboration with proactive marketing in an effort to make the most of your work and shape the way you are perceived.

The Big Picture

The various interactions that brands have with consumers add up to a collective experience that resembles a show in many ways. Just as you might lose your audience if a movie drags, or if the second act is totally disconnected from the first, you run the risk of losing a customer forever if the customer experience breaks down at any point. The idea that brands are creating a perpetual narrative, always entertaining and essentially putting on a show can be a helpful lens to look through when considering how to launch and market your fully-formed collaboration.

We touched on Austin Kleon's first book, *Steal Like an Artist,* in Chapter 9, but his second book, *Show Your Work*, is also relevant when it comes to marketing and collaboration. To put it simply, we need to share more than just the end product or service. We need to share more about our work. A similar idea has also been championed by Seth Godin, who speaks about branding and marketing as an art form. In *The Icarus Deception: How High Will You Fly?*, Seth explains, "the extraordinary thing about our revolution is that it is turning most business into show business." The world is "discovering that when they move from task to show, from spec to connection, they are adding far more value than ever before."

This show concept resonates with me because it's an approach that I have been observing for my entire life. I now realize why the examples of storytelling and entertainment from my youth that I shared in Chapter 1 feel so closely connected to the case for collaboration. It may also be why I have always romanticized the passion, attention to detail and customer service I observed at the locally owned businesses I frequented growing up.

My local butcher shop, Soltz Meat Market, was all about putting on a show. It was a family business run by four brothers and the main character, Jake, was straight out of central casting. His personality was larger than life, and although he was relatively unassuming (the bloody smock didn't exactly scream savvy executive), I now understand what a smart businessman he was.

Every time my mother took me in, Jake would slice a piece of salami or turkey and hand it to me over the counter. There were no plastic gloves, but I devoured it without thinking twice. Unsanitary, maybe, but that didn't matter. When we went to the Market I could count on Jake to ceremoniously deliver something tasty and give me his full attention. This made the experience more pleasant for everyone, as I was preoccupied by the treat long enough for my mom to actually buy something.

Jake and his brothers also knew exactly what kind of meat my family enjoyed, and they personalized their outreach accordingly. I can remember Jake calling our house to let my mom know he had some lean hamburger meat waiting for her. Not only did he know when we last came in, but he knew what we had in our freezer and exactly when it would be time to encourage us to purchase more. He must have had his own version of today's customer relationship management (CRM) software. But he didn't just sell, he told a story about the product and why it was special. Every third or fourth call he would offer something a little more exotic, and it would be done with a sense of urgency. "Tell your mother I've got a nice lean brisket in today, and I'll hold it for her if she's interested."

Jake had our full attention and we built a genuine relationship. As a result, he would map his offering to our preferences and buying patterns. He would even customize the in-store experience on the fly. Lastly, he was also involved in some of the same community organizations that we were, which furthered the connection.

Back then most of our interactions took place either in person or over the phone, but today marketers must consider many more points of entry and engagement where they can put on a show. Not to mention the increased competition that makes attention more difficult to receive and maintain.

If I were in the market for brisket today I could go to one of a dozen nearby grocery stores or I could have those same stores deliver the product to me through an online order. Alternatively, I could sign up for a subscription service like Omaha Steaks or I could hire someone to pick it up for me through the Taskrabbit app on my phone. Amazon is now in the grocery business, so they would provide yet another option. I could also visit the local farmer's market or go directly to a farm since many now have their own branded offerings. Last but not least, I could search Yelp or Zagat, the latter now owned by The Infatuation, and have the brisket served to me in a restaurant or from a food truck. You get the point. We have options. Our attention is being pulled in many directions and that means a brand must be intentional about everything they do. It also demonstrates how many opportunities there are to create and leverage collaborations before, during and after a purchase.

In some ways the increased competition speaks to Chris Anderson's now classic explanation of the "the long tail," which holds up extremely well more than ten years after he wrote his book of the same title. The long tail describes a world where we still have mainstream "hits" in the form of content, products, services and experiences that generate mass adoption (like watching the Super Bowl or shopping at Amazon), but also more opportunities for niche offerings to find audiences and flourish.

My favorite example of this playing out is the music industry. For many decades we lived in a world where consumers primarily heard music from a limited number of artists that were handpicked by a few large record labels. This was driven by the limited amount of shelf space available to physically stock albums. Then we shifted into the world of digital music and unlimited shelf space. In fact, there's no shelf at all. Combine this unlimited space with the new opportunities to distribute music (which are much less cumbersome than physical distribution), connections with social media, and you have the ability for niche music to reach niche audiences. If you want to put out a song every day, a mixtape every week, or a free album even though you know you could sell it, you can do it without anyone's permission. There are various other challenges with the modern music business, but it's hard to argue with the fact that more people now have a chance to share their art and possibly find an audience.

At this point, the long tail has impacted every industry and every brand. While this has been great for some artists and entrepreneurs, it has also resulted in a cluttered marketing and media landscape that only feeds our collective attention deficit.

> *"The most precious gift we can give*
> *anyone is our attention."*
>
> — Thich Nhat Hanh

Many of you already have integrated marketing strategies that attempt to overcome this challenge, and you carefully consider every step of the customer journey to capture and maintain attention. As more brands adapt, and technology further democratizes savvy marketing, the competition for consumer attention will continue to increase and force all of us to constantly rethink our efforts. Putting on a show will remain an appropriate way to describe the creativity brands need to put forth as this attention splinters further. You've heard this theme throughout the book, but if you want to ensure you reach your audience and deliver value, it's also imperative that your show is a co-production with other brands.

Food For Thought

Over the years food has become a show in more than one sense. From the emergence of the celebrity chef, to the Food Network, to the endless stream of cooking and mealtime photos on Instagram, we're all foodies compared to a generation ago. I can even remember when it was exotic to have sushi, as they didn't sell it anywhere in southeastern Connecticut where I grew up. It's wild to think that was just a few decades ago.

Today, food and everything related to it is a huge part of our culture and it's ripe for collaboration. I can only imagine what my old friend Jake the butcher would have thought of this new world. If he was marketing today he would probably have a butcher vlog featuring visits to local farms, recipes that were passed down from previous generations and tips for storing and preparing foods. He may have developed collaborations with sauce and marinade brands, sponsored a content series in partnership with local chefs or invited influencers to join him behind the counter. Perhaps he would have also hosted an educational series, or tested new products in collaboration with the the Spark makerspace that now exists in New London just across the street from his old market.

One modern food brand taking advantage of these opportunities and embracing collaboration is Sweetgreen. Salad bars are everywhere, and we can easily make our own at home, yet Sweetgreen, a chain of fast casual salad bar restaurants, has a long line out the door every time I visit their Boston locations for lunch. Yes, the food tastes great and it's locally sourced, but I believe people also line up for the show.

Sweetgreen was founded in 2007 by three guys in their early twenties, so it shouldn't be surprising that they regularly find ways to entertain and weave in subtle and overt nods to popular culture. This becomes evident the moment you walk in and read "Passion x Purpose" on the door, floor and wall. Their deliberate use of the "x", a visual cue that has become synonymous with collaboration, reinforces their youthful branding. Many locations also feature black-and-white photography of famous artists and bands that came up in the same city, along with those who have played Sweetgreen's annual music festival, Sweetlife. In the early years of the company, this festival became a platform that launched a variety of collaborations, provided a foundation for content and created an experience that reinforced the brand's values to its employees, partners and fans.

Like any great brand, they know how to successfully nurture collaborations and how to create an overall brand story that generates various points of entry and engagement for consumers. One example is the way they feature special menu items and corresponding merchandise inspired by chefs and artists. My favorite was the Beets Don't Kale My Vibe salad, named after a song by 2015 Sweetlife Festival headliner and Grammy winner Kendrick Lamar.

From a content and storytelling standpoint in the restaurants, they also place printed menus that look like newspapers along the line that forms while customers wait for food. In addition to the menu, the papers typically feature a number of other partners who provide seasonal ingredients, other brands they admire or work with, and stories that reinforce the social impact the company is trying to make.

Collaborative Content

As Sweetgreen and others throughout the book have illustrated, one of the most efficient and effective ways to put on a show, while increasing awareness, engagement and attention, is through collaborative content.

Marketers across industries have been touting "content is king" for years and although I've co-opted the phrase for the title of this book, the idea really goes hand in hand with collaboration.

One way to think about content in relation to your collaboration is through what the film industry calls beats. Essentially, beats equate to the important moments in a story, i.e. who you are and what you and your partners are doing, building, creating and launching.

Every story or show has an arc, made up of beats, and many of them rely on a similar framework. In his book *Creativity, Inc.*, Ed Catmull, co-founder of Pixar, mapped out the storytelling formula that drove the studio's box-office hits. It went like this:

> *Once Upon a Time...*
> *There Was...*
> *Everyday...*
> *Until One Day...*
> *Because of That...*
> *Until Finally...*

This may sound like a childish and simple exercise, but try mapping the story of your collaboration to this. Just like certain films and other performances, it just might surprise and inspire you. For example, "once upon a time" might draw upon the raw content you captured early in the collaboration courtship. "Until one day" reflects the the co-creation efforts and the a-ha moment when the new collaborative product or service was defined. Remember to let people know why you landed on this solution and how it was created. "Because of that" is your opportunity to creatively show the breadth and depth of what you'll offer, where, when and how people can get involved. "Until finally" is the launch, the purchase and the experience people have with the offering. The opportunities to be creative within this framework are endless, but the more you truly put on a show, the more you will reach and engage people.

One last but important point on this: the show may actually be a show. By that I mean your collaboration may not result in a product, service or in-person experience, but instead focus solely on content. This can come to life in so many different ways and there are endless partners to choose from when you consider the channels, publishers, platforms and individuals who are experts at producing images, videos, audio, articles, books, comics, magazines, games or interactive digital experiences.

We've talked about various levels of branded, native, sponsored and influencer content that you can explore, and as long as you rely on *fit* as your filter, you'll find willing collaborators who can help you create valuable content. By experimenting across these areas, and making sure your collaborations are apparent, you also take advantage of the fact that each distribution channel and point of consumption informs your story in a different way, not to mention reaching more people. Additionally, this process will reveal more of your brand personality, because you are showing up on each platform in a unique way, alongside a known entity and with the kind of self-awareness that makes your participation feel natural.

Even if your collaboration is built explicitly around creating content, you still want to build a story and marketing plan around the effort. Think about the creative ways a show or movie is launched and you'll find it's actually similar to creatively launching a brand of any kind. Not to mention, these days products, services and experiences are often created as extensions of great content.

As an example, in 2017 Netflix launched a merchandising division and partnered with Target—covered in Chapter 8 as a pioneer in retail collaboration—to offer a variety of products based on the series *Stranger Things*, including clothing, action figures, a co-branded Monopoly game and a Ouija board.

There's also an Eggo game that plays off one character's penchant for eating the brand's frozen waffles. For their part, Kellogg's-owned Eggo created a number of *Stranger Things* recipes, launched a food truck and sent co-branded toasters and waffles to influencers promoting the second season.

MODERN MARKETERS: **Cole Wassner**

Just like food, music, TV and film, there is no shortage of brand collaborations in fashion. And, as evidenced by Target and Netflix, Cheetos and Betabrand and countless other examples, fashion is also one of the most popular ways to create brand extensions for any product, service or content offering.

From a personal brand standpoint, fashion is also a great place to seek inspiration as it has always been driven by iconic designers. We all know who I'm talking about when I say Ralph, Tommy, Donna, Stella, Giorgio or Gianni in this context. Like so much of what we've talked about in this book, the number of individuals and brands entering this industry has increased due to the lower barrier of entry and DIY nature of everything. All of this has contributed to fashion becoming one of the most popular places for collaborations to occur. As materialistic as the industry may be at times, there's no denying the fact that fashion is also an outlet for creative expression.

To hear more about the evolution of collaboration in fashion, I connected with Cole D. Wassner, CEO of WMG (Wassner Management), a consultancy that specializes in fashion partnerships with brands and designers.

You focus primarily on fashion partnerships. What is unique about developing a collaboration in this space as opposed to other industries?

Fashion, unlike almost every other industry, is very emotionally driven. You literally wear your associations on your sleeve! Sports, music and Hollywood for example, can do endorsements that make no sense, because the brand is not as emotionally driven and perceived—i.e. Lebron × McDonald's or Sprite, we know, and he's been quoted saying that he does not eat or drink those types of foods/beverages, and it does not hurt him, his credibility or his brand. Fashion, as it is such an emotional purchase for consumers, is seemingly held to a higher standard. If a brand does a partnership which their core customer does not agree with (either for emotional, political, or association reasons) that brand just lost their customers for ever.

How do you develop a filter or criteria to evaluate potential partners if you're representing a product, service or entertainment brand?

Strategy, strategy, strategy. If it makes sense in my mind and my client's mind, then odds are it will make sense for the broader consumer. If there are certain touch points between the two partners, and there are ways to weave that into the storyline, then the potential partnership has more validity. People can now, easily, see through the bullshit that brands/products threw at them in years past.

Do you use the same process for developing a filter on the personal brand/designer side as you do when you're seeking other brands?

To an extent. There are brands which have names different than the designer, and some which share their designer's name. The latter adds a layer of emotional and personality to it which adds to the complexities of the potential partnerships. It is difficult to separate yourself from your brand if the name is the same (i.e. Michael Kors, Jason Wu, Derek Lam).

How do you know if a partnership should be formed as a licensing deal, sponsorship or collaboration and what are the key differences?

In my opinion, partnerships should hit on each of these silos. I think sponsorships should be a part of any collaboration and licensing partnership. I think that exploring a collaboration with a brand is a great first step to know if a licensing relationship is something viable.

What are the most common ways to think about structuring the compensation when two parties are entering into a partnership? Is one model preferred or becoming more common/advantageous in your mind?

It used to be that the minimum guarantee was the biggest focus for partners, but now, with the fear everyone has about putting so much upfront, I've been seeing considerably lower MGs and much larger royalties on the back end. The licensee obviously prefers the new approach, because it's less risk on their end, but the licensor always wants the upfront payment or MG. It's a learning curve to find the middle ground I think.

In addition to finding new revenue streams the other focus for you in all partnerships is acquiring a new customer base or demographic. How do you know the right new customer base or demographic to seek out? Is there a way to determine if a brand will resonate with these new audiences before you officially commit to a project?

It's an interesting question actually. I typically ask my clients seemingly mundane questions to better understand who the potential and existing customer is: What type of water does your brand drink (Fiji, Evian, Poland Spring, tap water), what music does your brand listen to, if your brand could eat at one restaurant in NYC which would it be, etc. These questions help not only me, but the brand owners to understand the associations for their brand and customer.

Any trends we should have our eye on?

I try not to focus on trends. Trends come and go, and in the age of Instagram, they come and go too quickly to be able to take advantage of. The goal for me is to be ahead of the trends...to set the trend! Take a brand like ALC for instance. Andrea Lieberman, coming to the world of design from being a celebrity stylist, has her finger on the pulse on her customer and typically is 1–2 years ahead of a trend that sweeps the nation from time to time. Brands and companies that are able to do that, and do it well, are the brands that will stand the test of time in my opinion.

How do you personally stay inspired and on top of your game creatively?

I live and breathe my job. I don't really consider it work actually. I love what I do and it's a part of who I am. When your work/life balance blends into the same thing, then I think you're always inspired. Of course you can't work 100% of the time, so finding those moments to get your head on straight is necessary... Personally, I go for a run and think of nothing but putting one foot in front of the other. But even when I'm on vacation, I work. I love it, it's who I am and that keeps me going and waking up with a smile everyday.

▼ ▼ ▼

Breaking Down The Stage

It's valuable to think about the show, and a mistake to think about elements of the customer journey as disparate experiences, but you can dig into each stage and identify opportunities to improve or add value. Earlier we touched on the idea of creating in public, and the awareness that approach can generate for your work. But regardless of how you get there, once you have an offering defined you must be deliberate about creating a pre-purchase experience that tells a story and invites consumer interaction.

If you anticipate demand, you may be able to build awareness by simply announcing the partnership to your existing customers and key partners. Even if that's the case, it's still in your best interest to create compelling content and exclusive opportunities for select customers and partners to gain access. Things like this can take demand and turn it into a breakout moment for your brand that may even transcend your industry.

That's a fortunate position to be in, but most brands need to proactively create demand by tapping into a range of different marketing initiatives just as you would with any launch or campaign effort.

HERE ARE A FEW QUESTIONS WORTH CONSIDERING:

- How can you add value and demonstrate the value of your offering before a purchase is even made?

- What can you do together to increase the number of people you reach and the quality of those initial experiences?

- Are you making content a key component of your work together?

- What does this look like online, in social media, at retail or during events?

- Are there opportunities to truly partner with artists and influencers by giving them early access?

The New Purchase Experience

Once you have built out your collaboration story, and the supporting content and experiences to generate awareness and consideration, it's time to think about how the narrative and value proposition will be reinforced during and after each sale.

When it comes to the purchase experience, begin thinking about where a product or experience is being purchased and whether you are directly employing the sales associates or relying on others. Either way they become part of the brand experience, so be sure to educate and empower these front-line brand reps. You also want to consider the different ways one or both partners will capture, share and leverage data around the transaction.

It's also critically important to think through the in-store vs. online experience. The latter presents many different opportunities, but at minimum think through the flow of the user experience (UX), the purchase confirmation, the tracking updates (if a product is being shipped) and the way data might inform future offers and interactions.

When you consider that sales records are being broken every year in terms of the frequency and volume of online transactions, it presents yet another challenge and opportunity in terms of how you form, manage and promote collaborations. In the weekly videos I create and share on Facebook to survey my friends, I often ask about shopping. Recently I wanted to know how shopping habits had changed around Black Friday, Small Business Saturday, Cyber Monday and Giving Tuesday. The overwhelming sentiment was confusion. That's because Black Friday has become as much of an ecommerce event as Cyber Monday. Buying online is now the default for so many people, but brands have yet to catch up when it comes to their marketing messages. This informal survey was obviously based on a small sample size, but it shows how much room ecommerce still has to grow, and how much trouble traditional retail is really in.

Shipping is yet another part of the buying experience that's ripe for improvement and collaboration. Opening packages has become so common it's even turned into a genre of content known as unboxing.

If you're not familiar, this is exactly what it sounds like, a term that describes the process of opening products. However, in modern parlance the word unboxing refers not only to opening, but also capturing the process with video, narrating the experience and sharing the content online. If you search You-Tube for unboxing you'll find millions of videos with a shocking number of views. Why are people so fascinated by these? That's a debate we can have another time, but for the purposes of this book, let's put aside the content part of this and focus on the fact that every single day the number of boxes that are delivered and opened by consumers is steadily increasing.

Ecommerce is a revolution that has forever changed the way we interact with brands during a purchase. You can split hairs and say the purchase is actually a different part of the experience, but there's no denying the direct connection between the box and whether or not you keep a customer. Sure, there's a short delay between the payment and the receipt of the product, but it's all part of the transaction. Not to mention the fact that delivery times are shrinking and a poor unboxing experience may increase the likelihood of a return.

> *"Do what you do so well they will want to*
> *see it again, and bring their friends."*
>
> —Walt Disney

In summary, take advantage of the growing medium known as the box. It's as old as commerce, and yet it's recently changed the "during" part of the customer experience. Unfortunately, too often it disappoints. But just like everything else, a number of companies are taking advantage and they are going to make you look bad if you don't step up. Our unboxing expectations are still relatively low, so this is also a great chance to surprise and delight, and literally overdeliver.

It's been years, but I can still remember the handwritten note and branded pencil I received in the mail from Imogene +

Willie. In the same shipment, my jeans were wrapped with paper that had an impressive weight and everything was tied up with scraps of denim. Another one of my favorite brands, Hiro Clark, shipped me a t-shirt with a few vintage Batman comics. It was completely unexpected, but quirky, fun and something I was eager to share.

Contrast these examples with products that show up in a box, wrapped in an generic plastic bag, buried in a sea of foam peanuts, or in a boring envelope. If this bland approach describes your current shipping experience, you may want to form a partnership or a series of cross promotions just to address this, independent of larger collaborations. The box is an increasingly popular medium, so find creative ways to develop mutually beneficial value.

This is just one example of how you can audit your purchase experience, demonstrate how much you care and show why you're different. When you and your partner collaborate be sure to leverage your respective resources to make this a thoughtful part of the journey. It's worth an explicit conversation as one of you will likely be leading the delivery and you're both invested in making it great.

After The Sale

Post-purchase is another great place for you and your partner to focus your collaborative resources and find ways to overdeliver, especially because so many brands fail at this stage. As we have cited a few times, listening to customers after their initial purchase, through social media or other channels, can provide ideas to improve future products, services and experiences.

In another one of my Facebook video surveys, someone commented about how happy they were with Chewy.com, especially how the company randomly inserts sample products into their packages. This requires additional time and money, but the return is proven when you read comments celebrating the brand. In this instance Chewy took things even further by liking the comment from my friend and sending them a hand-written note of appreciation. This shows an incredible commitment to social listening and a willingness to invest in long-term relationship building. Chewy is a huge brand with a ton of customers, and yet they took the time to find, acknowledge and follow up with one person. That's how you initiate post-purchase marketing and how you create a lifelong advocate.

> *"People will forget what you said, people will forget what you did, but people will never forget how you made them feel."*
>
> —Maya Angelou

I had an unexpected, but awesome, post-purchase experience with Kind Snacks after I shared a Tweet about an acai bowl I concocted in my parents' kitchen. I had tagged a few different brands that I used for ingredients and surprisingly received a response from Kind asking for my mailing address. I figured they might send a sample product or a coupon, but when a slick black matte box showed up I realized this would not be a typical product sampling.

Inside I found an illustrated book of "Kind Acts" that in a humorous, yet genuine way encouraged me to be nice to people. There were also a number of VIP cards that I was encouraged to hand others—empowering me to become a collaborator and advocate—so they could get a similar Kind Box. Last but not least were three new flavors of Kind bars to sample. Of course I did my own unboxing, sharing the experience through my social channels and with everyone who came into my office for the next month. I even took the box with me to a few meetings. Granted, I have the *Curse of the Marketer,* so I'm a bit abnormal, but the point is by deliberately investing in this post-purchase activity Kind found a unique way to turn me into even more of an advocate.

A loyalty program is another classic post-purchase approach that's proven to increase customer lifetime value and is ripe for collaboration. Regardless of the incentive or mechanism for reward, email is the most common way to maintain such a program. Many of us are inundated with spam, and reluctant to clutter our inboxes any more than we have to, which may lead marketers to overlook email as a viable channel. That would be a mistake as it remains a proven platform that's here to stay. Social media and messaging will certainly evolve, as will our overall adoption of voice and other technologies that aid communication, but our private email addresses are sacred and I bet they outlast most of our current communication habits. That doesn't mean we should ignore social media or these other advances, but we should recognize the power of permission related to the inbox.

Here are a few more questions to consider as you and your partner look for creative ways to collaborate around the post-purchase experience:

- Is there an automated follow-up of any kind that's triggered by the transaction or ongoing use? Can one or both brands make this experience better?

- How can you work together with your partners to encourage repeat purchases, cross-sells and up-sells?

- Are you providing an incentive that will increase the likelihood that a customer recommends the product or service and refers their friends?

- Is there an ongoing experience they are now eligible for because of the purchase? This could be in the form of exclusive offers, insider content, escalating discounts, event access, co-creation opportunities, previews of new offerings or a formal loyalty program from one or more partners.

Whether you have a box you mail to random customers, a loyalty program or simply pay attention to social chatter and recognize those who genuinely endorse your brand, the post-purchase experience represents a huge opportunity. Layer in a collaboration or two and you may be able to cut down costs, reach more people and deliver more value.

Keeping the Beat

As you work to turn your collaboration, your story and your corresponding content into a formal marketing plan, keep in mind that your efforts should always tie back to the shared goals and commitment of resources you agreed upon with your primary partner. The narrative and corresponding actions should reinforce the rationale for developing the partnership in the first place, reiterate the creative inspiration that led you down this path, exploit the differentiators that make your efforts unique and clearly articulate the functional, emotional and social benefits you hope to deliver. In the next chapter we'll look at a framework to help you layer in additional partners to push your collaboration over the top.

CoLAB: *Creativity*

The show you create must ultimately speak to the value you deliver to consumers with your core offering. While this can play out in all aspects of your marketing, let's think about developing a literal show.

To create a treatment for our show, start by thinking beyond the functional value and asking how someone feels when they interact with your existing product, service or experience. Now, what kind of show would deliver the same emotion?

Is your show about cooking, travel, history, fashion, culture, music, family, education, sports or adventure? Get really specific and once you have an overarching theme, try to come up with five different episodes.

To make it even more appealing and marketable, layer in some other brands that reinforce the value you aim to deliver. Put aside budgets for this exercise and have fun imagining who you would team up with.

Think about who you would want to produce this based on their personal brand. How about a host, if that works with your concept? What channel or distribution platform would reinforce your brand and the emotion and value creation you're after? What other brands would you want to feature in some way? Are there merchandising extensions or events that naturally tie into the show?

Finally, share your treatment and five-episode outline with a coworker or colleague and challenge them to do the same.

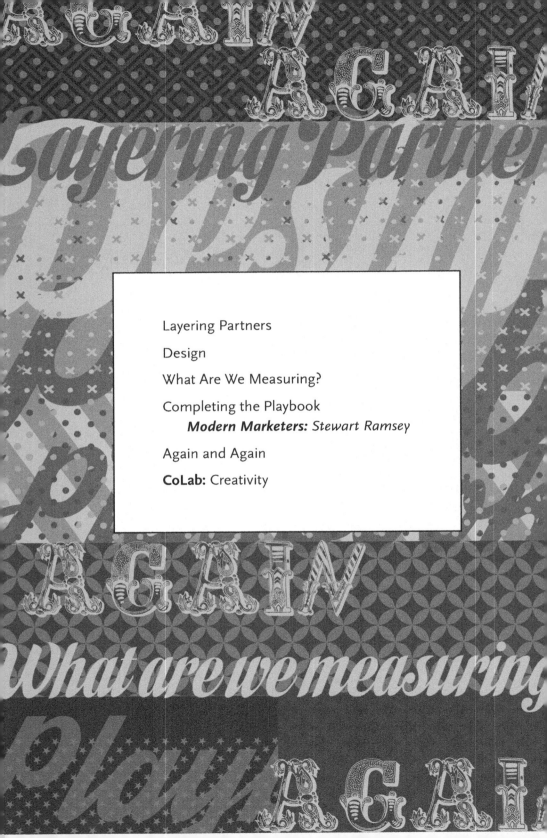

CHAPTER 12

Go-To Market(ing)

"A design isn't finished until something is using it."

—Brenda Laurel

DEVELOPING COLLABORATIONS PUTS you in a prime position to increase awareness for your brand and positively impact the way it is perceived. As long as you have established *fit*—shared values, shared goals and shared target audiences—you and your partners also have a built-in story worth telling. However, you must bring this story to life in every aspect of your marketing plan, including creating content, experiences, and in some instances, ancillary products or services that deliver value for consumers.

A philosophy similar to this kind of action-oriented marketing planning and implementation that I've admired from afar is that of co:collective, a strategy and innovation company in NYC. They sum up the need for brands to be more active and proactive through what they call storydoing:

"There are two kinds of companies in the world today: storytelling companies that convey the story of their brand, business or product by telling that story, usually through PR or paid advertising; and storydoing companies that consciously convey their story through direct action."

As co:collective co-CEO and co-founder Rosemarie Ryan expresses on the company's website when she describes the urgency for brands, "If they don't become disruptive themselves, they will be disrupted."

One of my favorite examples of a brand that has embraced "storydoing" and collaboration is Story. This gets a little meta, but that's why it's so interesting.

Story describes itself as "the store that has the point of view of a magazine, changes like a gallery, and sells things like a store." Their physical space, a retail store in Manhattan's Chelsea neighborhood, completely changes every few months with a different set of collaborations driving every element of the environment. There is a top-tier sponsor that in some ways mimics a naming rights sponsor, like you would see in an arena or ballpark, except that the brand is carried through the entire experience. Then other partners are layered in to help define everything from the interior design of the store, to the fixtures, to the collection of products and a multitude of themed events.

Story is a collaboration platform that lends itself to endless partnerships, audiences, points of entry and engagement. It also gives brands a place to take action, build relationships and surround themselves with other brands that help inform the way they are perceived. In reviewing an email announcing the launch of one of the store's themes I counted 18 different collaborations, including a top-tier partnership with Microsoft to promote their Surface tablet; personal brand collaborations with the likes of Sophia Amoruso, Martha Stewart and Iris Apfel; and a curated collection of emerging brands like Em John Jewelry. There were also a few completely unexpected but strategically sound partnerships with companies like Working Not Working, "an invite only community of the Universe's best creatives," that enlisted members of their freelance talent network to help customers design complimentary cell phone cases using Microsoft products.

In the spring of 2018 Macy's announced they had acquired Story, further illustrating the unique and significant value a collaboration platform can create.

Layering Partners

As you work to develop your collaboration, be sure to consider how you and your primary collaborator can leverage additional partners to help achieve your goals, uniquely activate your efforts and make an impact when you go to market. In doing so, think back to our thesis: you are the average of the brands you are most associated with. Remember that every experience and piece of information related to your brand factors into the way you are perceived. The same holds true of your collaboration. Explicitly ask, who else do we want to surround ourselves with to inform consumer perception and help bring our story to life?

This is a great time for a few more jam sessions aimed at coming up with ideas for these additional layers. Try assembling a few different groups of people within your organization and perhaps some people from the outside. It's not right for every project, but don't forget to consider including customers.

These layers typically break down into a few different categories, each with a set of distinct brands, resources and nuances to keep in mind:

RETAILERS

Additional retail exposure, often in the form of a shopper marketing program, is typically pay-to-play, but developing true relationships with online and offline retailers can lead to unique opportunities, as we saw with Story. This is especially true if you can provide something different than your competitors because of a collaboration. You may also be able to drive more traffic to a specific retailer by giving them early access or an exclusive, sharing content with them (they are certainly feeling the same pressure for more content as you are), lending someone from your team to participate in one of their promotions or hosting an event together.

INDIVIDUALS

Remember there are degrees of influence. While my mother may not come to mind when you think "influencer," today she has far more impact on the purchasing decisions of her friends and family than she did a few years ago. Similarly, who are the influencers who have deliberately built a following that's relevant to your offering and the creators who can help tell your story? There's nothing wrong with a celebrity endorsement or partnership with a social media star, just don't rule out micro influencers, especially those with audiences that map to yours. Above all, when you do align be sure to actually collaborate with these individuals, don't just place an order or treat the deal like a media buy.

CAUSES

Think back to your brand why and the collective vision of your collaboration. Is there a problem you're trying to solve, or a cause you want to bring awareness to that aligns with a specific nonprofit or community group? Are there existing brand platforms that give back and may want to cross-promote with your efforts?

EVENTS

Start by thinking about whether you plan to host your own events, join existing ones or both. Next consider what your brand can really bring to an event, or a party, to truly add value. Can you or your partner provide or sponsor entertainment in the form of music? Can you deliver an educational or inspirational message through a demonstration or a speaker? Who's bringing the food and drinks? These are simple and great opportunities for additional partnerships.

PAID MEDIA

Be sure to have your creative teams and media partners work together to develop ideas that explicitly take advantage of new platforms. Choose media channels that strongly align with yours from a brand standpoint, not just reach, and see if they are open to doing something beyond selling you traditional ad units. They may also have ideas for brands that you can team up with or their own in-house creators who can tell your story in a way that feels authentic to their audience.

DISTRIBUTION & SAMPLING

Think about the context in which your collaborative product or service will be most useful. Is it in the car, at the dinner table? Is it used solo or with a group? You get the picture, there are many different scenarios. Next, consider what other businesses, products or services surround that same experience. Perhaps they want to sell or sample your offering since it clearly aligns with theirs. The key is to deliver value by helping these other brands improve their own customer experience. Also consider straightforward collaborations in this vein, like product bundles or gifts with purchase.

TECHNOLOGY

Reach out to startup incubators and established players to learn about new tech, tools, apps or APIs that might complement your efforts or help them create a useful case study.

TRADITIONAL PR

If you're truly creating something unique there will be no shortage of journalists interested in covering it. They are being pressured to produce more content too, so if you have something remarkable don't be afraid to reach out. The important thing here is to do your research, target your outreach to journalists who specialize in your domain, and personalize your message by referencing something they wrote that made you think they might want to know what you're up to.

Design

As additional partners are brought into the mix, it's important to think about the visual treatment of the collaboration. You want consumers to immediately recognize that you have partnered with another brand, and by showing up in a consistent way you increase the likelihood that they will remember and share what you've created. That said, you probably don't need to reinvent the wheel or build out a completely new visual platform. After all, the existing equity in your respective brands is extremely valuable.

One way to approach this is to start with the existing brand standards for each company and then develop a creative treatment to lock-up the collaboration visually. The most commonly used device is an "×" placed between the two brand names or logos. In addition to literally standing for multiply, which is a nod to the exponential impact of a collaboration, this symbol has been used to market numerous collaborations. Therefore it's now a shared reference for many consumers and brings with it specific meaning, and often a progressive connotation.

Semiotics, or the study of signs and their meaning, plays a key role in marketing. Logos are the most obvious examples, but signs like the "×" used in many collaborations are more common than we might think and have the power to create understanding and efficiently convey messages.

Beyond this core design element, the visual and graphic treatment of your collaboration will vary based on your unique situation. The only other thing I'll say on this is don't get too caught up in classic branding challenges. Instead, focus design and creative resources on the assets you'll need to tell the story of your collaboration, namely content and anything that supports events or experiences.

What Are We Measuring?

At the end of the day whether you're serving a salad named after an artist like Sweetgreen, as we covered in the last chapter, launching a collaborative clothing line with the New York City Sanitation Department, as we discussed in Chapter 4, redesigning an entire retail experience like Story and Microsoft, or offering a pit stop and discount at Taco Bell through an app like Lyft, you can only improve what you measure. That's why it's important to define what you're testing, creating, and hoping to learn early in the relationship with your collaboration partner. To accomplish this, be sure that every idea you decide to run with, and tactic that you launch, has a corresponding metric, or Key Performance Indicator (KPI). Along with outlining the things you want to measure, define specific goals in terms of the actual numbers you hope to achieve. These can be online engagements (likes, follows, comments, shares), offline (in-store traffic, event attendance) and of course sales. You should also try to capture consumer sentiment and feedback even though it's not easily tracked. Lastly, make it clear who is responsible for tracking each piece and determine the cadence of reporting and sharing.

Completing the Playbook

You are now working with at least one outside partner, so your communication and leadership skills will become even more important. It can be easy to forget to make the extra call or write an email to ensure everyone stays on the same page. Documenting every element of your strategy and plan, and over-communicating with partners throughout the process, will inevitably lead to more impactful marketing and consistent consumer experiences.

Here are a few more things to consider adding to your existing Playbook:

- **Content Outline and Calendar**—detailing the raw content that exists, the new content that will be created, who is responsible for each piece and where it will be deployed

- **Creative Assets**—a list of designs, tools, materials and advertising assets that will be created to support the campaign

- **Media**—the brands you're paying or partnering with to amplify your message, including personal brand influencers

- **Key Talking Points**—the elevator pitch and boilerplate for your collaboration so everyone stays on message

- **Activation Ownership**—a designated project lead on both sides and clear assignment of responsibilities in terms of who initiates each part of the marketing plan—you, your partner, tertiary brands, media or agency resources

- **Timeline**—detailed schedule from pre-launch through public onsale and beyond, along with designated times for regular status calls

- **KPIs**—final list of exactly what you're each going to be measuring, what you're collectively capturing and when you'll be putting them together for review

- **Legal**—I'm not a lawyer, and every situation is different, but I'd be remiss if I didn't mention the need for some legal protection. You and your partner are investing resources into the collaboration and you want to make sure you're both truly committed and protected. This may not be necessary for basic social media giveaways

or event promotions, for example, but for anything
substantial you'll want to at least have a document that
outlines each brand's commitment and any limitations
on usage of logos, trademarks or other proprietary intellectual property. If your work turns into a more traditional licensing agreement, there are fairly standard practices
you can follow by seeking out an experienced lawyer.

MODERN MARKETERS: **Stewart Ramsey**

One of my favorite companies that represents what I think of
as a modern brand is Krochet Kids intl. They produce a variety of clothing and accessories, but they got their start making
crocheted hats. Women in Uganda produce the products and
personally sign the label inside each item. Upon purchase, consumers receive information about the production process and
the impact they have made, along with a personal touch in the
form of the signature of the individual who created it.

With each purchase consumers have the satisfaction of
knowing they supported an attempt to develop sustainable employment, while celebrating an individual's craft. It's also fun
telling others about the company when they inevitably comment on your rad new hat. These are the kind of socially conscious brand attributes people increasingly look for, especially early adopters and those who pride themselves on making
thoughtful purchases.

While their core business is truly remarkable, to gain additional awareness Krochet Kids intl. teamed up with a variety
of other brands, including the legendary skateboard company
Vans. For their part Vans brought additional product expertise, a focus on footwear (a category Krochet Kids intl. had not

entered), massive name recognition and marketing support. Together they co-branded a few exclusive lines that included shoes and a backpack. All of the efforts supported Krochet Kids employment programs in Uganda and Peru, and both brands benefited from the revenue, consumer engagement and press coverage, which included *Vogue, Marie Claire* and *SURFER Magazine.*

I caught up with Krochet Kids intl. co-founder Stewart Ramsey, who now helps build other brands through his company The R&D Dept, to hear more about his work on collaborations:

Can you share one example of a Krochet Kids intl. collaboration you're particularly proud of in terms of how it was creatively positioned or activated?

Our collaboration with VSCO, which at the time was a photo editing app for iOS, was one of our best and most surprisingly impactful. KK intl. is a non-profit apparel company so there were obvious and very natural collabs with other apparel brands, like Volcom and Vans. We met those brands at tradeshows so they seemed to unfold really organically over time as we built relationships. VSCO was an entirely different type of collaboration. Our Art Director at the time, David Garvin, was an early adopter of VSCO and was actively using VSCO filters to edit his personal photography. VSCO saw his stuff, loved it and what we were doing and wanted to start a conversation. VSCO became invested in KK intl. both on a personal level and as a company, and it's still a powerful relationship today.

But what was significant about the VSCO x KK intl. partnership was the access it provided to an entirely different and non-competitive audience. With the apparel collabs, while significant for exposure and bragging rights, functionally we were another hat or shoe in a sales rep's bag of tricks. While it made logical sense to make a beanie for Volcom or a shoe with Vans, we were at the same time competing against those brands, not only their other hat options but their entire catalog! With VSCO we were their one and only, which was special, unique and different.

KK intl. and VSCO share a lot of the same values and even mission to some extent of empowering and developing communities. They got on board in pretty big ways—producing content, sharing the content, creating custom product and we even had our own filter set for the length of the collab. Making exclusive apparel items for a technology company, who largely hadn't produced or sold apparel before, was significant for both parties. VSCO was so genuinely supportive and aligned I believe they allowed KK intl. access to engage with their audience in ways a big apparel company could not.

On a personal level, I witnessed the impact of the collab when creative professionals had heard of KK intl. through VSCO—these were people who cared about what we were doing but we wouldn't really have entered their realm before.

You developed collaborations with a number of established brands at Krochet Kids intl. while the company was still relatively young. What should marketers keep in mind if they are an emerging brand teaming up with a larger player?

I love this question. We were eager. If you're young and coming up it is easy to be swayed by a big brand. We are all seeking validation and credibility for ourselves and our businesses—those big brands can help you along your own path, but don't seek superficial validation. We didn't realize the power of what we were bringing to the table for these bigger brands, we were giving them access to fully transparent, measured and documented ethical manufacturing and access to marketing content (this is hard to come by or at least trust). There is a lot of value there, but we were so stoked that these guys were talking to us and sending us emails that we would do anything to make it happen—all in the hope these collabs would put KK intl. on the map! They didn't. Don't get me wrong, the collaborations we did helped us immensely, but where it seemed to have the greatest impact was on functional business and logistics of manufacturing. We got access to production calendars and sampling systems and sales and marketing cycles that KK intl. is still using today.

This either challenged us or validated decisions we'd been making. But our naive and hopeful expectations were that we'd see an immediate impact on sales—we didn't. Our sales grew but more as a natural progression and accumulation over time of collaborations as part of our marketing strategy. Advice if you're a small or emerging company working on big brand collabs: 1) Don't underestimate your value 2) Set your expectations low 3) A healthy collab is equally beneficial 4) Celebrate your collab by tastefully telling everyone and sharing your efforts; personally, digitally and with the other companies and retailers with whom you're engaging.

Anything else you can share with marketers who are looking to invest more in collaborations?

Collaborations are significant. They end up being huge for building community and relationships which is what drives any business. Invest in them? Yes! Your investment could be time, talent, or treasure, but I would set your expectations low—all of our collabs ended up being a lot of work and if we measured our time to dollars as an isolated economic decision I'm not sure they made any fiscal sense. However, relationships we built personally and for our business have been immeasurable and continue to pay dividends again and again and will continue to over time.

When you achieve true advocacy through relationship it is hard for others to ignore. We gained true mentors, received amazing amounts of advice and best practices, and have built new relationships because of the individuals involved with our collabs. In short, invest in collabs because it forces relationships to be worked out over time.

Where do you turn when you're looking for creative inspiration?

Without sounding overly cliché, I find creative inspiration is in nature, usually participating with her, whether surfing, climbing or riding. Creativity will sneak around and find me through music and film. I try to read a lot, history is insane. But I'm most inspired by other people; specifically their stories of perseverance or redemption or courage.

▼ ▼ ▼

Again and Again

Once your product or service is in the market, pay close attention and follow through on your plan even if the initial impact doesn't meet your expectations. It may take a little longer to catch on than you expected. At the same time, be prepared to make tweaks, shift resources or do other things to improve. If you're a few weeks in, and small changes aren't making an impact, there's no shame in pulling back on the efforts as long as all partners agree. Most importantly, maintain close communication with internal and external partners every step of the way.

The key for you is to experiment, learn, improve, evolve, rinse and repeat. Your aim is not just this one collaboration, it's shifting your company culture to one that prioritizes collaboration as a necessary and valuable brand and marketing tool.

CoLAB: *Creativity*

Creativity can often sound ethereal and separate from core business goals but in fact it's much more tangible and directly connected. That's why it's important to turn great ideas into actionable projects and plans. This transition can be tricky when you're working with partners as it can be unclear who's going to take the lead and whether or not there's full buy-in from decision-makers on both sides. Then there's the personal resistance described earlier which shows up every step of the way. Not just when we start—though resistance is particularly strong in the early stages of anything—but also before, during and after every milestone. So how do we personally step up, lead and keep things moving?

Keeping Yourself Accountable
To push through the challenges that often derail this kind of work, pick a buddy, otherwise known as an accountability partner. Your direct teammates and partners will be caught up in the details of the project and may be too close to see the big picture. That's why a trusted outsider can keep you honest and give you confidence when you experience setbacks. Tell this person what you're setting out to do and ask if you can update them on your project in accordance with the cadence you established for yourself and your team. Tim Ferris and others recommend layering in a public statement about your intent, so you feel compelled to follow through, or betting with a friend that you'll stick with the plan so you have a painful amount of money to lose if you don't.

If you haven't initiated an actual collaboration and you're still hung up trying to get your teammates on board, it may be time to dig into what's holding you back. A great way to do this is to ask your accountability partner—or anyone that you trust, respect and have established a real relationship with—to tell you what they perceive to be your greatest strengths, how you make them feel after an interaction and what they think is holding you back. It can be a bit embarrassing, but I've found doing this part through email takes away a little of the awkwardness while still providing significant benefit. Most people are honored to participate and their feedback will be priceless.

If you're really committed to investing in yourself, and open minded, consider hiring a coach. There's still a bit of a stigma around this for some, but when athletes, musicians, students and others want to excel they all hire coaches. Why then should we hold back from having one in our personal and/or professional lives?

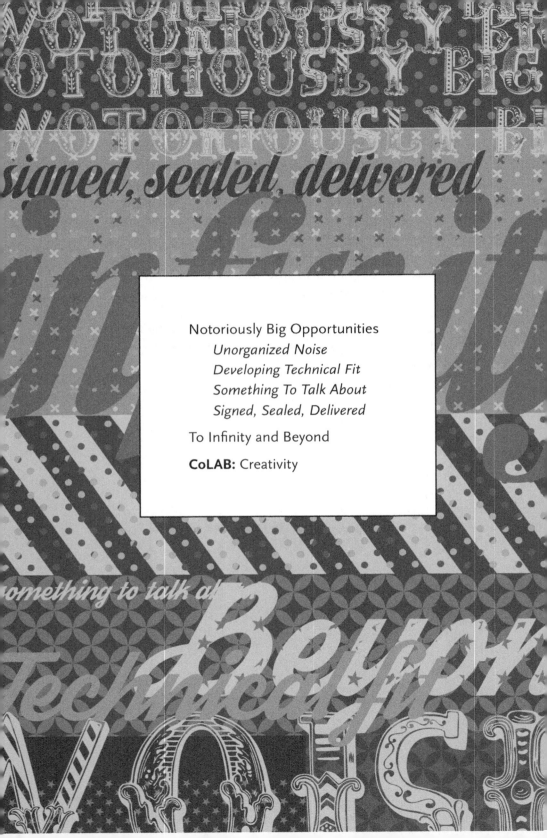

Notoriously Big Opportunities
Unorganized Noise
Developing Technical Fit
Something To Talk About
Signed, Sealed, Delivered

To Infinity and Beyond

CoLAB: Creativity

CHAPTER 13

A New World of Collaboration

"In world of limited choice, marketing is hyper-efficient. When choice is infinite, it's the reverse."

—Ian Rogers, Chief Digital Officer, LVMH, in
a 2017 interview with *AFR Magazine*

THE RAPID EVOLUTION of technology is often referenced through Moore's Law, a phenomenon first observed by Intel's co-founder, Gordon Moore. The theory states that the number of transistors in a dense integrated circuit doubles approximately every two years, driving down the cost of computing power and technology. For the most part this has proven to be accurate, and the theory is now commonly appropriated to describe the overall pace of change in business. Some call it disruption, but the fact is that every industry, especially the ones that enjoyed decades of relative stability, must now contend with a completely new competitive landscape.

The implications are different for every sector of the economy, but technology has directly and indirectly enabled competition across the board because it has made creating and launching a new company more accessible. At the same time, technology has also empowered individuals and brands to easily connect with one another and create and share their own media. Most of us recognize these shifts and have done our best to adapt, yet we know it's still early in the game.

One thing is for sure, these macro trends have resulted in everything being multiplied: the good, bad and ugly. For consumers this means the world is filled with more brands, more marketing messages, more media and more choice.

As this democratization of communication, creation and choice continues to unfold, it's not hard to envision growing consumer skepticism. It's already difficult to process everything that comes our way. Combine this with the likelihood that data breaches will get worse before they get better, and we may be entering a period where individuals are even more protective of their time, money and the degree to which they interact with brands. That said, there are competing forces at both ends of the spectrum. Technology enables us to streamline purchasing and in some ways automate loyalty, while similar advances make it easy to quickly switch to a competing brand at any time.

This emergence of technology certainly comes with business and societal challenges. However, for entrepreneurs, business leaders, marketers and artists, it also equates to an endless stream of new opportunities.

As first explored in Chapter 4, consumers have developed mental models and cognitive biases to navigate the world. Today's pace of change and creation will force all of us to depend on these shortcuts even more. By studying behavioral psychology and neuro-marketing, we know that some of the most common mental models and biases rely on familiarity and associations to help people determine if something is even worth considering. This is one of the main reasons I'm so bullish on brand collaborations and why I see room for them to grow in every industry.

Within this dynamic environment people need points of entry, references and trusted resources to help make sense of the world—including how we spend our time and money—and brands are in a prime position to aid in that decision-making. That's also why your brand is the average of the other brands it's most associated with. Marketers who harness this concept by proactively forming brand collaborations will have a better chance of reaching, engaging and building relationships with people.

Notoriously Big Opportunities

We've talked a lot about the pervasive nature of technology and a number of related trends, but the one thing that ties it all together is data. Moore's Law and the rapid growth of technology has given us the ability to track certain objects and actions for the first time in history, and at minimal cost. As our world becomes digitized and every device becomes a connected device, otherwise known as the Internet of Things (IoT), we will be creating an unfathomable amount of data, simply by going about our days. But the real power lies in combining data sets, and that requires collaboration.

"In short, software is eating the world."

—Marc Andreessen, *Wall Street Journal*, 2011

Depending on your phone settings, you may be generating data about a myriad of things that have never been automatically tracked before. The first mainstream example was tracking your steps. But think about when you pick up your iPhone or

Android device to request a car from a service like Uber or Lyft. You begin creating data. The pick-up and drop-off locations, the travel route, the time of day and the traffic are all captured by machines that will theoretically optimize your experience in the future. And this is where the intersection of psychology and the promise of machine learning and artificial intelligence (AI) becomes interesting for businesses, brands, marketers and consumers. My phone already recommends leaving early when it references my calendar and detects traffic on the route. This is based on real-time data it pulls through a collaboration with Google, which also owns the crowdsourced traffic app Waze. We're getting familiar with examples like this, but they are just the low-hanging fruit. Soon data, machine learning and AI will be used to transform and personalize a vast majority of the products and services we hire.

If this sounds scary to you, you're not alone. It's becoming hard to avoid articles, books, television shows and films about our collective lack of privacy, the negative effects of social media and the consolidation of power among a few large tech companies. Much like the infamous data breaches that seem to happen every few months, the drumbeat of these issues will get louder before they are dealt with in any kind of comprehensive manner. That said, the toothpaste is out of the tube, and the promise and value creation waiting to be unlocked by using data is too great to ignore.

"The price of greatness is responsibility."

—Winston Churchill

The good news is that it will soon become easier to distinguish between companies that responsibly leverage data versus those who are careless or malicious. Even then it will be challenging for brands and marketers who try to innovate—that's us—because we are perpetually in uncharted waters. The line between something feeling sketchy or pleasantly serendipitous may be gray, but this brings us back to the growing importance of company values and why they are the primary criteria we use when establishing collaboration *fit*. By starting with values alignment, respecting customers and offering clear opportunities to opt in or out of personalized experiences, we'll minimize mistakes while still making exciting strides forward.

What brand collaborations are worth considering given the emergence of connected devices and the ability to track related behavioral data?

Amazon clearly has a head start in the race to leverage personal data. But how did they build so much trust and attention? By providing immense value and connecting products that were often sold by different brands. In many instances this was not the result of a formal collaboration, but it still underlines many of the principles that will make collaborations increasingly viable. Not only did Amazon provide great customer service and lose money offering free shipping for many years, but they also raised the bar in terms of the variety of products and services offered by one company, not to mention the detailed information we could find about products and the customer reviews.

One of Amazon's most important innovations was their pioneering use of algorithms to provide recommendations, also known as collaborative filtering, or the wisdom of the crowd. This is the feature that suggests products, often from other brands, based on the intersection of your purchases and the purchasing patterns of others. Because this is based on actual consumer data, it can feel like Amazon knows what we want before we do.

What brands could you bundle or cross-promote with your products or services to take advantage of existing purchasing habits, just like Amazon has done with their algorithm?

As consumers, the more we experience the value of personalized, trustworthy and thoughtful buying experiences, the more we will want and come to expect them. Of course Amazon is the 800-pound gorilla in the room so it's easy to point to them, but every company has to figure out new and different ways to understand customers by leveraging data.

I joked about Jake the butcher's original customer relationship management (CRM) system in Chapter 11 because for most of his career the term didn't even exist. But now it's become table stakes to really know your customers and act accordingly. This sounds obvious—get to know your customers and rely on data to do so—but it's a perpetually moving target. As we've explored, psychology has always been central to marketing, but today understanding human behavior is more complex because of these new interactions we have with brands.

Back in one of my early jobs at the department store Macy's, we were incentivized to sign up customers for branded credit cards. We did this for the same reason we seek email addresses and other customer information today. We wanted to build relationships, communicate directly, collect data, present relevant offers and increase purchase frequency and volume. But this was just before online shopping really began to take off, and beyond tracking the in-store experience, the only other direct sales channel was the store catalogue. Today brands continue to incentivize consumers to share their data through branded credit cards and various other mechanisms, but online vs. offline shopping and other factors make the management and unification of customer data extremely complex.

Unorganized Noise

In addition to the challenge of getting in front of consumers for a first impression, and then finding a way to acquire data before, during or after a transaction, one of the major hurdles is the siloed and unstructured nature of data. A variety of companies have data about consumers that they keep private, unique to their own interactions and controlled by that company alone. In other instances, businesses don't even know they have certain data or they have no way to make it useful. According to Gartner, upwards of 80% of enterprise data today is unstructured. From a marketing standpoint, unstructured data is anything that isn't neatly organized. For example, transcripts of customer service phone calls or social media posts. Furthermore, Forrester estimates that 70% of a company's data goes unused, let alone combined with other brands to create more powerful and personalized experiences.

To understand the potential value, think about a common experience like traveling to a new city. It's still surprisingly cumbersome to find the right place to stay and the shops and restaurants you'll enjoy without cross-referencing multiple sites or finding a local expert. Even then, you need to personally provide that individual with your preferences so they can tailor their recommendations. Imagine what a travel or hospitality company could do if they teamed up with, or accessed data from, a series of brands you regularly interact with. By combining data from Uber and Spotify (already unified through their collaboration) with Amazon, OpenTable, Hotels Tonight, Ticketmaster, AMEX and Netflix, an entire weekend itinerary could be served up with incredibly relevant suggestions and offers. This may sound ambitious, but in reality it's already beginning to happen.

As we observed with the Lyft and Taco Bell collaboration in Chapter 4, when brands pay attention and mine unstructured customer data, in this case social media, they uncover *fit* that leads to unique collaborations that solve real customer needs. This approach is a great way to sneak up on the future* without machine learning or AI.

....

* *Sneaking up on the future is how entrepreneur, author and Stanford professor Dave Evans and others explain the power of design thinking. This approach focuses on designing to solve problems that have been identified through data, often by observing the way people interact with experiments or prototypes. In Dave's book with Bill Burnett, Designing Your Life, he applies the design thinking approach typically used by product engineers to lifestyle design. Among other things, he explains that people often think there's one path in life that's perfect for them, or an ideal career they must discover and commit to.*

In reality, most people go through a few periods of reinvention and have various mini careers. When considering a big decision like what industry to pursue, he suggests creating a number of prototypes rather than dealing with the all-or-nothing pressure that comes with that kind of decision. In this instance a prototype might be job shadowing, part-time work or a night class. Anything that puts someone in an experience that can generate tangible feedback. This is just one small piece of what Dave and Bill have uncovered, and I highly recommend the book. It's a unique tool that provides lessons in product development and career advancement at the same time.

....

Another collaboration inspired by consumer behavior and data is the partnership between the furniture company IKEA and TaskRabbit, a platform that connects people with individuals, or Taskers, who do odd jobs. IKEA's products come in many pieces and require at-home assembly. When it became clear that more customers wanted help with this, IKEA didn't start by building or buying a solution, they began by forming a collaboration with TaskRabbit. Why this service? According to data, TaskRabbit was already solving the problem for a subset of IKEA customers. Only after working together and experimenting with the alignment did IKEA decide to go all-in and acquire TaskRabbit. Now the primary decision for a consumer is whether or not they want a service to help with assembly, not which service is the most compatible or familiar with IKEA.

When it comes to embracing technology, data and collaboration, one of the most advanced consumer-facing companies is Domino's Pizza. They have been around for decades, relying on a proven and traditional model, which is probably what makes their recent commitment to innovation so unexpected and exciting. They have completely turned around their business by putting the customer first, increasing transparency, improving the product and leveraging data. In fact their CEO now calls them a technology company.

In Australia they launched the DLAB and Domino's Robotics Unit, which relies on partnerships with Flirtey and Marathon Robotics to experiment with drone delivery; with Navman Wireless for GPS tracking and fleet management; and with Nuance for voice recognition, to name a few. In the U.S., the Domino's Anywhere initiative has integrated technology and leveraged collaboration in a more direct-to-consumer manner. This service allows people to order pizza through Google Home, Amazon Alexa, Slack, Twitter, Facebook Messenger, several smart watches, Samsung TVs and Ford Sync. They are also testing delivery through autonomous cars with Ford. And when it comes to the business impact, the proof is in the pie. Over the past few years Domino's has achieved significant bottom-line growth, while leaving most of their competition scrambling to catch up. Now they are poised to leverage their technical infrastructure and data to further expand, and perhaps deliver much more than pizza.

Various companies are working to help brands like Domino's organize and leverage data, but IBM is arguably the most advanced. Their Watson platform has grown into a comprehensive solution that is already relying on AI to market products and services. At the heart of this is not only the ability to digest and process unstructured data—in a perpetually smarter way thanks to machine learning—but also collaboration in the form of marrying data sets from different sources. In partnership with Watson, brands have used real-time weather, tied to first-party loyalty data, location data and media consumption data, to deliver timely offers.

Another early use case is an interactive banner ad that relies on a dynamic ingredient database to deliver personalized recipes. It's easy to imagine how every element of this could become more personalized with brand collaborations and corresponding data. Why not have recipes that include products from different brands rather than just one brand and a number of generic ingredients? Especially if it means better targeting because of the shared data, and a better customer experience because of the comprehensive recommendations.

Now is the time to start thinking about the data you already own—most of which you are not yet using—the additional data you could be responsibly collecting and the related collaborations that might enable you to deliver even more value for consumers.

Developing Technical *Fit*

Personal data is being shared every day with or without explicit approval. In many cases it's anonymous and used for blind targeting that's not optimal. Even personalized ads have trouble keeping up with consumer activity. We all know what it feels like to have a banner ad chase us around the internet after we've already completed a purchase.

To effectively deploy personalized marketing, products and services, brands need to share data on the back end and collaborate on the front end to shape consumer experiences. That means brands not only need the kind of overall collaboration *fit* we've covered through the book, (shared values, goals and target audiences) but also *technical fit* in terms of their ability to integrate infrastructure. This is not a new idea as numerous businesses have application programming interfaces (APIs) that allow them to talk to one another, and according to industry leader Grand View Research, the systems integration sector will grow rapidly and eclipse $580 billion by 2025 (compared to approximately $300 billion in 2017). Today these services focus heavily on B2B solutions, but as ecommerce and other factors change purchasing behavior, every company is being forced to think deeply about how to transform their businesses.

From a consumer standpoint it remains to be seen how individuals might take more control of wrangling their data and putting it to use. The promise of a personal API that ties back to a record of our relationships, preferences, purchases and experiences could be interesting, as long as we have the right controls in place to throttle permissions, especially when it comes to the ability for brands to access our data. Today Facebook is the closest thing, and that's why it's one of the most popular, vilified, and arguably the most efficient, advertising platforms. They have mapped the social graph and know a lot about their users, which translates to more relevant ads, offers and content. However, they actually have just a sliver of the information needed to help inform and accurately personalize many of interactions we frequently have with brands. Whether Facebook, Amazon, Apple or another company manages to become our lead connection to other brands, one thing is for sure, collaboration will be at the heart of any solution that unifies and makes our data more accessible and useful.

Something To Talk About

As technology enables us to place certain things on auto-pilot for the first time, marketers and consumers will be outsourcing more decisions to brands. But what happens when technology makes those decisions on behalf of companies rather than humans? Can we trust an algorithm or API to understand a brand's values and act accordingly? This is an important consideration for marketers as they work to maintain consistency throughout the customer experience.

Virtual assistants are still a relatively new frontier for brands and consumers, but they will clearly rely on collaborations to make decisions and deliver value. For example, Amazon and Microsoft now allow their respective voice-enabled virtual assistants, Alexa and Cortana, to interact. Did this strike you as a major evolution when you heard the news? Regardless of what the two actually do, it's now a mainstream consumer experience to have virtual assistants in our homes that talk to each other on our behalf. Take a minute to ponder that with me and think about what this looks like in a year. How about five or ten?

This example advances our thesis and makes it even more literal. Your brand really is the average of the other brands it's associated with. If your brand is not friends with another brand, meaning there's no technical *fit* that allows them to interact, never mind why they might favor one brand over another, you will not be an option for that consumer.

As referenced earlier, the Internet of Things is also empowering decision-making and increasing the need for technical *fit*. For example, Amazon created "The Dash Replenishment Service" which allows connected devices, in the form of branded buttons and technology integrations with other products and services, to trigger purchases. Whirlpool has been one of the leaders in this area, as they not only connect to Amazon's Dash program, but also Nest (owned by Google), so your washer and dryer can automatically order detergent and it knows when you're home. If you represent another appliance company and you are not working on this kind of innovation via collaboration, there's a growing segment of consumers who simply won't buy from you because their machines can't talk to yours.

Can you identify a collaboration that positions your brand as a preferred or automated purchase in conjunction with the usage of another product or service?

Signed, Sealed, Delivered

One of my favorite entrepreneurs and business thought leaders is Ian Rogers, Chief Digital Officer for LVMH. You may not be familiar with LVMH but I'm sure you know the brands they own, which include Moët, Louis Vuitton, Hennessy, Dior, Fendi, Tag Heuer, Sephora and many more. Ian is widely recognized as one of the true pioneers in digital music, and before making a move into fashion and consumer goods he spent more than 20 years working on the shift from discs to downloads to streaming. His last position in music was with Apple, which he joined as part of the Beats acquisition where he led their streaming music service and advocated for human curation to supplement algorithmic recommendations.

In late 2011, Rogers gave a presentation to the Digital Music Forum West where he laid out his vision for the future of content, commerce and the need for curation. When Rogers speaks about the different stages of the internet and how it impacts consumer behavior, I listen. After all, he was there at the beginning when the thought of consolidating an entire physical record collection onto a mobile device was as futuristic as flying cars. In this particular talk he discussed the evolution of the internet, as explained to him by Andy Weissman of Union Square Ventures, which at a high level breaks down like this: In the early days we typed URLs into browsers, followed by portals like Yahoo, then search, and most recently what he called social distribution, where information comes to us because of the other people and brands we surround ourselves with. This social dynamic drives many of the themes and trends we've discussed throughout the book. But Rogers ended that talk with a prediction about how this would continue to unfold:

> *"FIFTEEN years from now we will all rely on a set of trusted brands to deliver us our content. Each of us will probably get more than 75% of our content from less than ten brands that we follow. What draws us to these brands is trust, trust that was hard-earned by honesty and the delivery of value in return for our precious time."*

As I'm writing this we're less than halfway into that 15-year stretch. Overall we have considerably more points of entry—products, services, platforms, channels, publishers, retailers, individual influencers and content—than we had in 2011 when Ian gave this talk. In some ways this makes his assertion that we'll need the help of brands to make decisions even more prescient. In fact, we may very well be on our way to the exact future he envisioned given the growth of Amazon, Apple, Google, Facebook, Disney and Netflix, to name a few leading brands that own a disproportionate amount of our attention and the corresponding content we consume. From a collaboration standpoint it looks like Ian may also be correct. If your brand is not friends with these top players by way of direct collaboration, curation or technical *fit,* you could be in trouble.

But how will this apply to the products and other services we consume? Will our purchases flow through a few brands just as they seem to do when it comes to content?

As Ian addressed, and we've explored quite a bit, humans look for help when it comes to decision-making. This is one reason subscription services are increasingly popular. They remove certain choices, or allow us to outsource them. Just like the gig economy, attention economy and other trending business memes, there's been a lot of buzz about the subscription economy. Do a quick subscription audit of your own life and you'll see how pervasive they have become.

In reality, we've been subscribing to things all our lives, and so have our parents and grandparents. Milk, eggs, newspapers and magazines were some of the most popular items delivered on a consistent basis during the last century. I'm sure you can close your eyes and picture a stack of old yellow *National Geographic* magazines, right?

Some of the traditional subscriptions remain, but many are being displaced, most notably cable television. Rather than subscribing through one provider, cord cutters opt for individual subscriptions to brands like Netflix, HBO, Amazon Prime Video, Hulu, YouTube and other over the top (OTT) streaming video on demand (SVOD) services marketed directly to consumers. These media and tech companies are the primary brands trusted to deliver content from a plethora of other brands they make deals with. And once again the data tied to our consumption allows these companies to understand us and tailor their collaborations, recommendations and overall services in ways that traditional media companies never could. A simple example is the welcome screen on Netflix. Not only does the service suggest specific titles you might enjoy based on your viewing habits, it also changes the type of content based on the time of day. If it's late in the evening they'll suggest you check out a shorter TV program, knowing you're likely close to bedtime, but earlier in the evening you'll be served up more films.

Beyond content, there are an increasing number of standalone products, services and "boxes" offered through subscriptions. If you're so inclined, socks, underwear, boxes of clothes, wine, beer, healthy or indulgent snacks, razor blades and more will automatically show up at your door on a regular basis. Perhaps the most popular example is Amazon Prime, a variation on the subscription model that has taken the concept in a variety of new directions by bundling incentives like free shipping with access to content and new technology that makes all of this more accessible.

Put simply, subscriptions are relationships, based on promises and expectations we have about what a brand will deliver.

Not only to entertain us, but also to make us more effective and efficient in all aspects of life. The subscription movement is especially relevant for marketers and for our collaboration thesis, because just like content providers, many of the individual subscription services rely on partnerships to deliver on their value propositions. In this respect, customers trust the primary brand to introduce secondary brands that *fit*. Increasingly, these services will also be driven by the combination of collaboration and data. When we add in the ability for connected devices to automatically share personalized information with these services, it's not hard to imagine entirely new buying experiences and business models emerging.

Let's take food as an example one more time. (Can you tell I get hungry when I'm writing?) In addition to regularly shopping at two different grocery stores, I get produce delivered through a subscription to Boston Organics. My wife shared a few of our food preferences on their website when she first signed us up and then a box of fruits and veggies started showing up every two weeks. We never know what will be inside until we open it. Although they sometimes insert stories about the farms where the produce comes from, the items are typically generic. However, periodically certain brands, like organic Dole bananas, make their way into the box. Somewhere along the line Boston Organics decided Dole was a trustworthy brand that *fit* and could be proudly delivered to its customers. It would be easy to discount this as a simple example of a distribution play, but in actuality it's built upon the principles of collaboration. We trust Boston Organics to only include items that are organic, fresh and tasty. If they insert a product from another brand that doesn't live up to the promise, it's not a good look and may lead us to delegate our produce selection and delivery to a different brand.

Now let's think about how their service might further leverage collaboration to evolve. To begin they could randomly insert branded products in the box. It wouldn't be difficult to get a brand of spices or dressings excited about this unique sampling channel. Looking even further into the future, Boston Organics might connect to my refrigerator and check whether I have a growing collection of unused turnips before doubling my issue with more of the same. They could also form a collaboration with Whole Foods, a brand that's increasingly connected thanks to Amazon, to automatically update my regular grocery delivery in a way that complements the produce they are delivering on that particular week. Perhaps even more straightforward, they could leverage AI and natural language processing via text or voice to ask what I want or need to round out a certain recipe. Of course that recipe could also be a recommendation from another brand partner.

Can your brand launch its own subscription or reach consumers by offering your product or service through a collaboration with an existing subscription platform?

To Infinity and Beyond

Effectively contending with technology will continue to be a key driver of change in our culture and businesses. By now I hope you can also see the direct connection between this and the advantages of brand collaboration. At the highest level this comes back to decision fatigue and the corresponding help consumers need evaluating and making choices. By teaming up, brands simply have a better shot of getting through, delivering valuable experiences and maintaining relationships.

> *"Choose your friends wisely—they will make or break you."*
>
> —J. Willard Marriott

As we've talked about throughout the book, it's important to regularly take time to reflect, personally and professionally. None of the recommendations here are meant to overlook the realities of running a business or managing a brand. These decisions are ultimately dependent on a variety of unique factors that you must consider. My goal is to simply spark your thinking and inspire you to proactively apply these concepts in your own way.

If you're ready to dive in, but anticipate the need to win over skeptical teammates, consider going back to Chapters 9–12 and playing with the framework until you find a path that feels appropriate.

If you're fortunate to already be part of dynamic company and team that welcomes the kind of intrapreneurial spirit we've talked about, make sure you're taking advantage and being proactive. Be careful not to kick off the next project, ship the next brief to your agency, pitch the next concept to your client, engage in the next planning cycle or apply for the next position simply because it seems like the logical path. At the same time, don't be paralyzed by indecision. Instead, push through the resistance and fear that we all contend with and make sure some element of your work, even if it's just a small percentage, feels a little risky. Do so with intention, leverage data when you can and track what you do, but experiment nonetheless.

If you're already an experienced marketer with a number of creative collaborations under your belt, hopefully this book stoked your confidence, while inspiring you to push even further.

Regardless of where you are on this continuum, our thesis applies: you and your brand are the average of those with whom you surround yourselves. Be deliberate and committed to aligning with a diverse range of collaborators who will make you better. Remember the point is not to do any of this alone. In fact, just the opposite. No woman, man or brand is an island.

CoLAB: *Creativity*

As marketers we have to work hard to keep up with the pace of change. Being insatiably curious and making time to explore helps us build the creative muscles and cultural awareness we need to succeed. It's necessary to do that on our own, but it's also critical, and fun, to make this exploration social. With that in mind, for this final exercise schedule time with a collaborator you admire, or convene a mix of people from inside or outside the company, and jam on some of the emerging trends impacting business. One way to organize this effort, and to keep everyone looking towards the future, is to do this on a regular basis—weekly, monthly or quarterly—and focus each session on one topic.

If you're really committed to leading the evolution of your brand, and frequently experimenting, this kind of regular discussion can be the catalyst. Then, the real key is to pick at least one idea from these sessions to chase down and prototype, even if that equates to simply doing additional research or having a quick conversation with a potential partner. You might quickly rule out the idea, but then move on to the next one. Just be sure you're meeting consistently and always pushing forward at least one idea until you hit a dead end and need to start over. Soon you'll gain traction and launch a meaningful new initiative.

Here are some emerging topics we've covered throughout, and a few we haven't. These are broad subjects, but they have at least two things in common. First and foremost, they are impacting almost every industry. Secondarily, they are ripe for you to explore through brand collaboration.

Use these as a jumping off point for your sessions or prioritize other forward-looking topics that seem most relevant to your business:

- The increasing transparency around every brand's ownership and production process

- The accessibility of direct-to-consumer sales and customer relationship management

- The ability to effectively target and personalize outreach based on data and technical *fit*

- The convenience offered by subscriptions, automation and connected devices

- The at-home delivery boom and the chance to enhance each unboxing experience

- The communities that passionately and publicly rally around every niche imaginable

- The content creation and distribution power of individual creators and influencers

- The expanded consulting and creative services offered by media brands and publishers

- The growth of text messaging apps as social networks

- The emergence of audio, podcasts and conversational platforms

- The education, escapism, entertainment and empathy enabled by virtual reality

- The opportunity to layer new experiences on top of everything with augmented reality

Acknowledgments

Throughout my life, I have been surrounded by a remarkable group of individuals who have provided love, friendship, support, encouragement, mentorship and guidance. I am eternally grateful for these relationships and the inspiration I continue to draw from them.

Darian

I have learned so much from you about life and love. You are incredibly smart, passionate, creative and hard-working. You have managed to build an impressive career, doing important work in healthcare, but you always keep things in perspective and prioritize friends and family. That is a beautiful gift. I love you and feel incredibly blessed to have you as my partner on this journey.

Mom and Dad

From a very young age, you instilled in me a set of core values that I rely on as my compass. Even when I veer off course, you are there with unconditional love, unwavering support and genuine belief in me. Thank you for making family a priority and ensuring Marla and I had everything we could possibly need, especially access to so many different creative outlets. You also set an incredible example by volunteering in our community and taking pride in your tireless work as career educators. I had the honor of witnessing the positive difference you made in the lives of so many children and parents and I couldn't be more proud of you.

Marla

Thank you for being a true friend and always cheering me on. You're an amazing woman with so many talents, most notably your creativity and passion for people. You bring joy and energy to everyone with whom you interact. I'm so grateful to have you as my sister.

Grandma

I'm always energized by our conversations and you never fail to remember a fun story from your youth in NYC. It's great to know I can count on your support, but also your unique perspective, especially when it comes to politics. I admire your volunteer efforts and appreciate you keeping everyone honest at the polls in Palm Beach County!

Debra Ellison

Your door was always open and your home was always filled with love. We shared lobsters when I was too young to have my own, you cooked Thanksgiving dinner every year when I was a kid and later you hosted my friends and did my laundry. Most importantly, you did it all with a sense of humor and grace. Thank you for being such a warm, comforting and supportive presence in my life.

Mark Silverman

You are a talented coach and an even better Uncle. I'm grateful for your friendship and your mentorship. From taking me on a road trip and teaching me to appreciate country music at a young age, to encouraging me to be myself and face my fears as an adult, you've been a true inspiration. I admire your bravery, your kindness, your passion for helping people and your commitment to being a great father. This book would not have been written without your encouragement and accountability.

Barry Silverman

You introduced me to city living and taught me about hospitality and customer service before I was ten. Those early trips to DC are some of the most exciting memories of my childhood because you were such a generous host. Later you showed me what it meant to be a true entrepreneur and how to get creative when faced with constraints. Your passion is contagious and you have a true gift for delivering unique and memorable experiences.

Adam Glazer

We've shared so many incredible experiences, from visiting Yankee Stadium with our fathers, to hanging in George Steinbrenner's office, to international road trips, to our respective weddings. You were also there for me when it came to this book, and your meticulous and thoughtful edits were invaluable. I'm extremely grateful for your friendship and support, and truly I admire the man, husband and father you have become.

Angelo Mazzella

You recognized my hunger and gave me an opportunity to prove myself. Then, you piled on additional responsibilities because you knew what I was capable of before I did. We worked harder and longer hours than I imagined possible, but I'm grateful that you pushed me because I learned so much. Most notably, how to really listen and then tap into my own creativity to develop partnerships that are truly win-win.

Brett Houle

When we met over 15 years ago, you explained the potential of the internet from a uniquely human perspective that I had not considered. You challenged my thinking, encouraged me to take risks and always boosted my confidence when I was feeling down. Most importantly, you lead by example—exploring, listening, questioning, empathizing, creating, risking, winning, failing and constantly reinventing. Thank you for your mentorship and friendship.

Patrick Griffin

You encouraged a culture of intrapreneurship, challenged me to step up and generously rewarded my efforts. I admire your many talents, especially your knack for communication and storytelling. I'm also grateful for the incredible education in politics, and the unique view you provided into our electoral process, from city hall to the White House.

Travis York

Thank you for asking me to join your team, empowering me to lead and encouraging me to focus on my unique abilities. Having the foresight to start me as an account executive was pivotal and enabled me to learn every element of the business. Together we discovered that being the most genuine version of ourselves, including sharing our collective passion for music, is always the right move. You are an extremely talented and creative person, but I admire you even more for your pride in family, heritage and community. I'm truly proud of our accomplishments and appreciate everything you taught me along the way. As you're fond of saying, onward and upward.

Heather Doyle Fraser

You are not only an incredible editor, but a great coach and friend. When I got off track or stalled for one reason or another, you always pushed me through with a perfect blend of inspiration, encouragement and reality. I learned so much from you and I can't thank you enough for your generous collaboration. You have a true gift for helping people find their voice.

Danielle Baird

You were a thoughtful, strategic sounding board in the early stages of this process and did an amazing job bringing the vision to life with your design. Thank you for your help making this book a reality.

Special thanks to the many friends, teachers, colleagues and family members who made an indelible impression and helped me grow:

Mrs. Kenyon, Mrs. Scillieri, Mrs. Abbey, Mr. Galvin, Dr. White, Matt, Jeffrey, Rick, Sam, Laine, Jeanne, Pete, Karl, Marc, Jim, Lucy, Jason, Ben, Josh, Heather, Mark, Bob, Sully, Dick, Steven, Don, CB, Zack, Jake, John, Sharon, Natalie, Jodi, Jeff, Ken, Josh, Katie, Dennis, Peter, Newton, Jeanine, Deb, Sophia, Lyndsey, EJ, Mike, Rose, Nancy, Gloria, Elaine, Jeff, Andrew, Cindy, Michelle, Deb, Kyle, Casey, Dan, Lucian, Terry, Don, Beth, Jess, Melanie, Scott, Kelsey, Michael, Luke, Alex, Matt, Josh, Tyler, Amanda, Jen, Evan, Fran, Jake, Micah, Carley, Tina, Nick, Adam, Seth, Dan, Chris, Andy, Shawn, Ryan, Max, Ralph, George, John, Sam, Adam, Zack, Ben, Gator, Michael, Jason, Bari, David, Marc, Lindsay, Meryl, Carrie, Ashley, Amy, Zack, Jake, Robbie, Steve, Eric, Kevin, Tyce, Aja, Justin, Joe, Joey, Dan, Tim, Jessie, Jeff, Bethany, Chad, Craig, Scott, Randy, Ben, Kristin, Michael, Brian, Colin, Ryan, Jarvis, Colin, Taylor, Sonny, Anthony, Rob, Steve, Matt, Jen, Ashley, Laura, PJ, Lee, Chris, Ian, Jamie, Isaac, Steph, Robert, Bonnie, Evan, DJ, Carson, Olivia and Scott.

Modern Marketers

Last but not least, this book would not have been possible without the contribution of so many individuals, especially those highlighted in the Modern Marketers feature. Thank you for sharing your experiences and expertise:

- Jay Acunzo, *Founder, Unthinkable Media*
- Julia Anderson, *Senior Manager, Brand Partnerships, charity: water*
- Mark Bollman IV, *CEO and Founder, Ball and Buck*
- Laura Cazatt, *Manager, Merchandising / Product Development, The Walt Disney Company*
- Alexa Christon, *Media Innovator, Co-host ADLANDIA Podcast*
- Chris DiPierro, *Director of Marketing, Boston Bruins*
- Chris Lindland, *Founder & CEO, Betabrand.com*
- Stewart Ramsey, *Owner, R&D Dept.*
- Melissa Rifkin, *Dietitian / Coach, Founder, Melissa Rifkin Nutrition*
- Chad Wagenheim, *EVP Strategic Development & Operations, Sequential Brands Group*
- Cole Wassner, *CEO, Wassner Management Group*

About the Author

Brady Sadler is an entrepreneur with a passion for building strategic partnerships that support business and the arts. He brings this to life through a variety of creative endeavors including consulting, advising and speaking.

Additionally, Brady is the founder of 1BAND 1BRAND, a global community of creators who study the intersection of art and commerce and champion collaboration between artists and brands.

Previously, Brady was the head of growth and innovation for GYK Antler, a marketing agency recognized as one of the top small companies in America. During his 10+ year tenure he worked with a range of client partners—from startups to Fortune 500 companies—across food and beverage, footwear and apparel, technology, healthcare, financial services, entertainment and gaming.

Before entering the agency world Brady worked in professional sports and for the Walt Disney Company, where he received extensive training in guest relations, storytelling and the creation of magical moments.

Brady is also proud to serve as a volunteer and advisor for a number of nonprofits including The Gratitude Network, an organization that identifies, nurtures, mentors and funds innovative social impact organizations; New Hampshire's Incredible Creativity Connection, an organization dedicated to fostering teamwork, creative problem solving, and innovation in students from preschool through college; and the Friends of CHaD (Children's Hospital at Dartmouth), where he was a longtime board member and co-chair.

Brady was named to the New Hampshire Union Leader 40 Under Forty and his work has been published in *Advertising Week, Fast Company, Food and Drink Magazine* and *The Huffington Post.*

CONNECT WITH BRADY

CollaborationIsKing.com

hi@BradySadler.com

Resources

INTRODUCTION

- CollaborationIsKing.com
- kylemosher.com, @thekylemosher

CHAPTER 1

- Kirby Ferguson, director. *Everything is a Remix*. 2010.
- Steve Stoute with Mim Eichler Rivas. *The Tanning of America: How Hip-hop Created a Culture That Rewrote the Rules of the New Economy*. Gotham Books, 2011.

CHAPTER 2

- Robert Kyncl with Maany Peyvan. *Streampunks: YouTube and the Rebels Remaking Media*. HarperBusiness, 2017.
- Edelman's 2017 Trust Barometer global study: https://www.edelman.com/global-results/
- Simon Sinek. "How great leaders inspire action." *TED.com*, 2010. https://www.ted.com/speakers/simon_sinek

CHAPTER 3

- Claudia D'Arpizio and Federica Levato. *Luxury Goods Worldwide Market Study*. Bain & Company. October 2017.

- Robert Williams. "Millennials in $1,400 Gucci Shades Lead Luxury-Goods Revival." *Bloomberg.com.* October 24, 2017. https://www.bloomberg.com/news/articles/2017-10-24/gucci-surge-boosts-kering-s-sales-as-luxury-revival-races-ahead

CHAPTER 4

- Daniel Kahneman. *Thinking, Fast and Slow.* Farrar, Straus and Giroux, 2013.

- Buster Benson. "Cognitive bias cheat sheet." *Medium.* Sept 1, 2016. https://betterhumans.coach.me/cognitive-bias-cheat-sheet-55a472476b18

- Jeff Beer. "Burger King's Five Tips For Marketers On How To Suck Less." *Fast Company.* June 26, 2017. https://www.fastcompany.com/40434873/burger-kings-five-tips-for-marketers-on-how-to-suck-less-as-a-client

- Clayton M. Christensen, Karen Dillon, Taddy Hall, and David S. Duncan. *Competing Against Luck: The Story of Innovation and Customer Choice.* HarperBusiness, 2016.

- Sacha Jenkins, director. *Fresh Dressed.* 2015.

CHAPTER 5

- Arun Sundararajan. *The Sharing Economy: The End of Employment and the Rise of Crowd-Based Capitalism.* MIT Press, 2017.

- Josh Luber. "Why sneakers are a great investment." *TED.com*, 2015. https://www.ted.com/speakers/josh_luber

- Kurt Kaufer. "The Podcast Ad Playbook: Baked-In Versus Dynamic Insertion Ads Explained," *Forbes. com.* December 1, 2017. https://www.forbes.com/sites/forbesagencycouncil/2017/12/01/the-podcast-ad-playbook-baked-in-versus-dynamic-insertion-ads-explained

- Richard Feloni. "An inside look at the life of T-Mobile's eccentric CEO, who wears only magenta and has a live cooking show." *Business Insider.* March 10, 2017. http://www.businessinsider.com/day-in-the-life-of-t-mobile-ceo-john-legere-2017-3

CHAPTER 6

- Kristin Houser. "The Internet Comes to Life at Complexcon." *iQ by Intel.* October 26, 2017. https://iq.intel.com/the-internet-comes-to-life-at-complexcon/

CHAPTER 8

- Elaine Watson. "Annie's enjoys explosive growth in household penetration, unveils new snacks campaign." *Food Navigator USA.* Oct 25, 2017. https://www.foodnavigator-usa.com/Article/2017/10/26/Annie-s-unveils-Your-House.-Your-Snacks-social-media-campaign

- Clayton M. Christensen, *The Innovator's Dilemma: When New Technologies Cause Great Firms to Fail,* Harvard Business Review Press, Reprint edition 2016.

- Paul Grimwood. "We're putting our money where your mouth is." *Linkedin.com.* October 23, 2017. https://www.linkedin.com/pulse/were-putting-our-money-where-your-mouth-paul-grimwood

CHAPTER 9

- Brené Brown. *The Gifts of Imperfection: Let Go of Who You Think You're Supposed to Be and Embrace Who You Are.* Hazelden Publishing, 2010.

- Chris Smith, director. *Jim & Andy: The Great Beyond.* Netflix, 2017.

- Austin Kleon. *Steal Like an Artist: 10 Things Nobody Told You About Being Creative.* Workman Publishing, 2012.

- Daniel H. Pink. *A Whole New Mind: Moving from the Information Age to the Conceptual Age.* Riverhead Books, 2005.

CHAPTER 10

- Eric Ries. *The Lean Startup: How Today's Entrepreneurs Use Continuous Innovation to Create Radically Successful Businesses.* Currency, 2011.

CHAPTER 11

- Austin Kleon. *Show Your Work.* Workman Publishing Company, 2014.

- Seth Godin. *The Icarus Deception: How High Will You Fly?* Portfolio, 2012.

- Chris Anderson. *The Long Tail: Why the Future of Business is Selling Less of More.* Hyperion, 2006.

- Ed Catmull with Amy Wallace. *Creativity, Inc.: Overcoming the Unseen Forces That Stand in the Way of True Inspiration.* Random House, 2014.

CHAPTER 13

- "Ultra-Fast Data Access Is The Key To Unleashing Full Big Data Potential: A Forrester Consulting Thought Leadership Paper Commissioned By SAP and Lenovo," January 2016, Forrester Research, Inc. http://www.thinkprogress.com/wp-content/uploads/2016/09/SAP-Forrester-TLP-FINAL-3-21-2016-update.pdf

- Bill Burnett & Dave Evans. *Designing Your Life: How to Build a Well-Lived, Joyful Life.* Knopf, 2016.

Made in the USA
Monee, IL
11 February 2020